MW01602453

FOOD FOR THE SOUL

FOOD FOR THE SOUL
Yonatan Raziel

A journey into the depths of Jewish mysticism,
its approach to food and the way it should be eaten.

Hebrew edition published by Steimatsky 2023

Book design: BenHerskowitz.com
Translated from Hebrew by Yechezkel Anis

ISBN: 978-1-60280-526-2

FOOD FOR THE SOUL

Yonatan Raziel

IN MEMORY OF OUR DEAR GRANDPARENTS

Sam & Sarah Rogansky

who lovingly fed generations of our family through
our weekly *shabbat kiddushim* in Hattons Lane,
wonderful *yomtaivim* meals and our early morning
walks home through the streets of Liverpool
after our *sedarim* finally ended.

The extended Rogansky clan nostalgically and fondly
remember their inspiring story
from a vanished world.

TABLE OF CONTENTS

CHAPTER 9: WHAT TO EAT AND TABLE ETIQUETTE

CHAPTER 10: BETWEEN SCIENCE AND FAITH

CHAPTER 11: SOCIAL IMPLICATIONS OF THE METAPHYSICAL STRUCTURE OF THE UNIVERSE

AN OPENING WORD

From the dawn of history to the present day, all living organisms are engaged on a daily basis with various aspects of food, starting with its procurement and preparation, and ending with its consumption and elimination. Fortunately, for much of humanity (and certainly for those reading this book), eating is no longer an existential challenge but has evolved into a global culture of gastronomical cuisine. In the last hundred years alone, thousands of recipe books, diet plans and restaurant guides have been published — testifying to a near obsessive interest that places food at the center of our lives, making it hard to escape its reach.

This book, unlike those just mentioned, does not deal in **what** to eat but rather guides us in **how** to eat, by revealing the mystical dimension of eating and its spiritual significance as understood in Kabbalah. Mindful Kabbalistic eating is an ancient discipline that describes the spiritual transformation that both the eater and the food itself undergoes, whilst combining these insights with a series of exercises in guided imagination. The objective of this practice, which is unfamiliar to scholars and laymen alike, is to introduce us to a nutritional experience more sublime and significant than any with which we are familiar.

In crafting this work, I hold hope that its pages will ignite curiosity and fascination among its readers, guiding them on a voyage of self-discovery and spiritual awakening through the simple act of eating. May this book serve as a beacon of insight and inspiration, enriching the lives of all who embark upon its enlightening journey.

LETTERS OF ENDORSEMENT

I hereby congratulate Rabbi Yonatan Raziel, who is a student in our Yeshivah, for having labored in the publication of a work dealing with the kavanot of eating as taught by the Arizal and the Rashash, of blessed memory (ob"m). The book is written in a style that is suitable for the general public and faithfully explains the wondrous wisdom that is inherent in the physical act of eating and its role in drawing down spiritual life-force into our world.

Rabbi Mordechai Attieh
Head of Yeshivat Ateret Mordechai for the Higher Study of Kabbalah, Jerusalem

The book is brimming with fascinating material. It deserves great success.

Daniel Matt
Professor of Jewish Mysticism, USA, translator of the Zohar, and author of additional works

I very much enjoyed perusing Rabbi Yonatan Raziel's book, which deals keenly and clearly with the important, yet neglected topic of the spiritual dimension of eating. I am sure that whoever reads it will find invigorating material to gladden both God and man alike.

Rabbi Uri Sherki
Teacher of Jewish Thought in Machon Meir, Jerusalem, and author of many books and articles

Your book is fascinating. I truly found it greatly interesting.

Rabbi Yitzchak Sheilat
Head of Yeshivat Maaleh Adumim

Eating is an ordinary daily activity but according to Kabbalah it not only nourishes our bodies but also elevates us and all Creation from a spiritual standpoint.

This book will expose you to the enchanting world of the Kabbalah as it relates to the act of eating, guiding you how to eat so that food will provide benefit and not harm, both physiologically and spiritually.

The Torah states: "He shall bless your bread and your water, and I shall remove illness from your midst." The curing of illness, according to this verse, ensues from the blessing that inheres in our bread and water.

The book is recommended for anyone who seeks out the inner dimension and depth of all things in life, with the hope that your meals will never appear the same after you read it.

Dr. Gil Shachar MD
Head of the Center for Rambam's Medicine, a center for
promoting natural science-based health

The topic is both very interesting and very relevant to the period in which we are living. The writing flows and the material is presented clearly for a broad range of readers, including those who are not religious or lack a faith-based education. The book's strength is its accessibility both at the beginning and end of each chapter. Especially noteworthy are the "Practical Implications" that close each chapter, as they render the conceptual material into a list of daily actions that the reader can learn to perform.

Kinneret Rubinstein
Writer, editor, and literary critic

FOREWORD

everal decades ago, amidst the ambiance of a joyous dinner gathering, an event unfolded before my eyes that would leave an indelible mark on my consciousness, igniting a spark within me that would later give rise to the creation of this very book. What was this pivotal moment that stirred me to the depths of my being? It was the simple act of observing a man engaged in the act of eating.!

I SAW A MAN EATING

Not an ordinary man, but a noble, dignified man — a great Torah scholar and an authentic Kabbalist, of pleasant demeanor, welcoming countenance, and enjoyable to converse with[1]. He did not just eat like you or I, but rather like a heavenly angel, like the priest bringing an offering in the Temple. Allow me try to describe what I witnessed:

> The plate in front of him contained about half the amount of food that was on mine. No meat or fried food; mainly fish and vegetables. When I asked about it, he replied that he only eats meat on the Sabbath and holidays. Rather than launch immediately into his food, he pondered his plate for some moments and then proceeded to cut everything into small pieces. He cut as tenderly as if he was holding a scalpel, laying his instrument to the side after completing his surgery, not to be used again. He then planted his fork in the first piece and slowly, in a light whisper, made the blessing before placing the food in his mouth. He lay the fork down, chewed for some moments, and then swallowed. He waited slightly before taking the fork in his hand and repeating the process until only one or two pieces of food were left on his plate. He then lay the fork and knife next to each other as if they were a loving couple, slowly drank a cup of cold water, and wiped his mouth with a napkin. The whole time he ate, a gentle smile adorned his face as he engaged those sitting around him in pleasant conversation in between bites.

I gazed at him, hypnotized by this aesthetic ritual. At the time it appeared to me that he was not feeding his body, but rather was nourishing his soul in the spirit of the verse (Proverbs 13:25), "The righteous one eats to satiate his soul." There was nothing about his style of eating that even vaguely resembled the way I eat or of anyone else I know. I was deeply impressed by the delicate hand movements, by the restraint and self-control. Mainly, I was thunderstruck to discover that such a common and base gastronomic action could be elevated to such a spiritual and uplifting accomplishment. I was absolutely convinced that he was not just an ordinary man, but a natural born saint, a special soul that had descended into the world.

His manner of eating was altogether different from the two types of eating that I was familiar with up until then, the ones I refer to as "oblivious" and "ravenous." Oblivious eating consists of the mechanical act of placing food in one's mouth and is predicated on the idea that eating is merely a necessary chore that enables us to accomplish far more important tasks, such as reading, watching television, listening to something, or at times even speaking — with a full mouth! Fast food is perhaps the prime example of oblivious eating. Ravenous eating, on the other hand, is characterized by complete concentration on the food being eaten in total oblivion of what is occurring around us. This type of eating is common among people who are either famished or faced with especially tasty food.

Many years passed and the memory of this event was relegated to a distant corner in my brain, until I was exposed to that wondrous and fascinating area of study called Kabbalah. After seven years of delving into its secrets, I arrived at the topic referred to in Hebrew as *kavanot he'achilah*, guided meditations on the act of eating. The memory of that dinner suddenly emerged from the recesses of my mind. In a flash, it dawned on me that the dignified scene I witnessed long before was not an expression of some inborn predilection, but rather the result of a deep and prolonged study in the *kavanot (kabbalistic meditations)* of the mystical tradition, accompanied by a concerted personal effort to cultivate the requisite traits with which to practice them.

This book endeavors to unveil those esoteric teachings of Kabbalah pertaining to the subject of eating, opening the gates of this ancient wisdom to a broader audience. Kabbalah, steeped in antiquity, delves into realms beyond the veil of apparent reality, offering insights into the metaphysical architecture of existence. It seeks to bridge the perceived gap between the material realm and its spiritual dimensions, illuminating the interconnectedness that binds them together.

Far from dismissing the material world, Kabbalah perceives the realms of nature and spirit as inseparable counterparts, akin to Siamese twins. It emphasizes the inherent harmony that resonates between these two aspects of reality, recognizing their symbiotic relationship and interconnectedness. Through the lens of Kabbalistic wisdom, the act of eating transcends its mundane appearance, becoming a gateway to deeper spiritual truths and a profound understanding of the unity inherent in all aspects of creation.

The Special Challenge Involved in Eating

It is a relatively easy task to reconcile physical actions with the spiritual realm when those actions are already somewhat spiritual in nature, such as praying or giving charity. However, reconciling an "animalistic" act with esoteric mysticism requires a whole new language. Thus, it states in the Talmud (Chagigah 15): "Man possesses six qualities, three of which he shares with the angels and three of which he shares with the animals: Like the angels, he walks erect, he speaks the Holy Tongue, and he possesses knowledge and understanding; like the animals, he eats and drinks, he procreates, and he eliminates waste."

In the Kabbalistic and ethical work *Reishit Chochmah*, which was written in the 16th century, the author addresses this point and distinguishes between natural, involuntary acts and those acts which man freely chooses to execute in a certain way. Thus, he states (*Shear HaKedushah* 4): "Behold, the acts of walking erect and eliminating waste are not in one's control — for this is human nature since the time of Adam. However, as regards eating, drinking, and procreating, acts that are apt to associate one with the animal kingdom, one must learn to sanctify these acts and not eat simply to sate one's appetite as does the animal. If one is able to sanctify and spiritualize willful acts of physical pleasure — which are common to the animal kingdom but are at the same time tempting and gratifying — then in the heavens one will be sanctified as well, as the angels proclaim, 'So-and-so is holy; no impurity will afflict him.'"

The import of the above citation is that Kabbalah calls upon individuals to exert a special effort in purifying actions that stem from primal, lustful urges, such as the desires for food and sex. This book introduces a novel perspective, drawing from the teachings of the Ari, which suggests that mindful and appropriate eating has the power to not only elevate the individual but also restore and uplift the entire world. This notion proposes that the act of eating, when approached with spiritual awareness and intention, possesses transformative potential comparable to traditional religious obligations like donning tefillin or blowing the shofar. Through this lens, the mundane act of nourishment transcends its ordinary significance, becoming a sacred opportunity for spiritual growth and global elevation.

THE STRUCTURE OF THE BOOK AND ITS SOURCES

The Torah of Kabbalah is exceedingly rich and varied. For the sake of presenting a clear and coherent review of the subject, I have limited myself to two principle sources: The Book of the Zohar, and the writings of the renowned Kabbalist, Rabbi Isaac ben Shlomo Luria — who is referred to as the Ari (**A**shkenazi **R**abbi **I**saac). The Ari, who lived in the Galilean city of Safed in the 16th century, was responsible for expounding the ancient and profound Kabbalistic teachings and disseminating them to the broader world. He forged a new system of Kabbalah that is called by his name — the Kabbalah of the Ari — and which has been adopted by most of the study halls that delve into both the conceptual and practical aspects of the mystical tradition.

The unique phenomenon known as the Ari is described by his faithful disciple, Rabbi Chaim Vital, in the introduction to his book, *Etz Chaim*:

> No one ever fathomed this wisdom in all its truth as he did, for he knew all the various facets of *Mishnah, Talmud, Aggadah*, and *Midrash*, as well as the *Pardes* tradition, the Work of Creation, the Work of the Chariot, and the dialogue of the angels. He would see souls as they departed the body and as they ascended every Sabbath eve to the Garden of Eden, and they would reveal to him the secrets of the Torah.

The Ari explained, elaborated upon, arranged, and refined the Kabbalistic tradition that he received from his teachers and from the ancient literature. On that basis, he constructed a new expository system that was arranged together into a series of books referred to as *Shmoneh Shearim*, the "Eight Gates." His theoretical approach is based chiefly upon the Book of the Zohar, but he also introduced many foundational doctrines, such as the secret of the *tzimtzum* (contraction), *shevirat hakelim* (breaking of the vessels), the concept of *partzufim* (sephirotic "personae"), the four *olamot* (worlds), and the connection between the *partzufim* and one's soul. Perhaps his most outstanding contribution was the translation of these abstract ideas into **practical guidelines** through his system of detailed *kavanot* (guided meditations). Further on in this book, I will present those *kavanot* in detail along with personal exercises, in the hope that the taste will remain long after you have finished this book.

THE NATURE AND THE PURPOSE OF THE BOOK

In this book, I aim to construct a mosaic of universally accepted concepts derived from a diverse array of disciplines, including cosmology, physiology, philosophy, and sociology. Through this interdisciplinary approach, I will weave these concepts into the profound Kabbalistic system of the Ari, particularly as it pertains to the act of eating.

What sets this work apart is its innovative fusion of disparate fields of knowledge, seamlessly integrating them into a cohesive and unified philosophical framework.

It is my fervent hope that this synthesis will not only pique curiosity but also foster a deeper comprehension of the concealed processes that underlie the superficial veneer of our daily experiences. While each topic explored within this tapestry could easily spawn an entire volume in its own right, I have opted to provide only the essential information necessary to elucidate the Kabbalistic dynamics inherent in the act of eating, hopefully leaving one with an appetite for more. Through the "Practical Implications" provided at the conclusion of each chapter (and at the end of the book), I aspire to empower readers to refine and elevate their eating habits. For those inclined to delve deeper, the kavanot of the Ari outlined in chapters 6 and 7 beckon, offering the prospect of experiencing the satisfaction and inspiration that many before us have derived from their implementation.

Ultimately, my aspiration is for readers to embark on a transformative journey, enriching their lives through the application of the insights presented herein. May this work serve as a catalyst for personal growth and spiritual awakening, illuminating the path toward a more conscious and enlightened relationship with nourishment and sustenance.

A Personal Testimony

My initial endeavor in this transformative journey was to adopt a mindful approach to eating, beginning with the simple yet significant act of refraining from eating or drinking while standing or walking, opting instead to sit and savor each morsel. This conscious shift in behavior required a deliberate effort, but it laid the groundwork for deeper engagement with the nourishment process.

Subsequently, I took steps to create a conducive environment for mindful dining by removing distractions such as screens or reading material from the dining table. This seemingly minor adjustment demanded a considerable degree of discipline, yet it served to enhance my focus and awareness during meals.

As I progressed along this path, I became attuned to the subtleties of my dining etiquette, including the way I wielded my silverware. Instead of treating utensils as mere tools for consumption, I learned to lay them down on the plate between bites instead of readying them for the next mouthful.

Each of these incremental changes served as preparatory stages, laying the groundwork for the eventual execution of the kavanot of the Ari outlined in Chapter 6—the apex of this transformative journey. These practices, rooted in ancient wisdom and spiritual insight, hold the promise of elevating the act of eating to a sacred ritual, imbuing it with profound significance and spiritual resonance.

It is possible to print on one A4 page of paper all the *kavanot* associated with eating and to perform them within two minutes, but in order to truly understand them, it is necessary to explain the concepts and the mechanisms — and this is my offering.

For Whom is the Book Intended?

Two imaginary readers looked over my shoulders as I was writing this book, and it is chiefly for them that I have intended this book. The first is the religious or traditional Jew who believes in a divinely revealed Torah and sees it as a guide for rectifying the world but possesses merely a fragmentary knowledge and familiarity with the world of Kabbalah. The second reader possesses an inquisitive intellect, familiar with modern science and yet holds ancient mystical wisdom in some regard. This renaissance person may not be convinced of God's existence and is perhaps especially skeptical of a Creator Who is involved with the trivial pursuits of man. On the spectrum between these two extremes, there exists a wide range of beliefs and my hope is to simultaneously appeal to them all, neither offending any particular group, whilst remaining relevant to all. The solution I adopted was to adopt a neutral style, presenting the sources in their own words without imposing my take on the reader. Here are a few examples: Instead of the categorical statement, "The universe is composed of four elements," I wrote "According to the Ari, the universe is composed of four elements." Similarly, I will often make a claim in the form of a suggestion as opposed to a certainty. For example, "It is possible to ascribe the sub-atomic motion to the will of the Infinite One," as opposed to "The Creator generates sub-atomic motion." Rather than try to convince the reader as to Kabbalah's exclusive path to the truth, I simply present the ideas and leave it for you to decide what is feasible and what is not.

ACKNOWLEDGEMENTS

On a personal note, I would like to express my gratitude to Yeshivat Ateret Mordechai for guiding me in the study of Kabbalah, and especially to its head, Rabbi Mordechai Attieh *shlita* and his students, who are my teachers:

From Rabbi Yoel Chakoun I acquired most of my knowledge in the Torah of mysticism (*Sod*), and I am especially grateful to him for the fundamental and didactic way in which he conveys every topic.

From Rabbi Yoel Blumenfeld I merited the pleasure of analyzing the Torah of the Ari in depth, although I am not always successful in understanding the material because of that depth.

From my first exposure to studying with these teachers, I have undergone significant internal changes: my prayer has become a palpable experience, my concentration has sharpened, and routine actions have become enveloped in an aura of holiness. Obviously, this exhilaration is not constant; it waxes and wanes in accordance with the insight, effort, presence of mind, hour, and muse that visit me — and of course, in accordance with a great deal of help from Heaven, the ingredient without which it is impossible to elevate oneself at all.

For forty years I was privileged to study alongside and learn from one of our generation's great Talmudic scholars — Rabbi Nachum Rabinowitz ob"m — starting with my academic studies in London and continuing after I followed him to Israel, where he was appointed as head of Yeshivat Maaleh Adumim. I found in him a rare confluence of qualities — genius alongside humility, creativity alongside conservatism, Talmudic erudition alongside scientific dedication and love of his fellow man. Of him it could truly be said, "Where you find his greatness, you also find his humility."

During my years at Jews College, I was also privileged to revel in the shadow of another spiritual and moral giant — Rabbi Lord Jonathan Sacks ob"m, who was a regular lecturer and dominant figure during my studies. His breadth of knowledge, fluent oratory, and constant passion for finding commonality in place of difference left their mark on me. His image and style of thought are sorely missing in our broken world. How sad to ponder these great figures whom once walked among us, but are no longer.

I am thankful to my dear friend and neighbor, Dr. Ron Wacks, a lecturer in Jewish thought at the Herzog Institute, for guiding me in my studies and encouraging me in the writing of this book.

The English edition you are reading was made possible through the generosity of my dear cousin Dr. Eric Ansell MD. Like his father before him, Eric has dedicated his life to improving the health and wellbeing of his many patients and friends. His fascination with these extraordinary ideas prompted him to enable me to expose them to a wider English speaking audience.

Most of all I owe thanks to my dear wife Judy, who encouraged me in the writing of this book and happily shares in the blessings that my Kabbalistic studies have brought. May it be God's will that we continue witnessing together for years to come both the material and spiritual success of our children Elisheva, Michal, Tzuf, Liora, Chanani, and their beloved families.

The name of this book is based on the verse permitting the preparation of food on Festival days (Exodus 12:16): "No work may be done on them, except for what is to be eaten by every soul (*nefesh*)." The use of the term *nefesh* implies that it is not the body alone but primarily one's soul that is nourished by the food we eat.

Chapter 1

THE SOURCES, AUTHORITY, AND NATURE OF THE KABBALAH

The objective of this chapter is to concisely describe the sources and authority underpinning Kabbalah. I will demonstrate how this esoteric tradition is an legitimate component of the recognized Oral Torah, indistinguishable from classical sources such as the Mishnah, Midrash, or Talmud.

TWIN TRADITIONS

In 2012, a fascinating battle of the minds took place between the great Jewish thinker, Rabbi Lord Jonathan Sacks and the well-known evolutionary biologist and atheist, Prof. Richard Dawkins.[2] At minute 18:00 the following exchange took place:

Dawkins: What is your opinion regarding the story of Adam and Eve in the Garden of Eden? Did it really happen or is it merely symbolic?

Sacks: There is no doubt that the Garden of Eden is a literary allegory.

Dawkins (visibly surprised by that response): I suppose, then, that the splitting of the Red Sea and the giving of the Torah are also myths.

Sacks: Certainly not; those are factual historic events!

Dawkins: You express a shocking lack of consistency regarding what you yourselves define as the "Holy Writings."

Sacks: Richard, the problem is that you are a "Christian atheist". If you were a "Jewish atheist", you wouldn't state things in such a way. A central tenet of

Judaism since its inception is that the Oral Law was given together with the Written Law and guides us as to how the verses are to be interpreted.

Dawkins: But how do you decide what is fact and what is merely folklore?

Sacks: Very simple. In the arsenal of the Oral tradition there is a principle that states: If a Biblical story contradicts confirmed scientific or historical facts, then it is forbidden to read it literally or simplistically; rather, one must interpret it based on the tradition!

These two systems of law — the Written Law and the Oral Law — complement each other. The written word without the benefit of its corresponding spoken word is entirely unrepresentative of Jewish tradition. The lack of understanding and appreciation as to the centrality accorded the Oral Law was the cause of indescribable harm and suffering throughout the millennia. One example among many is the verse (Ex. 21:24), "An eye for an eye," which has been referred to by the uneducated masses as "Old Testament Exact Retaliation."[3] Throughout history, Jews have been accused of maintaining a barbaric system of laws, more severe even then the Hammurabi laws (1800 BC) which established: "If a son should strike his father, his hands shall be cut off, and if a person should strike his friend and knock out his teeth, his teeth shall also be pulled out." The authentic interpretation of "an eye for an eye" is altogether different; the oral tradition, as passed on throughout the ages, explains the written word as an obligation to provide monetary compensation for physical injury[4] — a principled, moral judgement as opposed to a primitive law.

It may even be possible to empirically prove the authenticity and credibility of the oral tradition. A famous insider joke states that between two Jews there will always be at least three opinions. Indeed, Jews in general are an opinionated bunch who can hardly agree on anything, maintaining different customs based on lineage and community. But when it comes to the oral interpretation of the Torah handed down between teacher and disciple there is broad consensus among all groups. For example, the Torah commands Jews to perform the mitzva of *tefillin*[5] *daily* — (Deut. 6:8) "You shall bind them as a sign upon your arm and they shall be an adornment between our eyes." Despite the written command lacking any practical instruction, no Jew throughout history has ever donned *tefillin* that were not square black boxes made of leather containing scriptural parchments. Pairs of *tefillin* nearly 2,000 years old, uncovered in digs at Masada, are identical both inside and out to those in use today. This is the case, as well, regarding the commandment of Succot (Lev. 23:40), "You shall take for yourself…the fruit of a beautiful (hadar) tree." In the same vein, no Jew in the world ever took a pomegranate or a lemon instead of an *etrog* (citron), even though they are also 'beautiful' fruit.).[6]

THE TORAH OF *PESHAT* AND *SOD*

The Oral Law itself is comprised of various interpretive traditions, of which a comprehensive discussion is beyond the scope of this book. One can, however, roughly distinguish between two areas of knowledge — *peshat* ("simple meaning") and *sod* ("esoteric meaning").

The *peshat* tradition includes the straightforward and logical interpretation of Biblical verse, those laws that were conveyed in their entirety and not subject to disagreement (*Halachah l'Moshe miSinai*), and the hermeneutic criteria for interpreting inconclusive scriptural law (the Thirteen Rules for expounding the Torah). The classical rabbinic literature of *Mishnah*, *Beraita*, *Talmud*, and *Halachah* developed on the basis of these *peshat* components.

The *sod* tradition is comprised of metaphysical and esoteric interpretation of both Scripture and historical processes. Such interpretation cannot be grasped through one's senses or through rational or intuitive faculties; rather we receive it through ancient sources and prophetic inspiration. The *sod* tradition evolved in tandem with the *peshat* tradition, but in a much slower and exclusive fashion. The word *kabbalah* literally translates as "receiving" and refers to the unbroken chain of tradition that was transmitted and passed on by successive generations of disciples from their teachers. In contrast to *peshat*, the *sod* tradition is profound, obscure, and abstract. Out of fear that it would not be properly understood by the masses, it was only conveyed to a select few in every generation; hence, to this very day it has eluded popular adoption.

Thus, it is written in the *Mishnah* (*Chagigah* 2a):

> One should not expound upon *Maaseh Breishit* before two [students], or upon *Maaseh Merkavah* before even one [student], unless he be wise and able to understand on his own.

Maaseh Breishit (the "Act of Creation") refers to the natural and scientific laws, such as cosmology, particle science and evolution, that describe our material world. *Maaseh Merkavah* (the "Work of the Chariot") is a prophetic tradition that describes the Divine, metaphysical foundations and dynamics of the physical and spiritual realms.

The term *pardes* is also used in classical sources to refer to the Torah of *Sod*. It originates with the story related in the Talmud (Chagigah 14b) regarding the "four who entered the *pardes* (orchard)," an allegorical reference to the enticing realm of Divine secrets. The word *pardes* first appears in Song of Songs (4:13) where it refers to an exotic garden. Over time it found its way into Persian, Greek, and other languages, while preserving its esoteric allusion to the Garden of Eden — and is highly likely that the word "Paradise" is derived from Pardes. [7] A tradition found in the 12th century Tikkunei Zohar interprets the Hebrew word פרדס (*pardes*) as an acronym for the words פשט (*peshat*, "simple meaning'), רמז (*remez*, "allusion"), דרש (*drash*, "exegesis"), and סוד (*sod*, "esoteric meaning").[8]

For thousands of years until the 19th century, studying the Torah of *Sod* was only permissible under certain conditions: after having first mastered *peshat*,[9] in small study groups[10], by one with the requisite mental capacities, and only from a wise and understanding teacher in possession of the age-old tradition[11]. The term *sod* is **not** to be understood in line with its standard English translation as a "secret," something not to be revealed; rather, the opposite is true. The verse in Psalms (25:14) states: "God's *sod* belongs to those who fear Him, and His covenant is to inform them." *Sod* is something that is concealed and profound but destined to be revealed, not popularly, but to a select audience — those who are seriously in awe of Him.

In earlier generations, there was always the danger of the anthropomorphism that led the ancients to create graven images, as it is written (Deut. 27:15), "Cursed be the man who fashions a graven or molten image." Hence, the aversion to teaching Kabbalah publicly. However, from the 17th century onwards many prominent sages permitted and even encouraged the general population to study Kabbalah. This transformation coincided with modern man's increased capacity to differentiate between the figurative and the abstract. The Chassidic movement contributed to the popularity of Kabbalistic teachings by rendering them in more accessible psycho-spiritual terms. In our own day, the ubiquity of virtual technologies testifies even more to our capacity for simulating realities beyond our immediate reach without confusing them for the here and now. There is, therefore, no fear that the Kabbalistic ideas encountered in the coming chapters will lead to gross substantiations of the divine.

THE SOURCES OF KABBALAH

The sources for the Torah of *Peshat* are well-known and they include *Midrash*, *Mishnah*, *Talmud*, *Rishonim* ("Early Commentators"), and *Acharonim* ("Later Commentators"). The sources for the Torah of *Sod* are less well-known. The following is a partial list of the earliest writings that we have as sources for the oral tradition of Kabbalah:

The **Heichalot** (Palaces) — a general term for around 25 texts that were composed between the 2nd and 5th century CE by Rabbi Shimon Bar Yochai, Rabbi Yishmael, and Rabbi Akiva, as well as additional Talmudic Sages who are mentioned there by name. These texts document the mystical ascents of these Sages through the heavenly realms, or "palaces," and the revelations that they achieved there.

Sefer Yetzirah (The Book of Formation) — a mystical exposition of how the world came into being, focusing on the role played by the ten Sephirot and the twenty-two letters of the Hebrew alphabet. Scholars date its origins to as far back as the 1st century BCE, whereas tradition attributes it to our forefather Abraham.

Sefer HaBahir (The Book of Clarity) — attributed to the 1st century Sage, Rabbi Nechuniah ben HaKanah, it is a Midrashic treatment of the Biblical story of Creation, elaborating on the mystical significance of the Sephirot and Hebrew letters, as inspired by the *Sefer Yetzirah*.

Sefer HaZohar (Book of Splendor) is the most foundational text of Kabbalah. This collection of writings, which was first publicized in 13th century Spain, is traditionally attributed to the 1st century Sage, Rabbi Shimon bar Yochai. It is composed of various texts, many of which are Midrashic in nature, that explore Biblical verse as well as mystical teachings relating to God's Divine nature, the origins of the universe, and traditions received from Moses.

These compositions merited a host of respected commentaries by some of the greatest Torah scholars of the ages, such as Rabbi Saadia Gaon (9th cent.) Ramban (Nachmanides), Raavad (12th cent.), Moshe Kordevero & Ari (16th cent.)and the 18th century Gaon of Vilna. The fact that such esteemed scholars devoted their time and expertise to analyzing and interpreting these compositions serves as a testament to their importance within the realm of Jewish mysticism. Their commentaries not only shed light on the profound teachings contained within these texts but also demonstrate the enduring impact and reverence they command within the broader tradition of Kabbalah.

Through the meticulous examination and explication of these works by generations of scholars, their significance and relevance have been reaffirmed, ensuring their continued influence and study within the realm of Jewish mystical thought.

The Focus of Kabbalah

Many define the wisdom of Kabbalah as the soul of Judaism, while viewing *peshat* as the practical framework upon which Kabbalah is predicated. As the scholar and author Hillel Zeitlin states in his book *Pardes HaKabbalah* (ch. 1), "The ascent and descent of all worlds is contingent upon each and every aspect [of the material world]." Kabbalah maintains that its teachings accurately describe the way in which God's Infinite light devolves into the material realm. By way of study and special *kavanot* ("guided meditations"), the Kabbalist aspires to reveal the Divine spark that is concealed in every aspect of material reality. The relationship between the physical and spiritual realm was established at the time of Creation by a preordained and fixed law, resembling the relationship between the branches and roots of a tree.

According to the teachings of the great 16th century Kabbalist, the Ari (Rabbi Isaac Luria), there is a constant bidirectional flow of spiritual, metaphysical life-force (known as *shefa*) between the branches and the roots. It is this *shefa* which is identified as the most tangible and absolute reality, superseding even physical objects. For the sake of illustration, one who holds a wooden board in his hand feels with certainty that the wood is real, but in truth the wood is only a collection of absolute sub-atomic particles, about 99.9999999999996% of which is empty space, and these particles are the fundamental components of material reality. The analogue would be as follows: a spiritual life-force enveloping itself in a material mantle that stimulates the senses. The mission statement of Kabbalah is to describe the metaphysical constructs that constitute the universe and subsequently to ameliorate and vitalize the world by facilitating a heightened constant flow of life-force (*Shefa*) back and forth between the branches and the roots.

The primary message of this chapter which I wish to emphasize is that the Kabbalistic tradition in general, and the Kabbalah of the Ari specifically, are not new approaches that materialized over time; rather, they are an authentic and ancient link in the chain of teachings that comprise Jewish tradition.

A Great Surprise — Especially for Traditional Jews

The first encounter with the *kavanot* ("guided meditations") of the Ari is likely to astonish the myriads of traditional Jews for whom the term *kavana* (the singular of *kavanot*) hitherto applied to simply concentrating on the words of prayer or the performance of a *mitzvah* and avoid external distractions and wandering of one's thoughts. As we will see further on, avoiding distraction and concentrating are only the preliminary stages necessary before advancing to the main objective, which is guided meditation, coupled together with understanding the processes that the Ari established. This approach constitutes a veritable revolution in outlook for rabbis, scholars, and laymen alike. However, it is only in this prescribed manner that we are able to entice this spiritual life-force down into the world - that being the chief objective of *mitzvah* performance. If this strikes one as astonishing, it is only due the lack of familiarity with the writings of Kabbalah, which often and dismayingly has led to their derision.

Chapter 2

EATING: THE FIRST DIVINE MANDATE

The objective of this chapter is toillustrate the centrality that eating occupies in our lives and to propose that it is actually the primary reason for the creation of the world.

THE CENTRALITY OF EATING IN OUR LIVES

Throughout history and into the present day, food has remained at the core of daily life for all living organisms on Earth. From procurement and preparation to consumption and elimination, the cycle of sustenance is omnipresent. Bacteria thrive on organic carbon and minerals, plants harness gases, water, and light for energy through photosynthesis, and animals consume a variety of nutrients sourced from their environments.

In the Western world, individuals typically consume three substantial meals a day, punctuated by snacks and drinks in between. Research indicates that most people ingest between three to five pounds of food daily, typically within a two-and-a-half-hour window, amounting to approximately 1,760 pounds annually—equivalent to 37 consecutive days of continuous eating.[12] For the sake of comparison, a cow consumes on average 120 pounds of food a day (approximately 44,000 pounds a year), which, surprisingly, equals that of human consumption when taking body weight into consideration.

In the past couple of centuries, an abundance of culinary literature has emerged, ranging from popular works to scientific treatises. However, since 1960, this literary landscape has experienced a significant expansion, driven by advances in nutritional sciences and heightened awareness of animal rights and environmental issues. This proliferation of literature underscores society's near-obsessive preoccupation with matters of food. There exist more than 1,400 known diets, divided into various sub-groups: vegetarian, low-calorie, low-carb, low-fat, detox, faith-based, medical-based, etc.[13] Remarkably, a new eating disorder known as orthorexia has emerged, characterized and psychological well by an obsession with consuming healthy foods. The term "orthorexia" derives from the Greek words "ortho," meaning "correct," and "rexia," meaning "appetite." This condition underscores the extent to which society's fixation on healthy eating has permeated contemporary culture, highlighting the complex relationship between food, health, and psychological well-being.![14]

The culture of food resides at the core of our lives and as such is very difficult to avoid. Restaurants, reality cooking shows, cookbooks and recipe websites, festive meals — all these are just a small part of the gastronomic arc of life, from the hysterical cry of a hungry baby, through the diet crazes that pursue us through adulthood, to the loss of appetite that afflicts both the ageing and ailing population alike.

The subject of nutrition extends beyond individual health to encompass far-reaching global implications, significantly impacting relations between nations. In 2016 alone, nearly a billion people endured malnutrition and hunger, while almost two billion individuals grappled with overweight or obesity. This disparity in nutrition is reflected in a staggering 45-year discrepancy in life expectancy among different nations: a child born in Guinea, West Africa, may expect to live to only 48 years old, while a child born in the affluent principality of Monaco on the French Riviera may anticipate a lifespan of 93 years.[15] Throughout history, some of the most violent conflicts and revolutions have erupted due to disparities in access to food. The profound inequity between the hungry and the well-fed has served as a source of grievous injustice and global tension. Furthermore, approximately 45 million Americans embark on a diet each year, collectively spending a staggering $33 billion on weight loss products. These figures underscore the pervasive impact of nutrition on individual lives, societal dynamics, and geopolitical relations on a global scale.[16] In spite of this, nearly two-thirds of Americans are either overweight or obese.

This brief introduction is intended to highlight the unique status of food and eating, which transcends borders and cultures and is common to all of humanity.

"In the Beginning God Created" — Why?

To embark on our journey into the mysteries of human consumption, we will start by examining the Biblical verses that address the subject of eating. These verses hold relevance not only for those with religious inclinations — and I will explain why. Four and a half billion Christians and Muslims and a sprinkling of a few million Jews, almost half the world, believe that the Torah[17] was given to Moses by God in the 14th century BCE, and view the Bible as a source of authority and divine inspiration. No one holds this to be an absolute truth more than the Jewish people — who are justifiably known as "the people of the Book." Scholars, poets, and philosophers have all drawn inspiration from its text, and even if one accepts the position that the Torah was written much later[18], it is nevertheless the oldest work in existence still being read. Indeed, it has been voted as the world's most influential work.[19] In addition, between 1815 and 1975, five billion copies were printed, a statistic that crowns it as the bestselling book of all time.

The first three chapters of Genesis describe the creation of the world and the living creatures that populated it. An inspection of these chapters reveals the purpose of Creation. A fresh reading of the relevant verses suggests an unexpected approach to this question, directly touching upon the topic under discussion. After concluding the account of Creation, God reveals to man his mission in the nascent universe (Gen. 1:28-30):

> God blessed them and God said to them: "Be fruitful and multiply, fill the earth and subdue it, and **rule over the fish of the sea and the birds of the sky and over every living thing that crawls** on the earth." And God said: "Behold I have given you every **plant that propagates seed** on the face of the earth, and every **tree with fruit that propagates seed**; it shall be yours **for food**. And to every beast of the earth, and to every bird of the sky, and to everything that crawls on the earth, which possesses a living soul — every green vegetation shall be **for food**." And so it was.

The phrase "and God said to them" marks the first time that the Creator addresses Adam and Eve, serving as the source of inspiration for Michelangelo's iconic rendering of God's finger meeting that of man. What monumental lesson does God communicate to the first man and woman at this awesome event ? Surprisingly, not religious rituals or even a moral dictate, rather it is the demand that mankind occupies their rightful position at the head of the food chain by partaking of all the sustenance that the earth has to offer.

Let us take a moment to reflect on the profound implications of the ideas expressed in the preceding paragraph. Indeed, they may signal a paradigm shift in thought and faith, challenging established religious norms and conventions to which we have grown accustomed.

What could possibly be the rationale for such a directive? The urge to eat is an inborn instinct shared with all living things, similar to breathing and just as we are not commanded to breathe, we need not be commanded to eat. Furthermore, eating is a means of survival; what logic is there in turning the means into an end?

The mystery only deepens upon reading the next verse (Gen. 2:9):

> The Lord God made sprout from the earth every tree that was **a delight to behold and good for food**.

The nourishment that the Creator brought forth were attractive to the eye as well as tasty and healthy. What role does aesthetics play here? Human physiology demonstrates that the five senses can initiate hormonal processes that profoundly impact mood. For instance, the power of music to uplift one's spirit showcases how auditory stimulation can trigger positive hormonal responses. Similarly, other sensory stimuli, such as the sight and aroma of food, can elicit emotional and physiological reactions that contribute to overall well-being and mood regulation.

The sense of taste takes effect from the moment that food enters one's mouth and contacts the thousands of taste buds on one's tongue. Each bud contains taste receptors that can detect five basic tastes — bitter, sweet, sour, salty, and savory. In addition, the nasal cavity contains smell receptors that can detect thousands of complex odors.[20] It follows that taste is of paramount importance and is neither physically or spiritually a marginal subject.

Nutritious food that lacks taste is not absorbed in the digestive tract to the same degree as food that possesses the attractive qualities of aroma, color and taste stimulating one's senses.[21] The significance of taste is even discernible in the complaint registered by the newly liberated Israelites as they erroneously recalled in the wilderness what they left behind in the land of their bondage:

"We remember the fish that we ate in Egypt for free, the cucumbers, the melons, the leeks, the onions, and the garlic. But now our lives are bland, there is nothing, nothing to look forward to but the manna." (Num. 11:5-6)

In direct contrast to these mouth-watering reminiscences, the thought of once again consuming the nutritious but bland manna left them despondent. Hence, they cried out (ibid. 21:5), "Our soul is revolted by this abominable bread!"

The way that food is served also affects one's natural desire to eat. These appetite triggers are based in those areas of the brain that are responsible for memory, pleasure, and reward recognition. An imbalance of hormones, such as dopamine, serotonin, and endorphin, can trigger an irrational and unbridled hunger for food.[22]

The nutritional facts noted above indicate that the Creator not only established eating as the reason for creating the world, but also engineered and designed the human body accordingly. His desire that man gain pleasure from eating appears again in His permitting Adam and Eve to partake of all that the Garden had to offer (Gen. 2:16), "From every tree of the Garden you may surely eat." Rather than restrict them to a narrow diet, the Torah offers a rich and varied menu that includes all the elements of Creation that were fit "for you as food."

The Creator prepared a vast table laden with all the diverse abundance that the new world had to offer. This bolsters our claim that eating is not just one aspect of God's purpose in creation, but rather it is a fundamental tier occupying a central place in man's purpose on planet earth. This claim is further strengthened by the first commandments that appear in the second chapter of Genesis (Gen. 2:16-17):

> The Lord God commanded the man, saying: "**From every tree of the Garden you may surely eat.** Yet, from the Tree of Knowledge of Good and Evil, **you may not eat**, for on the day you eat from it, you shall surely die."

Although these are possibly the best-known verses of the Bible to millions of people, especially to the People of the Book, awareness in the field indicates otherwise. I once conducted an experiment, asking over 100 religious high-school students the following question: What was the first commandment that God addressed to man? The vast majority (97%) answered that the first commandment was the prohibition against eating from the Tree of Knowledge. It's reasonable to believe that this result would be no different among other populations, from non-Jews to Yeshiva students. However, it is the wrong answer! **The first directive was that adjoining them to eat and enjoy the fruit of every other tree in the world.** Indeed, the one and only prohibition directed at Adam and Eve in the Garden of Eden was to restrain themselves and avoid eating the fruit of one solitary tree — all the rest was theirs to enjoy!

Let us ponder again the words of that verse:

And He commanded —The first mention of God "commanding," indicating a formal directive, appears here in context of eating.

From every tree of the Garden — The command to eat applies to every tree in the world, apparently without exception.

You may surely eat (*achol tochel*)— Throughout the Bible, the appearance of a reiterated verb, such as *achol tochel*, indicates forcefulness and importance and appears here first in relation to eating.

From the Tree of Knowledge of Good and Evil, you may not eat, for on the day you eat from it, you shall surely die.

The consequences of Adam and Eve deviating from their culinary mandate were catastrophic:

"To the woman He said, 'I will greatly increase your anguish and your gestation; **in pain will you bear children.** Your desire will be for your husband, but he will rule over you.' And to Adam He said, '…Cursed be the earth on your account. With anguish shall you eat from it all the days of your life. Thorns and nettle will it sprout for you, and you will eat the plants of the field. **By the sweat of your brow you will eat bread,** until you return to the earth from which you were taken. For you are dust, and to dust shall you return.'" (Ibid. 3:16-19)

"The Lord God banished him from the Garden of Eden, to work the soil from which he was taken. He drove Adam out…" (ibid. 3:23-24)

As a result of their eating from the Tree of Knowledge, Adam and Eve were driven out of the Garden of Eden and punished with mortality. In no time, the course of mankind underwent a polar reversal, deviating from its original path. Even on the personal level, Adam and Eve were punished terribly: Woman was sentenced to the agony of childbirth — "In pain will you bear children," while man was sentenced to grueling labor — "Thorns and nettle will it sprout for you, and you will eat the plants of the field. By the sweat of your brow you will eat bread." This last decree directly links the sin with the punishment: Before the sin, the earth offered up its yield with minimal effort on the part of man; afterwards, man was forced to labor harshly before the earth produced its yield.

What Is So Special About Eating?

The question begs to be answered: What is so special about eating that it was chosen as the reason for Creation? Were there not more worthy candidates for this distinction? Could it be due to the fact that every living organism, from bacteria and flora to animals and humans, is dependent upon it from its very inception. This urgent need locks man into a constant war for survival, dominating his life even more than the aggressive sex drive. The challenge of gaining control over one's base desires carries with it a great moral potential for mankind. For if one could tame, restrain, and even dignify this feral compulsion, then there is no unseemly trait or disposition that one could not vanquish.

In addition, the way one eats reflects one's inner state and is influenced by one's prevailing mood. One who is frustrated or disappointed seeks out candy or chocolate as a source of comfort; one who is stressed or depressed may lack appetite altogether and need to be reminded or encouraged to eat. It is not the body alone that eats, but the soul of a person as well, as repeatedly seen in the Torah's association of eating with the *nefesh*, or soul (see Lev. 7:18-27).

The Spiritual Harm from Junk Food

In recent generations, junk food has presented an almost insurmountable challenge to our ongoing pursuit of good health through nutritional moderation. In the not-so-distant past, manufactured sweets were rare commodities. The enjoyment of sweetness was usually attained through the consumption of a fruit, such as a pineapple or an orange, which possess a natural mechanism that prevents their over-consumption. Modern science learned to isolate the chemical components of sweetness and saltiness and succeeded in concentrating them into a form that infuses them, almost intravenously, into the body. It is impossible to eat a dozen oranges at once, for fruit naturally satiates; however, when you extract the pleasurable ingredient and circumvent this natural defense, it encourages an unbridled addiction. The consequences of such food engineering are disastrous for entire generations of children who are bound to suffer from obesity, attention disorders, and numerous other illnesses. Salty snacks, commercial baked goods, sausages, sweetened soft drinks, frozen pizzas, chicken and noodle snacks — they all contain sugar and sodium in quantities up to thirty times more than the minimum found in nature. The pancreas and the endocrine system experience shock and are unable to process the insane amounts with which they are assaulted. Addiction to sugar and sodium causes inflammatory response, metabolic collapse, cardiac and vascular disease, cancer, diabetes, Alzheimer's disease, and other disorders.

This type of food becomes a serious problem when it becomes a permanent fixture on the family's table, for the cumulative damage it wreaks is almost irreversible. One need not take the extreme route of banning junk food entirely; it may be consumed in small amounts without causing significant harm, either bodily or spiritually. (See Chapter 9 for more on this topic.)

THE PROHIBITION AGAINST EATING FROM THE TREE OF KNOWLEDGE

The exercise of self-control ought not to be an impossible task, especially in between meals when one is normally not very hungry or thirsty. Ostensibly, that was the case in the Garden of Eden when all its trees were permissible to eat from. The biblical account describes how the serpent promised Eve a radical transformation - if she would only dare nibble from the Tree of Knowledge, as stated in the verse (Gen. 3:5): "On the day you eat from it, your eyes will be opened and you will be like God."

According to the Midrash, the Tree of Knowledge was no different from any of the Garden's other trees, nor did eating from it have the magical power to make one like God.[23] The Tree of Knowledge of Good and Evil is so-called on account of the ultimate outcome linked to it. The prohibition against eating from it was not related to the qualities it might impart. Indeed, prior to their sin, it was known simply as "the tree that was in the center of the Garden" (ibid. 3:3). Rather, its name points to its purpose, which was to teach man the benefit of obeying God's command regardless of the good or evil he sees in the act.[24] It was not only permissible, but a commandment, to derive pleasure from all the Garden had to offer, except for the fruit of one solitary tree. But of course, it was this one arbitrary prohibition that fired man's senses to the point of irrationality, in the spirit of the verse (Proverbs 9:17), "Stolen waters are sweet."[25]

A similar concept can be found regarding other commandments, such as the prohibition against eating pork on which the Talmud comments: "One should not say, 'I have no desire to eat pork,' but rather, 'I certainly have the desire, but what can I do — our Father in Heaven has forbidden me!'"[26] In other words, the reason for avoiding forbidden foods is for no other reason, health or otherwise, than the simple fact that they were forbidden — just that. This arbitrariness naturally makes it harder to control one's impulses and to defer gratification, for one lacks a rational motivation. It is quite probable that such self-control is the basic human goal that the Torah seeks to inculcate in us, as expressed in the prohibition against eating from the Tree of Knowledge

.

THE CONSEQUENCES OF THE PRIMORDIAL SIN OF INCORRECT EATING

We can summarize the severe results of Adam and Eve's sin as the fall from a state of balance to one of imbalance. The account of their sin demonstrates the shift from a state of overwhelming harmony in the Garden of Eden — between Adam and Eve, as well as between them and God — to one of fragmentation, division, and estrangement, characterizing the new order in Creation. We will now detail the consequences that ensued for humanity:

- **Mortality** — From the moment man and woman ate from the Tree of Knowledge, they became mortal. Even if they were to subsequently eat from the Tree of Life, they would not merit eternal life. Their sin precluded that possibility.

- **Estrangement between the sexes** — Originally, Adam and Eve were "as one flesh." After the sin, a rift formed between them. Adam answers

God's query to them, "Where are you?" in the singular (Gen. 3:10): "I was afraid, for I am naked, and so I hid." Indeed, he lays the blame on woman (ibid. 3:12): "The woman who You gave to be with me — she gave me from the tree, and I ate."

- **Estrangement from one's body** — The practical significance of their having eaten from the fruit, subsequently knowing good and evil, can be summed up in one verse (ibid. 3:7): "The eyes of both of them were opened, and they knew that they were naked, and so they stitched a fig leaf and fashioned for themselves sashes." man and woman went from being oblivious to their nakedness to being conscious of it. From a state of freedom and absence of shame they discover the body and seek to conceal it. With the introduction of mortality, man reverts to the raw matter from which he was formed, causing him to ultimately disassociate from his body.

- **Estrangement from the earth** — Instead of working to preserve the naturally fruitful earth of the Garden, as intended when God placed him there "to work it and preserve it" (ibid: 2:15), man was now fated to work the harsh and unyielding earth of "thorns and nettle." In this confrontation with the earth, man is in a position of weakness, for he must inevitably be buried in the earth while it remains eternal: "Until you return to the earth from which you were taken. For you are dust, and to dust shall you return" (ibid. 3:19).

- **Estrangement from God** — Ironically, man and woman hide from God amid the trees of the Garden: "Man and his wife hid from God amid the trees of the Garden" (ibid. 3:8). God seeks man out, calling "Where are you? — testifying to the broken lines of communication between them. man is fearful of God and acts like a hunted beast: "And he said: I heard Your voice in the Garden, and I was afraid" (ibid. 3:10). Out of fear he denies culpability and even implies that God was responsible: "The woman who You gave to be with me — she gave me from the tree, and I ate." Adam and Eve are driven out of the Garden and forbidden from ever returning: "The Lord God banished him from the Garden of Eden...He drove out man and posted to the east of the Garden of Eden the cherubs and the flare of the revolving sword to guard the way to the Tree of Life" (ibid. 3:23-24).

These fateful tragedies were the result of the primordial gastronomic offense committed by the forebears of humanity in the Garden of Eden, causing a breach in the covenant of trust between God and man.

Chapter Summary

A fresh reading of the Bible's first three chapters clearly reveals the centrality of eating as the prime reason for the creation of the universe, even though it is ultimately responsible for the reversal in the fortunes of mankind. The sin associated with eating brought disaster to man, affecting his relations with his mate and his God. This may be a surprising realization for many, perhaps even a bit revolutionary relative to the accepted interpretations, both classical and modern.

Practical Implications

In accordance with the premise that eating is the prime reason for the creation of the universe, we ought to reevaluate our attitude towards food:

- The act of eating should be viewed as a sacred service, on a par with prayer and Sabbath observance - not just as a means of satisfying one's urges and preserving life.

- One should avoid occasional snacking while otherwise distracted, as well as eating while standing, walking, talking, reading, or listening to something that requires concentration.

- One should take care that most of one's daily cuisine be composed of home-cooked, natural foods, keeping to a minimum the consumption of processed or industrial food, especially those containing excess sugar, sodium, or preservatives.

Chapter 3

THE SPIRITUAL STRUCTURE OF THE UNIVERSE AND THE FOOD CHAIN

The objective of this chapter is to present and explain the Kabbalistic structure of the universe, a vital topic to cover in order to understand the spiritual processes that take place when food is metabolically broken down and digested. The key Kabbalistic concept to be discussed is that of Aliyat HaOlamot, the "Ascent of Worlds."

BETWEEN KABBALAH AND PHILOSOPHY

The common denominator shared by Kabbalah and general philosophy is the desire to analyze with depth and exactitude the changes that influence humanity and the world.[27] Both disciplines demand critical thinking, intimate reading of text, and clear, logical analysis — techniques necessary in order to fathom our place in the universe, and we will soon see that there is a significant amount of correspondence between them. The main difference, of course, is Kabbalah's inclusion of the Divine element in its deliberations. The following quote from the Book of the Zohar lays down the conceptual foundation for Kabbalah's foray into the issues here to be discussed. It is familiar to millions of Jews, especially Sephardic Jews who recite it from youth before every prayer:

> Master of all worlds! You created heaven and earth and produced from them the sun, the moon, the stars, and their constellations; and from the earth — trees, grasses, the Garden of Eden, vegetation, animals, birds, fish, and humans; so that through them we may learn about the upper realms and how the upper and lower realms operate and interact.[28]

This last sentence holds a most important message for mankind, a Divine message in a bottle for those who despairingly ask: How can a lowly mortal, who is but a microscopic speck in the universe, ever begin to understand the nature of an infinite Creator? Indeed, the prophet states (Kings I 8:27): "Behold, the heavens and the highest of heavens cannot contain You"; as well as (Isaiah 55:8), "For My thoughts are not your thoughts and your ways are not My ways."

The Zohar's determined reply is that by deeply contemplating the physical, scientific universe one can indeed unlock its metaphysical mysteries; the nature of the spiritual realms can be comprehended by physical beings — "through them we may learn about the upper realms and how the upper and lower realms operate and interact." Just as the preparation of a gourmet meal demands a prior familiarity with its ingredients and their properties, so does the proper understanding of eating and its mystical significance demand a prior familiarity with its metaphysical components and their hierarchic arrangement.

DEFINING THE ELEMENTS AND DOMAINS OF CREATION

From the Zohar's above list of created entities, the Ari identified four elements and four domains which account for every material entity:

> Fire, Air, Water, and Earth are the four elements that support life, but which exist as fixed and static components.

> Inanimate, Vegetable, Animal, and Human are the dynamic and variable domains into which all created things fall.

With regard to the static elements, the Zohar states as follows:[29]

> Come see: Fire, Air, Water, and Earth ... which are the elements of the Lower World ... are integrated and bonded one with the other and there is no separation between them.

With regard to the dynamic domains, the Ari taught:[30]

> Behold, the World of Action (i.e. the physical) is composed of four domains, namely from the lowest to the highest: *Domem* (Inanimate), *Tzomeach* (Vegetable), *Chai* (Animal), and *Medaber*[31] (Human).

The above classifications are ancient in origin and apparently were first articulated in the 5th century BCE by the Greek philosopher Empedocles and later adopted by Aristotle. Similar classifications explaining the nature and complexity of matter appear in other ancient cultures such as those of Persia, Babylonia, Japan, Tibet and India.[32] Kabbalah recognized their fundamental truths and adopted them for its own purposes.

It should be noted that Zohar's above reference to the "Lower World" signifies much more than just planet Earth on which we live, but rather includes the entire universe — that is, space-time, the stars and planets, the galaxies, all forms of matter or energy and all the various spiritual domains. There is broad agreement as to the approximate size of the visible universe: tens of billions of light-years. Its dominant component is mineral (*Domem*), especially the elements of hydrogen and helium that together comprise 99.9% of the universe. Virtually all the heavy elements were formed in the stars, afterwards propagating through space as gas and dust. Hence, the cosmologist Carl Sagan's immortal words: "We are all made of stardust."[33]

It is also important to note the essential difference between the elements: Fire, Air, Water, and Earth are **fixed in nature and can never spontaneously metamorphose**. Fire cannot spontaneously become water just as air cannot morph into earth. In contrast, the diverse and dynamic representatives of the mineral, vegetable, animal, and human domains can naturally **shed one form and assume another**, blending and combining with each other, as we will see further on. Ingestion and digestion are perhaps ultimate prototypes of naturally occurring dynamic processes, whereby the food that we take in from all four of these domains is metabolized. It is thus logical that these domains should serve as the basis for the Kabbalistic *kavanot* of eating. The four eternally fixed elements of Fire, Air, Water, and Earth are less applicable to these organic processes and thus are virtually absent from the Ari's writings. From here on in, I too will relate only to these four domains of Creation, known collectively by the acronym *datzcham* (see glossary).

DOMEM, TZOMEACH, CHAI, AND MEDABER

Regarding these domains, the Ari writes:

Behold, the World of Action (i.e. the physical) is composed of four domains and they are, from the lowest to the highest: *Domem* (Mineral),

Tzomeach (Vegetable), *Chai* (Animal), and *Medaber* (Human). There is no doubt that even the mineral domain — earth, rocks, metals, and so forth — must possess a spiritual life-force that sustains it, a supernal *mazal* (medium of influence) that cultivates and preserves it. The vegetable domain possesses an even greater spiritual life-force than the mineral, insofar as it has the ability to grow and to nourish and to engender new growth. Animals are superior to vegetables, and humans occupy the highest of all four domains.[34]

In the short excerpt above, the Ari establishes the basic principle that flows throughout all his writings: At the root of all four physical domains there inheres a **spiritual life-force** (often called their *mazal*) which is the ultimate reason for their existence.[35] The life-force of each domain permeates those domains that are above it in the food chain, as the Ari explains in *Etz Chayim* (50:2):

The *Domem* is exclusively *Domem* both in body and soul. The *Tzomeach* possesses a portion of the *Domem*'s body and soul, in addition to its own body and soul. Hence, the *Tzomeach* supersedes the *Domem*, which it incorporates. Subsequently, the *Chai* incorporates the body and soul of both the *Domem* and the *Tzomeach*, in addition to possessing its own body and soul. Finally, man (the *Medaber*) incorporates the body and soul of all three — *Domem*, *Tzomeach*, and *Chai* — in addition to possessing his own soul **which is composed of them all.**

The Ladder of Being - Naturae Scala

From the 18th century on, science ceased relating to the four classical elements Fire, Air, Water, and Earth as the four unique material bases of the physical world. that we perceive via our senses. They were replaced by the chemical elements of the periodic table, which were classified by their atomic numbers. This switch does not invalidate the relevance of the Kabbalistic teachings, for Kabbalah deals in **value-based** criteria rather than scientific criteria and these offer two very different perspectives. According to classical criteria, all created beings can be ranked in accordance with their spiritual qualities, with man — the crown of Creation — at the top of the chain.

Some two thousand years before the Ari, Aristotle, in his *Historia Animalium* (History of Animals),[36] formulated the well-known thesis referred to in Latin as *Naturae Scala*, "The Ladder of Being."[37] According to this thesis, which is also referred to as the Great Chain of Being, all created beings can be ranked according to their degree of spiritual perfection as well as their ability to move, feel, and propagate[38]. Professor Loren Eisley, an American anthropologist, argues that the principle lying at the basis of this thesis is the ***immutability*** of Creation, such that the place occupied by each being on the cosmic ladder is constant, incapable of either ascending or descending[39]. According to this principle, a *Domem* being, such as a rock, could never become a *Tzomeach*, such as a flower, in the same way as a frog could never become a prince, despite all those fairytales we were told as children.

THE ASCENT OF WORLDS

The Kabbalah of the Ari posits a doctrine diametrically opposed to the inflexible *Naturae Scala*, known as *Aliyat HaOlamot*, the "Ascent of Worlds." It should be noted that the Ascent of Worlds is the **core principle** behind the Kabbalistic concept of *Tikkun Olam*, "cosmic restoration." This concept is derived from the ancient *Aleinu* prayer wherein we beseech God that He rid the earth of idolatry "and restore the world through the Almighty's Kingship."[40]

What is the Ascent of Worlds? In broad terms, it occurs when a lower spiritual entity ascends the ladder of Creation and upgrades itself to a higher rung. An example of this is when the soul of a *Tzomeach* ascends to the level of a *Chai* or *Medaber*. Worlds can ascend in this way by means of two possible tracks:

» By way of free-willed human initiative; in particular, the *kavanot* of the Ari.

» Through an automatic, time-based process, independent of human intervention.

This latter, time-based track derives its power from the inherent sanctity built into Creation, such as the Sabbaths and Festivals which occur automatically with the passage of time and do not depend on individual human action. By Divine design, the prayers and festive meals eaten on Sabbaths and Festivals automatically elevate the eater on to a higher plane. The quality of ascent achieved through the prior track — voluntary human action, such as praying or giving charity — depends on two factors: 1) the source of the act (e.g. one of the torah commandments or merely rabbinical) 2) the cognitive and spiritual purity of the one executing it. This book deals exclusively with this human initiated form of ascent.

It is important to emphasize the following principle embodied within the Ari's doctrine of 'Ascent of Worlds': Whenever a spiritual entity from one domain is elevated to a higher domain by way of ascending the food chain, **the essential identity of that spirit remains present and immutable.** Rather, it retains its original nature which is then enhanced by virtue of the ascent. For instance, when one consumes the meat of an animal that has fed on vegetation which is fortified with minerals, the unique life-forces associated with each of those domains are incorporated into the person who consumes them. While each domain is refined and purified in the course of its ascent, it never loses its original identity. This can be illustrated by way of a parable: an aspiring high-school student who is accepted into a university and ascends the academic ladder, from bachelors to masters to doctorate and eventually professorship. The professor is an upgraded version of that aspiring high school student whose essential character remains the same, while being edified at the various stages of his or her career.

The Kabbalistic approach argues that shifts in the hierarchy are not only permissible and possible but essential and desirable in order to achieve the goal of *Tikkun Olam*. This thesis is reinforced through the following quote of the Ari regarding the nature of the *tikkun* (restoration) achieved when man elevates the four domains:

> Man possesses the power and ability to refine, rejuvenate, and elevate all four domains to a higher level than the one they originally occupied. [For example,] it is possible to refine the *Domem* and restore **all of its components**, and thereby raise it to successively higher levels until it reaches the uppermost rung. By consuming that particular soul domain, we rarify its power and boost the goodness and nourishment it inherently possesses; while its refuse, impurities, and toxins are refined by way of elimination through the bowel.[41]

The Ari hereby establishes that it is in man's power to refine (*birur*) and restore (*tikkun*) the constituent elements of the four domains and thereby elevate them to the "uppermost rung." (The concepts of *birur* and *tikkun* will be further explained in Chapter 5.) This power is unique to humans and challenges us to realize our destiny by taking advantage of this special capacity.

Pay attention to the Ari's exacting language when he describes the ascent of each domain **itself** ("all of its components") from a lower to a higher rung without those components having to undergo any kind of internal transformation. The ultimate result is that the life-force of the *Domem* (for example, water or earth) rises and combines with that of the *Tzomeach* (e.g. grass) which is then consumed by the *Chai* (e.g. cattle) so that the spiritual essence of all three domains combines into one. The pinnacle is then achieved when the *Medaber* (a human) consumes the *Chai* while practicing the Kabbalistic *kavanot*. All throughout the process, the unique and independent character of each domain is preserved.[42]

CHAPTER SUMMARY

Creation divides into four domains — *Domem, Tzomeach, Chai,* and *Medaber* (Mineral, Vegetable, Animal, and Human) — in that hierarchic order. Underpinning each domain, there exists a spiritual life-force. It is this spiritual hierarchy that characterizes and defines the Ladder of Being, with man, the crown of Creation, occupying its highest rung.

Philosophers viewed this Ladder as static and fixed, with no possibility of moving between rungs. In contrast, the Ari promoted the idea of *Aliyat HaOlamot*, the Ascent of Worlds. Every element in Creation is capable of, and intended to, elevate itself to a higher rung.

PRACTICAL IMPLICATIONS

- Humans are the pinnacle of creation and as such we should express gratitude for the privilege of being the crown of Creation.

- One should pay attention to the type of food one ingests so as to determine which category it belongs to.

- One should bear in mind the simple meditation that eating elevates each individual domain from which the food derives to the level of *Medaber*, that of human beings who were blessed to have been created in the "image of God."

Chapter 4

THE SECRET OF GROWTH
AND DEVELOPMENT

The objective of this chapter is to explain the reason for physical growth as rooted in the structure of the four domains discussed in the previous chapter.

THE ASCENT OF WORLDS AS THE BASIS FOR GROWTH

Nothing warms the heart of a Jewish mother more than the sight of well-fed, sated children. Hence the familiar tribal refrain, even from the cradle, that they must finish everything on their plate! The incontestable fact is that the more we eat, the more we grow. Still, few know how food actually nourishes and strengthens the body. I will now summarize how this vital and wondrous system functions physiologically, and then demonstrate how it mimics and corresponds to the metaphysical mechanism step by step.

As we saw in Chapter 3, a foundational principle throughout Kabbalah is that every phenomenon in the material world occurs on two parallel planes: the physical and metaphysical, or the material and the spiritual. The phenomenon of growth is a classic example of this principle at work. I will open with the unique explanation offered by Kabbalah for why growth takes place and then follow with a summary of the biological reason, thereby allowing us to appreciate the points of concurrence between these two processes.

THE KABBALISTIC EXPLANATION OF GROWTH

Classical philosophy ascribes a basic duality to all existence, between the essence ("whatness") of a thing called Form (*eidos* in Greek, translated as "idea") and the stuff that the thing is made of, which is called Matter. This approach is referred to as hylomorphism.[43] The combination of matter and form confers substance to the object itself ("being"), whilst the myriad interactions the souls of the four domains bears responsibility for the changes that occur within it. In place of the term Form, Kabbalah employs the term *nefesh* (pl. *nefashot*) or soul and claims that the *nefesh* of a *Domem (inanimate)* object (e.g. a rock) is what confers upon it the qualities of passivity and solidity. Alternatively, the *nefesh* of a *Tzomeach (vegetative)* object (e.g. wheat) is what gives it its physical form and nutritional capacity. It goes without saying that man's build and physiology are also dictated by his *nefesh*, rather than the other way around.

The *nefashot* of these four domains are an integral part of their physical counterparts, thereby producing the variety of entities that exist in the earth's ecological system, from rocks to plants to animals and eventually humans. Scientists estimate that there are more than nine million types of plants and animals.[44] According to Kabbalah, each category has a unique *nefesh* that sustains and distinguishes it. When someone eats meat and vegetables and drinks water, the *nefashot* that reside within the *Chai* (meat), *Tzomeach* (vegetable), and *Domem* (water) are released from their respective "shells," combining inside the one who eats.

The key to understanding this process is the central Kabbalistic doctrine of *Aliyat HaOlamot* "The Ascent of Worlds" that is laid forth by the Ari in the book *Etz Chayim* (50:2). Here is an excerpt, modified slightly for ease of understanding:

> When a *Tzomeach* (such as a grass) is nourished by a *Domem* (such as soil, water, or salt), the *nefesh* of the *Tzomeach* **joins** the *nefesh* of the *Domem* and **grows**, thus **surpassing** the *Domem*. When a *Chai* (such as a cow) subsequently eats the *Tzomeach*, it incorporates the body and *nefesh* of both the *Tzomeach* and *Domem* while adding its own body and *nefesh* to the mix. It, too, grows as a result and surpasses its predecessors. Finally, when the *Medaber* (a human) eats and is nourished by the *Chai*, he **becomes connected** with the body and *nefesh* of the *Chai*, which contains the body and *nefesh* of the *Tzomeach* and *Domem*. He then grows too, and having merged his own *nefesh* with those of his antecedents, achieves the highest level of all.

Notice the words in bold: **join, grow, surpass, connect.** As our food metabolizes and integrates itself into the body, the *nefesh* of each domain ascends the Ladder of Being, ultimately blending into a greater spiritual entity. **Their ascent and integration are the factors responsible for growth in the physical world.** Hence, the Kabbalistic significance attached to the verse (Deut. 8:3): "Not by bread alone does man live, rather it is by what issues from God's mouth that man lives." Physical bread sustains life only in partnership with its spiritual essence (the issue of God's mouth), invested in it by the Creator.[45]

THE SIMPLE AND KABBALISTIC INTERPRETATION OF *BOREI NEFASHOT*

This thesis figures nicely in the wording of the ancient (1st century) and unusual blessing known as *Borei Nefashot*, recited by millions of Jews after consuming foods, such as meat or dairy produce, that are not derived from the family of wheat crops. The blessing reads as follows:

> Blessed are You, God our Lord, King of the Universe, Who **creates numerous souls (*borei nefashot*)** together with all that they lack, upon all that You have created with which to sustain the soul of every living thing. Blessed is the Life-source of all worlds.

The simple meaning of this curious blessing, as proposed by the 13th century classical legal work *Baal HaTurim*, is that God created numerous and varied creatures and provided them with all their vital nutritional requirements ("all that they lack"). In addition, He has created many edibles that are not essential for maintaining life but whose purpose is to delight ("to vitalize every living thing").[46]

The Ari's explanation of this blessing, however, is very different:

> The *Borei Nefashot* after-blessing alludes to the *tikkun*, "restoration," that is afforded the ***nefashot*, "souls"** of the many vegetative and animal foods. man praises the One who creates the many [and distinct] souls of the nutrition which His creatures need in order to vitalize every living thing — and by dint of this blessing, the *tikkun* takes place [leading to the fitting conclusion] "Blessed is the Life-source of all worlds." A tremendous accomplishment is achieved by the one who recites this blessing in the proscribed manner.[47]

This is the clarification of these words of the Ari:

Blessed are You, O God, Who rules over the universe ("King of the Universe"), Who created the four types of souls (*nefashot*) — *Domem, Tzomeach, Chai,* and *Medaber;* and when they are supplemented to and combined with the underlying *nefashot* residing within the person who eats ("in addition to all that You have created"), the necessary and desired consequence is the vitalization of all creatures ("to vitalize every living thing") and even the upper worlds themselves (Life-force of all worlds").

Just as the proliferation and intertwining of souls ("in addition") brings life, so too does the breakdown and fragmentation ("what they lack") of these souls cause demise. An increase in spirituality translates into more vitality and presence, as opposed to a waning spirituality that translates into cessation and death.

According to the Ari's explanation, it is by way of eating and blessing that one joins together the souls that inhere in the various types of food, thereby vitalizing both the one who recites the blessing and the physical and spiritual worlds that he occupies.

A small but significant difference between the simple and Kabbalistic interpretation of the blessing relates to how we parse its words — note the placing of the bold comma in each of the versions::

According to the simple (*pshat*) interpretation, it reads:

"Blessed is He Who creates numerous living things, alongside all the nutrition that they [would otherwise] lack." and in Hebrew –

Baruch atah ado-nai elo-hai-nu melech haolam, borei nefashot, rabot v'chesronan, al kol ma she'barata, l'hachayot bahem nefesh kol chai, baruch chei ha'olamim.

According to the Kabbalistic interpretation, it reads:

"Blessed is He Who creates the souls, and enables them to combine, increase and grow or conversely fragment, decrease and wane." and in Hebrew –

Baruch atah ado-nai elo-hai-nu melech haolam, borei nefashot rabot, v'chesronan, al kol ma she'barata, l'hachayot bahem nefesh kol chai, baruch chei ha'olamim.

THE SPIRITUAL REASON FOR WASTE ELIMINATION

The spiritual component of the four domains, what we have referred to as their *nefesh* (pl. *nefashot*), is itself made up of various sub-elements, which are called *klipot*, "shells," *sigim*, "impurities or shards," and *nitzotzot*, "sparks" (see Chapter 5 p. 55). According to the tenet of *Aliyat HaOlamot* (the "Ascent of Worlds") the *nefashot* of the four domains are purified, both quantitatively and qualitatively, during the process of being eaten. "Quantitatively," since only the portion of food that is organically and spiritually healthy is elevated whilst the dregs are expelled; "qualitatively," since only the life-giving soul elements are passed up the chain. The *nefesh* that has been elevated no longer "tolerates" the inferior spiritual elements that it contained prior to being purified, and so they are expelled as waste. What remains in the body after this elimination is the pure and unadulterated *nefesh* which is assimilated into one's own flesh while its rejected elements become sewage.

This is how the Ari in *Etz Chaim* (50:2) describes the above process:

> Man's *nefesh behamit*, "animal soul", is crafted from a similar place as the *nefesh* of lower animals. When man nourishes himself, the *nefesh* of the *Domem* he eats is incorporated into his own *Domem*, which is superior to it, and they grow together. Afterwards, when he eats from the *Tzomeach*, its *nefesh* joins with its superior counterpart in man and grows with it. It is only the body of the *Tzomeach* that is expelled as residue. Similarly, when he eats from an animal, the waste is expelled and the *nefesh behamit* of the animal is joined with man's own superior *nefesh behamit*, and then grows together with it. This is the secret of bodily nutrition, for the *nefesh behamit* of man is still referred to as his body and not his soul.

The Ari reveals in this excerpt a most important idea: **Spiritual activity triggers physiological processes of growth, both quantitative and qualitative, including even the elimination of waste from the body.** Given that every physical entity possesses a spiritual root, the growth and development of all four material domains is dependent upon their spiritual development. In other words, it is not the physical matter in food that advances bodily growth, but **the spiritual components of that food** that are elevated and bring about the desired outcome of healthy growth and development.

The fact that human life is dependent upon nourishment derived from the three lower domains necessitates a spiritual mechanism for sifting the desirable from the undesirable and the superior from the inferior. This spiritual *birur*, or "sifting and extraction," sparks the biological process whereby food is broken down and refined and the residue eliminated from the body.

I will now present the scientific explanation of digestion that faithfully mirrors this Kabbalistic process of *birur*.[48]

THE SCIENTIFIC PROCESS OF *BIRUR*

The development of life in general, and the digestive process in particular, are wondrous and fascinating biological phenomena. The mechanical breakdown of food begins in the mouth with mastication of the food by the teeth and continues in the stomach which churns the food like a cement mixer. The key phase of the process takes place in the intestines where the desirable nutrients are absorbed and the residue passed into the colon for elimination.

Chemical breakdown begins with salivary enzymes and intensifies in the stomach where strong gastric juices convert proteins and carbohydrates into amino acids that break down starch (poly-saccharides) into simpler sugars (di-saccharides). The main part of digestion takes place in the small intestines, with the help of bile, produced by the liver for the breakdown of lipids, and pancreatic juices. At this point, there is no similarity between the food we just consumed and the sticky, grey mass that continues its 20-foot journey through the small and large intestines. The intestines serve a dual function: continued breakdown of the food mass into its simplest constituents and absorption of nutrients into the bloodstream through the intestinal wall. These nutrients convert into the smallest molecules known to us — proteins, carbohydrates, and fats — and are carried by the blood into every cell of our body.

After the breakdown of food into its basic molecular components, the true magic reveals itself in all its wonderful glory, and that is the conversion of proteins, carbohydrates, and fats into the energy that nourishes our cells. This physiological process, which is well known and even taught in schools, is called "cellular respiration" and occurs in **every one** of the 30 trillion cells that comprise our body. This process creates stores of available energy in two stages that are referred to as glycolysis ("sugar-splitting") and Krebs cycle.[49] These are metabolic pathways that enable the production of energy in every living organism. Organic compounds, mainly carbohydrates, break down and release energy that results in the formation of a compound called ATP (adenosine triphosphate), referred to as the "energy currency" of all life.[50]

The Synthesis Between the Metaphysical and the Scientific

This brief description of the digestive process was intended to illustrate the huge difference between the food we eat for lunch and the molecular elements that are absorbed in our body's tissues and cells a short time afterwards. In Chapter 10, I suggest that these sub-atomic particles are the closest physical interplay between the analogue to the *nefesh* of the food we eat. It is not the chemical ATP that is responsible for cellular proliferation in the eater's body, but the metaphysical *nefashot*. Indeed, it is the spiritual *nefesh* that drives the chemical process that causes the Kreb's cycle to occur in tandem with the metaphysical process.

The Ari defines the process as one of spiritual elevation and the sanctification of matter, intentionally using words like "restoration," "elevation," and "growth" in order to underscore the upward flow of forces. This upward flow is responsible for physical growth along with a metaphysical ascent in the food chain. In the process of eating, the *Domem* rises to the level of *Tzomeach*, just as the *Tzomeach* rises to the level of *Chai* and the *Chai* to the level of *Medaber*. These ascents are not necessarily incremental, but can skip a step or two; one may partake of *Domem* (e.g. water) and *Tzomeach* (e.g. vegetables) but then jump over the *Chai* and go straight to *Medaber*.

For Humans Only

The capacity for this kind of metaphysical food-based *birur* (purification or refinement) is found solely in humans, by virtue of their being created "in God's image." It occurs as soon as one partakes of food while simultaneously practicing the prescribed meditations that we will introduce in detail in Chapter 6. This is not to say that without these Kabbalistic meditations normal physiological function is arrested; rather, it is driven by nature, in the same way as the lower tiers of the food chain ascend without our intending it thus. The difference between a process directed by nature and one directed by God will be addressed later (Outer *Shefa* and Inner *Shefa*) — for it is not only humans who are able to "select" what is beneficial to them in the process of eating, but the *Tzomeach* and *Chai* as well when consuming their nutrition, as pointed out by the Ari:

At first the *Domem* ascends to the level of *Tzomeach* by enclothing itself in that which sprouts from the earth. Afterwards, the *Tzomeach* is consumed by grass-eating animals and thus ascends to the level of *Chai*.[51]

There is however an immense difference between the automatic, unintentional ascent that the inanimate and vegetable soul undergoes immediately upon consumption by an animal, as opposed to the contemplated elevation that is initiated by a thinking human. The Creator established a natural order in which the grass that sprouts from the earth and is nourished by its minerals causes the *nefesh* of the *Domem* to enclothe itself in the *Tzomeach*, just as the animals that graze on that grass cause the *nefesh* of the *Tzomeach* to envelope itself in the *Chai* — all without any conscious intent. This idea is alluded to in the in the words of the Ari:[52] "By eating something, **we extract** the power of its goodness."

The Elimination of Waste

It was suggested earlier that the **metaphysical** *birur* that transpires as a result of eating constitutes the catalyst for the parallel **physiological** *birur* that occurs during digestion. Hence, the Ari even references it ("the bowel's waste") at the conclusion of his above description.

Given that the elimination of human waste corresponds to the conclusion of the above metaphysical process, our Sages instituted a special blessing to be said after every visit to the toilet. Granting spiritual significance to a bodily function considered base and distasteful must surely provoke wonderment, if not total bewilderment. To the best of my knowledge there is no parallel for this in any other culture.

This is the wording of the *Asher Yatzar* blessing:

Blessed are You, God our Lord, King of the universe, Who formed (*asher yatzar*) man with wisdom, and created within him many orifices and cavities. It is manifest and known before the Throne of Your Glory that if one of them should become punctured, or one of them should become blocked, it would be impossible to survive for even one hour. Blessed are You, O God, Who heals all flesh and acts wondrously.

Barukh attah Adonai, Eloheinu melekh haOlam, asher yatzar et haadam b'chokhmah, u'vara vo n'kavim n'kavim chalulim chalulim. Galu'i v'yaduah lifnei kisei k'vodekha, she'im yifateach echad meihem, o yisatem echad meihem, ee efshar l'hit'kayem v'la'amod l'fanekha afilo sha'ah echat. Barukh attah Adonai, rofei khol basar oomaf'li la'asot.

In the work *Shaar HaKavanot* (*Drush Birkat HaShachar*), the Ari explains the sublime intent hidden in this blessing. I will cite the thrust of his explanation in order to illustrate how every physiological function of our digestive system reflects a parallel metaphysical process.

An Interpretation of the *Asher Yatzar* Blessing

"Who formed (*yatzar*) man" — This special blessing is intended to restore man in the World of Formation (*yetzirah*)[52]. Hence, the blessing itself contains 45 words, the *gematria* (numerical value) of the word *adam*, "Man." The *chochmah*, "wisdom," with which God formed man alludes to the World of Creation (*beriah*). Hence, "He created (*bara*) within him many orifices and cavities." This refers not only to the excretory orifices, but also to the seven openings in the human head that allow the flow of spiritual life-force (*shefa*): two eyes, two ears, two nostrils, and the mouth. If these orifices should become blocked, "it would be impossible to survive for even one hour."

The conclusion of the blessing, "Blessed are You, O God, Who heals all flesh and acts wondrously," can be interpreted as alluding to the Kabbalistic concept of *hamtakat dinim*, the "sweetening of harsh judgements." *Dinim*, "judgements," are those restrictive forces in our lives that are often viewed negatively. They actually have their source in the Divine *sephirah* of *Gevurah*, "Might," which itself is a force of good, as it confines God's boundless benevolence (*chesed*) to the viable boundaries of the created realm, thus allowing it to thrive. Within the created realm, those boundaries may be experienced as restrictive and bitter *dinim*. When we "sweeten" those *dinim*, we reveal the source of good from which they derive, thereby neutralizing their bitterness and endowing them with a sweet taste.

By emphasizing the way in which the human body is designed to maintain just the right equilibrium between God's boundless *shefa* and the limits of its own materiality, the *Asher Yatzar* blessing highlights the wondrous process of *hamtakat hadinim*. Hence, the blessing concludes, "Blessed are You, O God, Who heals all flesh and acts wondrously." The word for "wonder" — *peleh*[53] — refers in Kabbalah to the supernal conduit that conveys God's *shefa* from the uppermost World of Emanation (*atzilut*) — which contains His "Throne of Glory" referred to earlier in the blessing — to our own world, endowing us with the ability to "sweeten His judgements."

According to the Ari, the engine driving every physical action in the universe — from the motion of the galaxies to the movement of our bowels — is the metaphysical *nefesh* that directs it. All the laws of nature that science, in its profound wisdom, articulates in such detail, are just the last link in the chain of *shefa* that devolves from God's Infinite Being, through the intervening spiritual realms, until it reveals itself in our own material world.

Even so it is important to emphasis that the Ari is not writing a biological text when he describes the breakdown of foods into their **spiritual** components,[54] the elevation of their goodly elements, and the purging of their **spiritual** dross. The functioning of the digestive system, in general, mimics the metaphysical *birur* just described, but is not intended to mirror the anatomical mechanism in every detail.

Outer *Shefa* and Inner *Shefa*

Aside from a small cohort of Kabbalistically enlightened people who are familiar with these metaphysical dynamics and employ the Ari's meditations in their own eating, the rest of the world's population partakes of its food with characteristic indifference. Unsurprisingly, no physiological difference has ever been observed in their respective digestive functions. That being the case, one may ask, what is the advantage to employing these meditations?

I will provide three possible answers:

- There is indeed an expectation that one who eats (with moderation) and performs the Ari's meditations will achieve a healthier and more wholesome body than someone who eats without regard to what, when, how much, or in what frame of mind he eats.

- Spiritual processes accrue in influence over time and their results are only felt after a long course of persistent effort.

- The most accurate answer however relates to the distinction between two types of *shefa* through which God sustains His world: "External" (*chitzoni*) *shefa*, which is associated with the laws of nature and operates independent of our own behavior and actions; and "Inner" (*pnimi*) *shefa*, which is contingent upon our own service and infuses our world with additional spiritual force, **privileging especially the one who meditates.**

Such an individual is edified and rewarded spiritually through the inner *shefa* generated by one's own actions rather than by the autonomous laws of nature. At times the advantages incurred by those who employ the Ari's meditations are obvious to all, while at other times they accrue to one's benefit over time like a long-term investment.[55]

CHAPTER SUMMARY

In this chapter, I elaborated on the profound connection between the spiritual and the physiological. I explained how the very essence for one's growth and development reside in the coupling and synthesis of the *nefashot* that inhere in the four domains of Creation achieved through the meditative act of eating. At the root of each domain there exists a spiritual force — a *nefesh* — that sustains and directs it, and upon which all growth and physical development is dependent. The process of integrating these various *nefashot* (pl. nefesh) during the act of eating translates directly into physiological function.

PRACTICAL IMPLICATIONS

- One should pay attention to the external aspects of food — its color, taste, and texture because these are the physical expressions of its inner spiritual essence.

- Whilst eating, one should have in mind to integrate the unique spiritual aspect of each class of food (inanimate, vegetable, or animal) and to absorb it into one's organs and limbs:

  » When drinking water or consuming salt, one should have in mind to elevate the *nefesh* of the *Domem* (including that of the soil) and upgrade it to the level of *Domem* that especially exists in every human.

  » When eating fruits or vegetables, one should have in mind to elevate the *nefesh* of the *Tzomeach* and to upgrade it to the level of *Tzomeach* that especially exists in every human.

  » When eating fish, fowl or meat, one should have in mind to elevate the *nefesh* of the *Chai* and to upgrade it to the level of *Chai* that especially exists in every human.

Chapter 5

THE FOUNDATIONAL PRINCIPLES
OF *SHEVIRAH* (SHATTERING)
AND *TIKKUN* (RESTORATION)

The purpose of this chapter is to elaborate on several important Kabbalistic concepts, such as partzufim (personae), nitzotzot (sparks), and klipot (shells). This elaboration is necessary in order to fully grasp the Ari's philosophy on the topic of eating. The content of the next two chapters is drawn from the Ari's teachings in the foundational Kabbalistic works, Etz Chaim and Otzrot Chaim.

Caveat
Even though the material covered in this chapter is extremely pertinent, the reader who wishes to remain solely within the topic of eating should feel free to skip this chapter and return to it at a later opportunity.

THE COSMOLOGICAL VIEW

Physicists and cosmologists are both united in their opinion that we are in possession of sufficient reliable data to provide an exact description as to the state of the universe at any given moment from 10^{-36} seconds after the Big Bang. Despite this impressive achievement, science will **never** be able to definitely describe what occurred prior to the beginning of creation. According to cosmologist Dr. Steven Hawking, the reason for this inherent limitation is due to the unique conditions that prevailed prior to the Big Bang, referred to as the "gravitational singularities."[56] At that juncture the entire universe was concentrated inside an infinitesimally small point, such that the laws of nature as we know them did not exist, precluding measurement of any sort. The nature of existence was enveloped in obscurity, and like Aristotle, Hawking proposed that the universe had no beginning; although unlike him, Hawking prophesied its demis.[57]

THE KABBALISTIC VIEW

In contrast to the scientific stance, the Kabbalah of the Ari sets forth an unequivocal position regarding what existed prior to these singularities:

> At the very beginning, all of Being manifested itself as a [boundless] "Uniform Light" (*or pashut*) known as *Ein-sof*, the "Infinite." No void or vacuum existed; rather, the Infinite Light was everything. When **it arose within His primordial Will** to emanate "independent" beings so that He may be [recognized and] addressed [by His distinguishing qualities] — [such] as the Compassionate One, the Gracious One, He Who is Slow to Anger, etc. — He **contracted** (*tzimtzem*) Himself at the center of His Light, creating a **vacant space (***chalal***)** ... At the periphery of this circular *chalal*, He extended His light via **a single, linear, and narrow ray (***kav***), a type of conduit from the Infinite penetrating the vacant space, filling it [with Divine emanations]**, whilst the original, Infinite Light (*Or Ein-sof*) continued to **surround** the circumscribed *chalal*.[58] See *Figure* 1

An elucidation of the above: Prior to the beginning (possibly synonymous with the Big Bang), there existed nothing other than a Divine energy referred to as the "Infinite, Uniform Light" that constituted all of reality, devoid of any physical characteristic by which it might be described. This Light provides us with the most proximate description of the Creator Himself, of Whom it is said (Isiah 64:3): "Never heard, never perceived, never beheld by an eye." And as the Talmud states: [59] "Do not seek out that which is unfathomable to you, and do not investigate that which is concealed from you. Ponder only that which has been permitted to you; you have no business in secret matters."

The Infinite Light (*Or Ein-sof*) is NOT a created entity; it does not possess atoms or photons[60] nor is there a term in the human lexicon that could define it[61]. The unique *Or Ein-sof* that existed prior to the *tzimtzum* ("contraction") infiltrated itself into the *chalal* and subsequently split off and multiplied into both straight vectors (*kavim*) and concentric circles (*igulim*) – see *Figure 2*:

> The chief connection to *Ein-sof* Itself is perpetuated by way of the *kav* that penetrates [into the *chalal*] and through which the *Or Ein-sof* descends and propagates itself in concentric circles (*igulim*). The [original, pristine] *Ein-sof* encompasses [the *chalal*] and surrounds it [externally] on all sides, essentially making the *kav* alone the sole point of entry radiating into the emanated Creation.[62]

As cited in the Ari's earlier words, at a certain point it "arose within His Will" to create an "independent" realm whose core purpose was to receive benefit from God's benevolence. What purpose does Kabbala see in such a formation? Its objective is to produce living creations that are capable of recognizing and acknowledging His greatness and accept His Kingship, thereby promoting mankind into a junior partner in His creative work. There is however a formidable theological obstacle to overcome before attempting to achieve this goal: It is theologically impossible to create an autonomous man possessing free will whilst still basking in His Infinite Light. "This would be akin to expecting a child to be independent and make his own decisions whilst the parent nis constantly perched on his shoulder like a guardian angel!" It became vital to withdraw His own essence from the arena of creation, achieved by retracting His light and forming a vacant space which would still be surrounded on all sides by the original *Or Ein-sof*. This primordial stage is that of creation *ex nihilo*, or in Hebrew parlance, *yesh m'ayin*, the creation of "somethingness from nothingness."

THE PROBLEM OF CREATING SOMETHING FINITE OUT OF THE INFINITE (OR HOW TO REALLY GET SOMETHING FROM NOTHING)

Infinity ∞ is a boundless value, larger than any natural number. It is mathematically agreed that one cannot add to or subtract from infinity. Philosophically, the idea of a finite world emerging out of infinity is wholly untenable. It is also seemingly untenable to suggest that there may be an infinite subset of infinity. We thus must inquire: Is there a way to reconcile the Kabbalistic tradition of a finite Creation emerging out of *Ein-sof* with existing scientific knowledge?

The answer is "most certainly"

At the beginning of the 20th century, a revolutionary mathematician by the name of Georg Cantor proposed the Set Theory, which now is firmly established as a foundational system for the whole of mathematics. Cantor's theory of transfinite numbers proved through a well-established mathematical formula that an infinite set of real numbers (numbers that can be used[56] to measure a continuous one-dimensional quantity such as distance) is greater than a corresponding infinite set of natural numbers (whole positive integers). The existence of an infinite number of sets of infinite sizes has immense philosophical implications and was considered so counter-intuitive — even shocking — that it provoked extremely disparaging opposition by his contemporaries, even his own professors, Leopold Kronecker and Henri Poincare. Ludwig Wittgenstein raised philosophical objections. Indeed, it probably was this brutal opposition was responsible for his spending his last years in a sanatorium. Today, his proofs are accepted and taught in all institutions of higher learning where he is touted as a genius and a pioneer in his field.

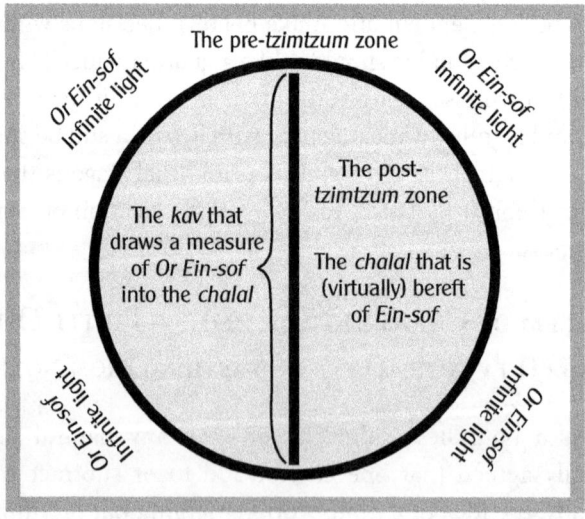

Figure 1: The metaphysical structure of the primordial universe.

Cantor's views on mathematics are understandingly associated with their theological implications. He himself identified the Absolute Infinite as God the Creator and viewed the "lesser" infinities as Divine manifestations within the material universe. This approach concurs in many aspects with the Ari's doctrine of the *tzimtzum* whereby a relatively infinite cosmos is derived from the absolute infinity of the Creator, whose celestial expressions are revealed within the universe at every turn.

The Ari's revolutionary thesis of *tzimtzum* can be a key factor in understanding the inherent paradox between the transcendent and immanent relationship between man and his Creator. Immanence affirms, while transcendence denies that God is contained within the world, and thus within the limits of human reason. The conundrum can logically be resolved if we accept that His infinite light is just concealed but still present, allowing a human being to exist and yet perceive Him at the same time.

The spherical space, or *chalal*, appearing in this diagram should not be confused with the planet Earth, but rather it is a metaphysical representation of the entire created universe, containing both material and spiritual entities. The *chalal* was formed to facilitate the emergence of a finite Creation external to God's nullifying *Or Ein-sof* (Infinite Light) — a kind of cosmic womb. Yet just as a tree must surely die if its nourishment from the earth is severed, so too would all created beings cease to exist if they were completely severed from their Divine source of life. In order to perpetuate and expand life, Kabbalah teaches us that the Creator introduced a concentrated beam of His *Or* into the *chalal*, which took the form of a thin conduit called the *kav*. The Light channeled through the *kav* is what sustains all of creation, kind of like a Divine umbilical cord. The further into the *chalal* that the *Or* penetrates, and the greater its distance from its source outside the *chalal*, the less its intensity and force.

The *Reshimu* ("Impression") of God's Initial Light

Many have pointed out that there is a logical contradiction in the Ari's assertion that God "contracted (*tzimtzem*) Himself at **the center** of His Light." How could the *Or Ein-sof* possess a center before the *tzimtzum* even allowed for Space and Time to come into existence? The Kabbalistic interpreters[63] explain that "the center" refers to the center of the future universe, implying that after the *tzimtzum* an "impression," or *reshimu*, of the *Or Ein-sof* uniformly filled the entire space of the *chalal*. This description invites comparison to the physical phenomenon of the Cosmic Microwave Background (CMB) which uniformly fills the cosmos. This 'fossil' radiation was released soon after the 'Big Bang' and scientists consider it as an echo or 'shockwave' of the Big Bang, the furthest that any telescope can see. At that first moment, when the cosmos erupted out of gravitational singularities, this radiation filled the universe instantaneously, leaving us with an impression, or *reshimu*, of its state at the time.

THE SEPHIROT

The further that the *Or Ein-sof* descends into the *chalal* via the *kav*, and the greater its distance from its source, the weaker it becomes. At various junctures in this process of descent, Divine emanations referred to in Kabbalah as *sephirot* are created. The term *sephirah* finds Biblical expression in two prophetic visions describing God's Heavenly Throne. In the first, at Mount Sinai, the elders of Israel ascended the mountain and "beheld the God of Israel, and beneath His feet was a brickwork of sapphire gems (*sapir*), and it was like the essence of the heavens in its purity" (Ex. 24:10). In the second instance, Ezekiel's vision of the Chariot, he beholds God's attending angels, the Chayot, "and above the firmament that was over their heads, was the appearance of a stone of sapphire (*sapir*) in the likeness of a throne" (Ezek. 1:26). In both visions, we have an unmediated prophetic encounter with God's Heavenly Abode. At its bottommost tier, "beneath his feet" and "over [the angels'] heads" a blindingly pure light emanates from a sapphire stone. This may be the first allusion to the Divine emanations known as *sephirot*.

There are various other interpretations of the word *sephirah*, some of which are also quite ancient. Its first appearance as *sephirah*, in the foundational Kabbalistic work *Sefer HaYetzirah*,[64] links it to the root *s-p-r*, which means, amongst other things, "to count." Perhaps this is meant to suggest that the ten *sephirot* mentioned there were God's instruments in "enumerating" the sequence of creation. Additionally, the word *sephirah* is phonetically similar and etymologically related to the word sphere, as exemplified in the commonly used expression, "Sphere of Influence," indicating the influence the *sephirot* have on the created realm.

Kabbalistic texts over the millennia have concentrated on the *sephirot* as the metaphysical bridges mediating between *Ein-sof* and a bounded, material Creation. The ten *sephirot* individually and in tandem draw the Divine life-force (*shefa*) down in to the lower worlds are identified as: *Chochmah* (Wisdom), *Binah* (Understanding), *Daat* (Knowledge), *Chesed* (Kindness), *Gevurah* (Stength), *Tiferet* (Beauty), *Netzach* (Victory), *Hod* (Splendor), *Yesod* (Foundation), *and Malchut* (Kingship). Working together, they give expression to God's creative Will and through them He and man advance that creation.

Each *sephirah* is composed of *or*, "light," and a *kli*, "vessel." The *or* is

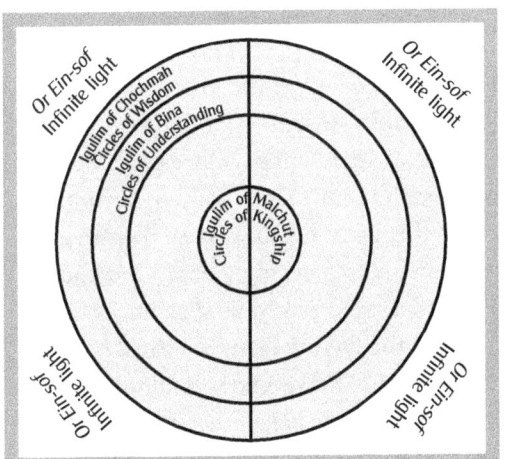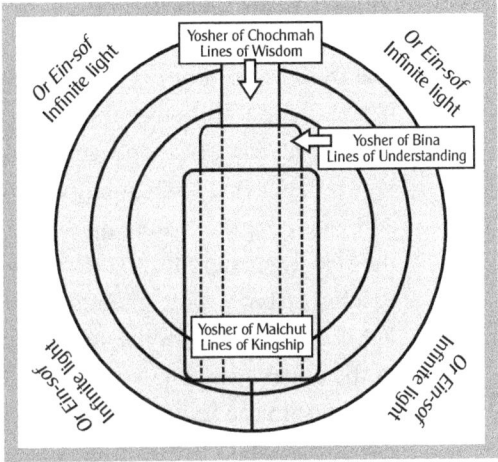

Figure 2: Structure Formation after the Tzimtzum

the "soul" of the *sephirah*, residing within it and consists of an immutable *or* alongside a dynamic *or* that varies in accordance with human action, referred to as *tosefet mochin* or "enhanced enlightenment."[65] The unchanging *or* of the *sephirot* is referred to as *igulim*, "circles" or "rings," representing the established laws of nature that govern Creation; while the dynamic *or* is referred to as *yosher*, "straightness" or "linearity," representing God's individualized providence over His creatures in accordance with their deeds.

A fundamental rule of Kabbalah is that the *or* of a *sephirah* can **only** be revealed through its *kli*, such that no light can exist without its corresponding vessel. Despite their mutual dependance, *Orot* (pl. *or*) and *kelim* (pl. *kli*) represent two contrasting attributes, since light by its nature is ethereal and spreads out unchecked, while vessels are coarse, bounded objects. Unbounded light contains inexhaustible, immense spiritual energy which cannot be grasped through man's limited faculties. In order for this light to be revealed (which is its very raison d'etre), the only solution is to dim its intensity by enshrouding it in a vessel that will filter out some of its rays.[66] The *kelim* themselves derive from the *reshimu* of the *Or Ein-sof* that preceded the *kav* which introduces the *or*.

THE WORLDS OF *TOHU* (CHAOS) AND *TIKKUN* (RESTORATION)

The initial repository of the ten *sephirot* is referred to as the World of *Tohu* (Chaos), for at that stage they existed as ten wholly unstable and undeveloped concentrations of Divine energy, incapable of interacting with each other. When the Divine Light attempted to enter the immature *kelim* of these *sephirot* and when the *kelim* were unable to contain this light due to its great intensity, the vessels shattered into countless shards, in an astonishingly organized and specific fashion. This phenomenon is famously referred to as *shevirat hakelim,* the "shattering of the vessels" and caused the Divine Light to retreat back to the upper worlds from whence they originated. However, the multitude of shards from the *kelim* retained residual "sparks," - *nitzotzot*, of that primordial, pristine Light. Only the lower seven of the *sephirot* — from *Chesed* to *Malchut* — were actually affected by the shattering — *shevirah*, whilst the higher three *sephirot* — *Chochmah*, *Binah*, and *Daat* — were indeed able to tolerate the Light by virtue of their more refined nature.

Immediately following the *shevirah*, the World of *Tikkun*, or "Restoration," emerged with the purpose of receiving the fallen shards and enabling the possibility of cosmic repair. The World of *Tikkun* is composed of four sequential realms, each providing an intermediate berth for the Divine Light as it seeks to ultimately infuse material reality. These four realms are referred to as the Worlds of *Atzilut* (Emanation), *Beriah* (Creation), *Yetzirah* (Formation), and *Asiyah* (Action) — collectively referred to by the acronym *ABY"A*.

The shards of the lower seven *sephirot* descended immediately into the lower three of these worlds, while the intact *sephirot* of *Chochmah*, *Binah*, and *Daat* remained in the World of *Atzilut*. The essential difference between the

World of *Atzilut* and the three lower Worlds is that the *Or Ein-sof* so thoroughly suffuses the World of *Atzilut* that the *sephirot* there are completely nullified in its Light, bereft of any "self-awareness." The World of *Atzilut* radiates Divine Will into the lower three Worlds where that Will is actualized in accordance with the guidance of *Atzilut*. As the Divine Will passes through the chain of lower Worlds, it undergoes successive transformations until it ultimately manifests itself in the World of *Asiyah*, which is the spiritual prototype of our own physical world.

An apt metaphor for understanding the above could be the transmission of military orders through an army's chain of command. It may begin at the top, by the minister of defense, as a general, strategic objective framed in one short sentence. At every level however, it expands into more and more detailed, specific instructions, until it reaches the soldiers in the field as a comprehensive and exhaustive set of instructions, many pages in length.

An alternative metaphor can be described as microscopic drops of water in the upper atmosphere condense and fall, becoming more tangible in nature, until the turn onto a flood of water. So too, the *orot* and *kelim* of the *sephirot* as they descend through these worlds become denser and the *orot* more tangible as they proceed toward their destination in the lowest World of *Asiyah*.

The Ari established a very important principle in respect to the propagation of God's creative Will through the chain of Four Worlds: Every World has its source, and is actually generated by the World above it in whose image it is created. Hence, the ultimate World of *Asiyah* benefits from the influence of all Four Worlds, neatly explaining the correspondence that we have seen between physiological processes in our own world and their metaphysical antecedents.

PARTZUFIM, SEPHIROTIC "PERSONAE"

What distinguishes the World of *Tikkun* from the World of *Tohu* with regard to the *sephirot* is that in the World of *Tikkun* the *kelim* are robust enough to contain their *orot*. This not only renders each *sephirah* more stable and mature, but also allows the aggregate of *sephirot* to interact with each other in accordance with the Divine Will at each level of creation. The alignment of all ten *sephirot* into a particular configuration for such a creative purpose is called a *partzuf*, or "persona."

There are five primary *partzufim*, or personae, in each of the Four Worlds. From the highest to the lowest, they are referred to as follows: *Atik Yomin*, "Ancient Days"; *Arich Anpin*, "The Long Countenance"; *Abba*, "Father"; *Ima*, "Mother"; and *Ze'ir Anpin*, "The Small Countenance."

Just as the face is made up of discrete elements — eyes, ear, mouth, etc. that in unison leave a singular impression, so, too, do the *sephirot* that comprise the Kabbalistic *partzuf* combine harmoniously to produce a singular effect on the evolution of created reality.

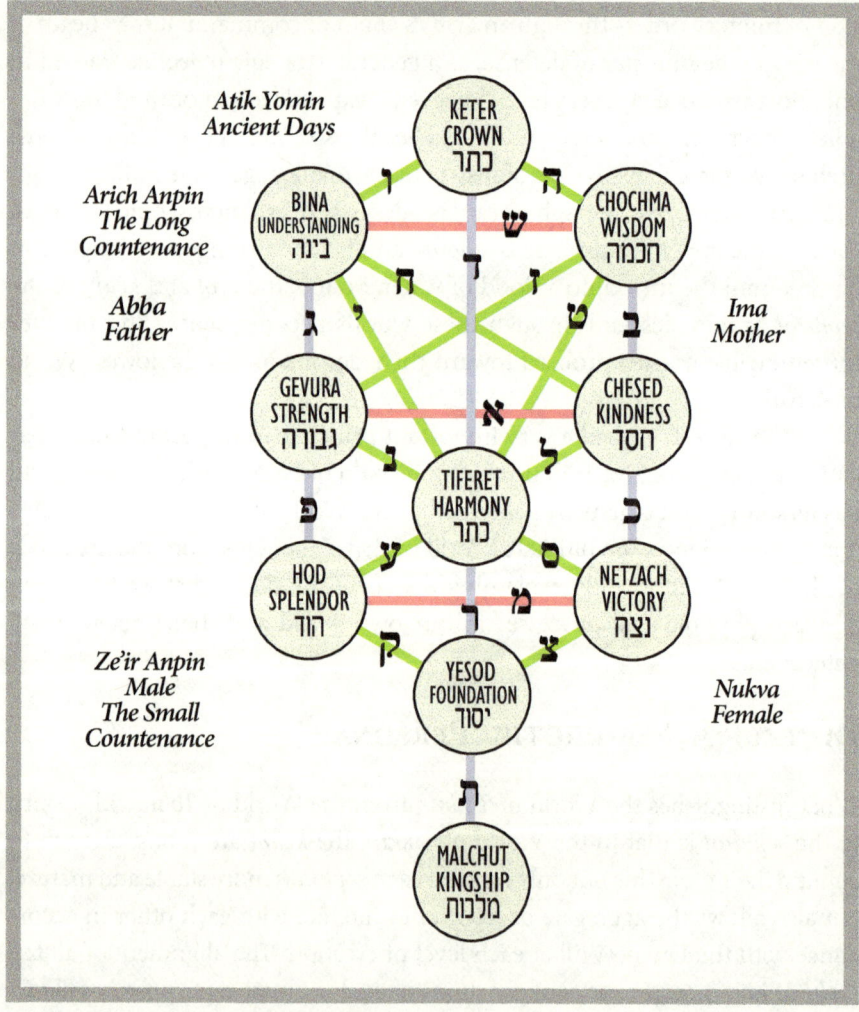

Figure 3: Sephirot and Partzufim Interaction

SPARKS, SHARDS, AND SHELLS

The plunging of the fallen shards of *kelim* into the three lower Worlds distanced them from their original *orot*, leading to the formation of spiritual impurities referred to as *klipot*, "shells," or *sigim*, "dregs." In the higher World of *Atzilut*, the *orot* are still strong enough to nullify these impurities entirely. Hence, if the *kelim* had only fallen into the World of *Atzilut*, these impurities would have been imperceptible, just as the light of a candle is imperceptible in the midday sun.[67] However, once the *kelim* descended into the lower Worlds, these impure *klipot* revealed themselves actively and brought about a domain of evil referred to as the *sitra achra*, "other side."

Detachment from their original *orot* should have led to the demise of the fallen *kelim* together with their *klipot*. That is why God in His Goodness impressed into these shards "sparks," or *nitzotzot*, of that primordial *or*. Their purpose was two-fold: a) To sustain the lower Worlds and all that was in them, and b) To enable man to repair those broken Worlds by releasing these Divine sparks from their captivity in the fallen shards so that they could reunite with their ultimate source in the *Or Ein-sof.*

PERFECTING THE WORLD *(TIKKUN OLAM)* THROUGH HUMAN ACTION

The intricate depiction in Kabbalah of the above cosmic drama is meant to enlighten us as to the path Creation must take if it is to achieve its intended perfection. The mission of "perfecting the world," *tikkun olam*, is too great for any single individual, or even generation, to undertake. That is why the Creator, in His great Wisdom, split this overwhelming mission into a myriad of small tasks to be shared by all of mankind through the course of human history. Every individual is invested with a unique "soul," or *neshamah*, that is charged with executing a battery of *tikkunim*, "rectifications," that he or she alone is suited to carry out. Every person ever created has a mission, a specific and unique set of rectifications, that **he or she alone**, can carry out in order to perfect the world. Each person born receives a singular soul never to appear again in the course of history. This soul is accorded an arsenal of *tikkunim* under its exclusive charge to be carried out every day it is on earth. To use a computing analogy, it is like saying that each unique soul combined with each unique day is allocated a unique IP address that is used to identify his or her activities and accomplishments throughout their lives.

The Kabbalah of the Ari provides us specific guidelines for carrying out our own individual *tikkun olam*. The 613 commandments of the Torah are the basic active framework, while the Ari's doctrine of *birur hanitzotzot*, "extracting the sparks," guides us in leveraging those practical *mitzvah* acts for the purpose of rectifying the higher spiritual Worlds.

As stated earlier, the actual *tikkun* takes place when we release the holy sparks from the shards in which they are held captive so that they could reunite with their source in the *Or Ein-sof* that preceded the *shevirah*. This "raising of the sparks" is accomplished through Kabbalistic meditations undertaken at the appropriate time and place while engaging in the performance of a *mitzvah*. The purpose of every *mitzvah* act is to "extract" sparks that have heretofore never been released. This is the reason that we are obligated to pray at specific times of the day, for each prayer carries within it new and unique potential for effecting change. As the Ari states:

> There is a major difference between today's prayer and tomorrow's prayer; the effect applicable to one is not applicable to the other. **From the dawn of creation to the end of time, not one of the myriad prayers may be compared to another** (because each one is unique).[68]

The awareness that a personalized and unique series of *tikkunim* awaits each and every one of us every day of our lives should inspire a revolution in how we relate to our mission and destiny in life. Every prayer — indeed, every meal — represents a **one-time opportunity**, never to recur, for rectifying a small aspect of both the human and cosmic condition. Hence, the following Midrash:

> (Gen. 24:1) "Abraham was old, advanced in years; and God blessed Abraham with everything", although the literal Hebrew text for 'advanced in years' is actually 'came with his days' i.e. every day in his life was counted and meaningful. This implies that Abraham completed the entire set of *tikkunim* accorded him in the world and no tasks assigned to him to be performed in this world were left undone.[69]

THE MECHANISM FOR *TIKKUN OLAM*

Considering all we have described so far, it is now possible to present the Kabbalistic plan for perfecting this broken world. These rules for *tikkun olam* are valid for all *mitzvot* and acts of human comportment — from the meditations for eating to the blowing of the shofar (the rams horn) on Rosha Hashana (the new year). Simply put, the task of *tikkun olam* awaits every one of us each day anew, as implied in the following verse from the account of creation (Gen. 2:5): "The shrub of the field was not yet on the earth and the grass of the field had not yet sprouted, for the Lord God had not made it rain upon the earth and there was no man to work the soil."

It goes without saying that this belief has the potential to be a gamechanger in the way that we look upon the meaning of our lives and provides us with optimism in amending our ways and reconnecting with our spirit. This tailored individualistic approach is positioned in direct and stark contrast to the hopelessness and insignificance found in latter day and modern atheists. For example, the 1st chapter of Noah Harari's book 'Sapiens' is ominously titled "Sapiens - An Animal of No Significance". See also Richard Dawkins in his book 'The God Delusion' "We have simply evolved from bacteria; we are nothing more than glorified monkeys. There are no gods, no goals, and no goal-oriented superpowers of any kind. There is also no life after death. No ethics, no meaning to life, and no human free will. "

The mechanism for *tikkun olam* consists of **freeing the sparks from their *klipot* and elevating them back to their source in the *Or Ein-sof* that preceded the *shevirah* of the *kelim*.** If this *tikkun* is successful, the Divine life-force flows from the upper Worlds down into our own material world.

The process of *tikkun olam* takes place in three stages:

1. Identifying the spark by its unique marker, as provided to us by the Ari as described in the next chapter.

2. Isolating the spark from the mixture of *klipot* entrapping it.

3. Freeing the spark entirely so that it could return to its supernal source.

THE TANGO BEGINS

Rather than viewing the spiritual and material as parallel forces that occasionally and randomly intersect, Kabbalah sees them as inextricably bound up in each other, to the degree that they substantiate and empower one another. The reflection of the supernal in the mortal is expressed by the very name Adam, which alludes to the Biblical phrase **adameh l'elyon**, "I will liken myself to the Most High" (Is14:14). This idea is expressed as well by Job when he states, "From my flesh, I shall envision God."[70] The human form — its complex of limbs and organs — provides a model for understanding the Divine structure of the upper realms.

We are like marionettes, with every one of our limbs controlled by a corresponding limb of the Primordial man (*Adam Kadmon*),[71] the very first *partzuf*, or "persona," whose limbs are controlled by the Creator Himself. When God moves this *partzuf*'s hand, we move ours, as intimated in the verse (Psa. 121:5), "God is your shadow at your right hand." God is the invisible presence that shadows our every action.

This metaphor also works in the opposite direction: Just as our movements mimic His, so have we the power through our actions below to impact the upper realms, to activate the corresponding "limbs" of the supernal *partzuf*. And thus, the system is constructed, with man's composite parts corresponding to metaphysical antecedents.[72]

According to the Kabbalistic view, small meritorious acts — such as donning tefillin, eating matzah on Passover, or committing an act of kindness — when accompanied by the appropriate meditations, have the power to shake the heavens and influence the farthest reaches of our physical and spiritual universe. Imagine a truck carrying forty tons of earth traveling down a highway. It is not the driver's foot that propels that truck, but rather its massive engine that was designed to react to the pressure of the driver's foot. The analogy is clear: Our actions in this world indirectly bring about dramatic changes in the universe, and this very mechanism was designed and implemented by the Creator himself.

Kabbalah's assertion of a mutual influence existing between the mortal and the Divine suggests a kind of tango dance between the spiritual and physical realms.

Indeed, Kabbalah teaches us that man possesses various levels of soul that correspond to different levels of his anatomy. Those levels of soul are called *neshama*, *ruach*, and *nefesh*. The *neshama* is the level of soul most rooted in the Divine and hence unique to intelligent beings. The *nefesh* is the animating soul which man shares with all physical creatures. The *ruach* is an intermediate level of soul associated with man's emotive functions. Hence, the Ari teaches us (*Etz Chayim, Shaar* 6:5): "The *neshamah* radiates from man's head and brain; the *ruach*, from his heart; and the *nefesh*, from his liver and flesh."

The following quotes are additional Kabbalistic examples that emphasis the symbiotic relationship between one's body and the different levels of soul:

- The *nitzotzin* (sparks) are the *nefesh* of one's external limbs, including one's flesh, tendons and bones. The *orot* are the *nefesh* of one's internal organs, such as the heart, lungs, kidneys, and liver. (Ibid. *Shaar* 20:1)

- The liver is found in the lower torso and includes ten *sephirot*; it enclothes itself throughout the body by way of the veins. The heart is positioned higher than it and includes ten *middot* (emotive traits); it enclothes itself in the liver through its pulse and spreads throughout the body. The brain is higher than them all and includes ten *middot*; they enclothe themselves in the heart by way of the nerves that extend from it and spread out throughout the body. (*Nehar Shalom* p. 41b.)

We have traced, in broad terms, the transfer of the Divine life-force between the upper and lower realms of Creation. Now it behooves us to focus in greater detail on how that Divine energy actively manifests itself in our own realm of existence. I emphasize, once again, that this level of detail may be overwhelming for some at this stage, and can be skipped for now to be returned later on.

THE HOLY NAMES OF GOD

In his introduction to the Book of Genesis, Nachmanides, (The Ramban) writes:[73]

We possess an authentic tradition that the entire Torah is entirely composed of the Names of the Holy Blessed One.

In accordance with this tradition, Kabbalah establishes the mechanism of *tikkun* as one that is driven by the Holy Names whose source is in the Bible. It is through them that we free the sparks and bring down Divine life-force.

There are seven Holy Names for God that appear in the Bible, the most preeminent one being the ineffable Four-letter Name *Y-H-V-H*, known as the Tetragrammaton. **This Name may not even be pronounced as it is written.** Hence, the verse (Ex. 3:15): "This is My Name *l'olam* (forever); this is My enunciation for generations," upon which Rashi comments as follows:[74] "The word *l'olam* is written without the letter *vav*, as if to say: This is My Name 'to be concealed (*l'haalim*),' and not pronounced as written."

The Talmud elaborates:

> Rabbi Avina raised a contradiction: The verse states "This is My Name," but also states, "This is My enunciation ('how I am to be remembered')." The Holy Blessed One is hereby telling us: "Not as I am written (My Name) am I pronounced (My enunciation). I am written with the letters *Yod-Heh-Vav-Heh* (Havaya), but I am pronounced as if written *Alef-Dalet-Nun-Yod* (*Adonai*)."[75]

Even this substitute pronunciation *Adonai* is reserved exclusively for use in the recitation of prayers and blessings. When raised in everyday conversation, the Tetragrammaton is referred to simply as *Shem Hashem*, "the name of the Name." Indeed, *Hashem*, the Name, is how Jews refer to God in their daily parlance. Hence, when asked "How are you?" we reply with the words "*Baruch Hashem* (Blessed be the Name), which is the equivalent of "Thank God."[76]

The power of God's Names as they appear in the Bible is what circumscribes their use, mandating caution as if one was handling explosive material! That is why there are various other prohibitions regarding these Names, both as spoken and as written: The prohibition against erasing them, uttering them in vain, defacing them or handling them disrespectfully. Texts containing these names cannot be disposed of normally but must be buried in a special repository called a Geniza for that very purpose.[77]

In Kabbalah, there are additional Names ascribed to God which are used for the purpose of meditation aimed at drawing His Divine life-force down into the world. Each Name is like a garment allowing us to grasp an aspect of His Divinity. Just as garments allow us to face our surroundings while at the same time concealing our nakedness, so do God's Names disguise His inexpressible Essence, while affording us a narrow and limited look at Who He is.

The following are just a few verses illustrating the importance attached to knowing the Creator's Names:

"Those who know Your Name will trust in You" (Psa. 9:11)

"I will exalt him, for he knows My Name" (Ibid. 91:14)

"Let them place My Name upon the Children of Israel and I shall bless them" (Num. 6:27)[78]

Perhaps the best-known reference to God's Name is found in the Kaddish memorial prayer that has been recited by Jews throughout the centuries:

"May His great Name be magnified and sanctified. May His great Name be blessed forever and for all eternity. Blessed and praised…be the Name of the Holy Blessed One."

ILLUSTRATING THE SIGNIFICANCE OF NAMES AND SYMBOLS

Meditating as proscribed upon God's Names causes His life-force to be attracted to and permeate among the *sephirot*, which in turn, guide the universe toward its creative purpose. The modern mind may find this concept more understandable through some examples from our own contemporary experience:

- The atomic sequence C6H12O6 is the chemical formula for the glucose molecule, which contains 6 carbon atoms, 12 hydrogen atoms, and 6 oxygen atoms. This formula allows the chemist to manufacture sugar in the laboratory.

- A DNA sequence composed of four proteins appears like this: ATTGAAGGTGCGG. With these proteins a geneticist can create new life in a test tube.

- A musician can play Beethoven's Ninth Symphony by looking at staffs, lines, and notation that are inscrutable to laymen. The signs and forms are an agreed-upon language that enables people to create various pieces in accordance with their profession.

- A radio receives a broadcast from a particular station on condition that it is set to the right frequency of electromagnetic radiation, ranging from 3 kilohertz to 300 gigahertz along the electromagnetic spectrum.

These are just a few examples familiar to us by which we can grasp the importance and power of the language and symbols employed in different fields for the purpose of creating something tangible in the physical world. For those who employ the Ari's meditations, the Names of God — together with their cantillation and punctuation signs — are the interface that allows one to recognize the Creator and commune with Him, as implied by the Zohar's statement: "He [God in His Essence] together with His *orot* [the *sephirot*] and *kelim* [His Names] are one."[79] For example, the Name *El* is the *kli* (vessel) for the *sephirah* of *Chesed*; the Name *Elokim* is the *kli* for the *sephirah* of *Gevurah*; the Name *Adonai* is the *kli* for the *sephirah* of *Malchut*, and so on.

According to Kabbalah, the Holy Names provide the most authentic means for establishing an intimacy in this world between the Infinite One and His creatures. This is expressed by the following Midrash:

> (Ex. 6:2-3) "God spoke to Moses, and said to him: 'I am *Y-H-V-H*. I appeared to Abraham, to Isaac, and to Jacob as *El-Shadai*, but by My Name *Y-H-V-H* I did not make Myself known to them.'"

> Moses had just requested that God make Himself known by His Great Name [the Tetragrammaton]. God said to him: "My Name you wish to know? I am called as befits My actions... When I judge My creatures, I am called *Elokim*; when I wage war against villains, I am called *Tzevaot*; when I suspend punishment for the sins of man, I am called *El-Shadai*; and when I have mercy upon My world, I am called *Y-H-V-H*.[80]

Since the Name composed of the letters *Yod-Heh-Vav-Heh* is not to be pronounced as written, the custom is to refer to it by way of its anagram, *Havayah*. That is how I will refer to it from hereon in.

THE NAME *HAVAYAH*

The Name *Havayah* is a proper noun and it appears an astonishing more than 6,000 times in the Bible. Aside from being called the Four-letter Name (Tetragrammaton), it is also referred to as "the special Name" (*Shem hameyuchad*) or simply as "the Name" (*Hashem*).

The four letters of the Name *Havayah* correspond to the four stages whereby created reality emerged from God's Infinite Light, *the Or Ein-sof*, and progressed through the Four Worlds: *Tzimtzum* (contraction), *Hitpashtut* (expansion), *Hamshachah* (Extension), and once again *Hitpashtut* (expansion).

- The first letter, *yod* ׳, is basically a dot, but with a tiny spike in its upper left corner. The spike symbolically points to the hidden *Or Ein-sof* which precedes the emergence of the Name altogether. The dot shape represents the *tzimtzum*, whereby God contracted His Infinite Light so as to allow a prototype of Creation to occupy the initial World of *Atzilut* (Emanation).

- The second letter, *heh* ה, is composed of three lines forming the borders of a square space. It represents the expansion of the contracted light in the uppermost World of *Beriah* (Creation).

- The third letter, *vav* ו, is a single vertical line, representing the extension of God's Light into the World of *Yetzirah* (Formation).

- The last letter, another *heh* ה, represents the final three-dimensional expansion of God's Light into the World of *Asiyah* (Action), which is the metaphysical equivalent of our own material reality.

CALCULATING THE *GEMATRIYA* OF THE NAME *HAVAYAH*

Since every Hebrew letter has a name which itself is composed of letters, the four letters of the Name *Havayah* can be expanded in various ways which affect the way we calculate the numerical value, or *gematriya*, of the Name. In its simplest and most basic form, called *pashut*, the Name *Havayah* consists of the initial letters themselves — *yod*, *heh*, *vav*, and *heh* — whose numerical value is 10, 5, 6, and 5, giving it a *gematriya* of 26.

By calculating the additional letters that appear in these letters' names — thereby spelling *Havaya* in "full," or *malei* — we arrive obviously at greater values. For example, the letter *yod* is spelled *yod-vav-dalet*, whose numerical values are 10, 6, and 4, producing a *gematriya* of 20. The remaining letters, *heh* and *vav*, can each be spelled in more than one way. The *heh* can be spelled *heh-aleph*, *heh-heh*, or *heh-yod*, thus giving it a possible *gematriya* of either 6 (5+1), 10 (5+5), or 15 (5+10). The *vav* can be spelled either *vav-vav*,

vav-aleph-vav, or *vav-yod-vav*, giving it a possible *gematriya* of either 12 (6+6), 13 (6+1+6), or 22 (6+10+6).

Of all the possible combinations afforded by these different spellings, the Kabbalah of the Ari chose four as representative of the Four Worlds and their corresponding *sephirot*:

The combination amounting to **72**: *yod* (20) + *heh* (15) + *vav* (22) + *heh* (15) — corresponding to the World of *Atzilut* and the *sephirah* of *Chochmah*.

The combination amounting to **63**: *yod* (20) + *heh* (15) + *vav* (13) + *heh* (15) — corresponding to the World of *Beriah* and the *sephirah* of *Binah*.

The combination amounting to **45**: *yod* (20) + *heh* (6) + *vav* (13) + *heh* (6) — corresponding to the World of *Yetzirah* and the *sephirah* of *Tiferet*.

The combination amounting to **52**: *yod* (20) + *heh* (10) + *vav* (12) + *heh* (10) — corresponding to the World of *Asiyah* and the *sephirah* of *Malchut*.[81]

These four combinations of the Name *Havayah* are Kabbalistically referred to by their *gematriyas* as the Names *Av* (72), *Sag* (63), *Mah* (45), and *Ban* (52). Together, they represent the diverse scale of values introduced by Kabbalah.

There are two other approaches to calculating the *gematriya* of the Name *Havaya*, referred to as *malei d'malei* and *achorayim*, which are not germane at this point.[82]

The Four Variant Spellings of the Name *Havayah* and their Correspondences

Spelling:	יוד הי ויו הי	יוד הי ואו הי	יוד הא ואו הא	יוד הה וו הה
Corresponding:	Yod Hey Vyv Hey	Yod Hey Vav Hey	Yod He Vav He	Yod Heh Vv Heh
Name	*AV* עב (72)	*SAG* סג (63)	*MAH* מה (45)	*BA* בן (52)
Filler Value[83]	46	37	19	26
World	*Atzilut*	*Beriyah*	*Yetzirah*	*Asiyah*
Partzuf	*Abba*	*Ima*	*Ze'ir Anpin*	*Nukva*
Domain	*Medaber*	*Chai*	*Tzomeach*	*Domem*

The Unification *(Yichud)* of Male and Female

Aside from the centrality of the Name *Havayah* in advancing Divine life-force through the Four Worlds, we must mention the vital role played by the male and female principles at work in Creation. In the symbolic systems of both philosophy and Kabbalah, we find the male principle associated with active, seminal influence, as rooted in the male's biological role as the provider of seed, and the female principle associated with receiving that influence and then cultivating it into full-bodied form, as rooted in her procreative role.

In Kabbalah, the male is also associated with the *partzuf* of *Abba* (Father) and its corresponding *sephirah* of *Chochmah* (Wisdom). The word *Chochmah* permutes into the words *koach mah*, "the power of essence," once again alluding to the conceptual spark that triggers the creative process as if "out of nowhere." Kabbalah finds a basis for this in the verse (Job 28:12), "As for wisdom *(chochmah)* — from where *(meayin)* can it be found?" As reinterpreted Kabbalistically, the verse actually posits that the *sephirah* of *Chochmah* has its source in the absolute "nothingness," or *ayin*, of the Infinite One, emerging from it like a bolt of lightning that suddenly illuminates the dark and vacant space of Creation. Hence, *Chochmah* is experienced cognitively as a sudden intuitive flash, like the Eureka phenomenon.

Conversely, the female is associated with the *partzuf* of *Ima* (Mother) and its corresponding *sephirah* of *Binah* (Understanding).[84] Cognitively, *Binah* is what takes the abstract seed of thought provided by *Chochmah* and then cultivates it by "understanding one thing from another." Our Sages teach us that "the Holy Blessed One granted Woman an extra measure of *binah*, relative to man, as it is written (Gen. 2:22), 'And the Lord God fashioned *(banah)* the side that He had taken from the man into a woman.'"[85]

The union of the above male and female *partzufim* gives birth to a male "child," associated with the *partzuf* of *Ze'ir Anpin* (The Small Countenance). This union of *Chochmah* and *Binah* activates within *Ze'ir Anpin* a range of Divine attributes that are emotive in nature, corresponding to the *sephirot* of *Chesed* through *Yesod*. It is within *Ze'ir Anpin* that the process of *birur* (extraction) takes place, whereby the sparks of holiness are released from their captivity in the shattered fragments of the fallen *kelim* and returned to their source in the *Or Ein-sof*.

The *yichud*, or "unification," between the male and female aspects of the *sephirot* and their related *partzufim* is the core element in the practice of the Ari's meditations. It forms the basis for drawing down new Divine life-force into the world.

CHAPTER SUMMARY

We have briefly introduced in this chapter several Kabbalistic topics, including creation *ex nihilo* (*yesh m'ayin*), the shattering (*shevirah*) of the vessels *(kelim)*, and the process of evolving a finite, material world out of God's Infinite Light. We have seen how sparks of that primordial Light are trapped within the material components of our own world, with our role being to redeem them through the practice of Kabbalistic meditations focused on God's various Names. The result of such practice is the enticement of Divine life-force from the most supernal realms into our own physical world. This life-force translates into an profusion of both material and spiritual blessing for the practitioner, in accordance with his or her spiritual caliber and the timing of their practice (weekday, Sabbath, or Festival). Proper meditation on God's Holy Names, as prescribed by Kabbalah, both ameliorates and rectifies the catastrophic *shevi-rah* that occurred at the dawn of Creation. The most powerful rectifications (*tikkunim*) are achieved while engaging in the physical pleasures of this world, such as eating. Hence, those are the meditations that we will explore in the next chapter.

PRACTICAL IMPLICATIONS

Whilst eating, one should have in mind that one is not just satisfying a random, fleeting hunger, but also one is rectifying the worlds that were corrupted through the primordial shattering of the *kelim*. The *tikkun* that takes place at that specific moment is exclusively intended for you and is accomplished by extracting and releasing the sparks that inhere in the food you are eating, enabling them to return to their source.

Chapter 6

MEDITATIONS FOR EATING — A PRACTICAL GUIDE

The purpose of this chapter is to present a step-by-step practical guide for implementing the Ari's meditations for eating. This chapter is divided into two parts: Part 1 describes how to properly prepare for executing the meditations, while Part 2 provides specific instructions, with accompanying diagrams, to employ when performing them.

PART 1

THE *REAL* REASON WE EAT

The topics covered thus far should enable the reader to implement the Ari's meditations and even understand them. As previously learned, in addition to their physical constituents, all foods possess various spiritual elements - sparks of the primordial *Or Ein-sof* that were trapped in the *klipot* and shards of the shattered vessels *kelim*.[86] Whilst the immediate physical goal of eating is to sate our hunger, **the true spiritual aspiration of eating is to liberate these sparks and elevate them back to their supernal realms**. According to Kabbalah, the task of "extracting" these sparks is the primary purpose of eating, whereas hunger and appetite are there only to prod us toward that end. This insight definitely resonates with the theme elucidated in chapter 2 : Eating as the reason for creation.

The act of eating is the best example of a routine action that, due to its great regularity and our inattentiveness, becomes rote, rendering us virtually oblivious to its many stages. We eat under any possible condition: standing, walking, reading, watching TV — even while carrying on a conversation! Countering this heedlessness, the Ari's meditations attempt to harness our attention, asking us to make the act of eating a unique experience by concentrating on its order of execution.

Our morning cup of coffee liberates a unique, spiritual spark that is different from that of our afternoon cup. Every action, great or small, provides an unparalleled opportunity to extract good from our activities in the world, such that nothing is insignificant and so we should aim to make our actions meaningful and try not to "kill time". From the information presented thus far, it should be apparent that Kabbalah intends for mankind to heal this fractured and flawed world. In fact, **spiritual *tikkun* is *the* raison d'etre for Creation and all that transpires within is directed to fulfill that goal.** Through the mechanism of recurring hunger at specific times, the Creator furnishes everyone with their own unique list of *tikkunim* and indicates His desire for us to engage in redeeming those particular sparks. Our craving or hunger facilitates the opportunity to engage **in eating for the purpose of rectifying the spiritual realms**. In such a manner, we elevate the act of eating from a animalistic necessity to a holy, cosmic service - no different from any other formal *mitzvah*.

THE APPETIZER APPROACH

As we will soon see, performing the Ari's meditations requires a great deal of study and practice, and since one may be overwhelmed at the prospect, I have seen fit to preface this section with the words of the Ari himself, indicating that even the smallest effort is beneficial:

> If one succeeds in performing these meditations throughout the course of one's meal, that is indeed a great thing. However, **at the very least**, one can perform a meditation while eating the initial slice of bread upon which one recites the blessing of *hamotzi*.[87]

The Ari is establishing here a very important principle, which applies not only to the meditations of eating, but to all the myriad Kabbalistic meditations employed in daily living. The best way to illustrate this principle is to quote the words of my revered teacher, Rabbi Mordechai Attiah, who once said that one should relate to Kabbalistic meditations as if they are spiritual appetizers or tasty nibbles — there to be enjoyed even in the smallest quantity. Under no circumstances should one delay implementing Kabbalistic meditations until having mastered the practice in all its depth and breadth; rather, one should apply it immediately — regardless of the level achieved. If one does not have the time or state of mind to perform three meditations, then just carry out one. This golden advice has saved many who could not see themselves withstanding the burden of studying and implementing this important practice. Having pursued it daily in small measures, many found their ability increasing steadily, to their great satisfaction.

On a personal note, I try carrying out the meditations once a day, usually while dining alone or when circumstances otherwise allow; sometimes with just a cursory and generalized contemplation, while at other times covering all the stages through a sustained act of guided imagining. One thing I can say with certainty: The more one attempts the process, the easier it becomes to execute and the more meaningful the act of eating becomes. many others can testify to this as well.

As explained above, the overriding purpose of the Ari's meditations is to coax a Divine life-force (*shefa*) to descend from Heaven above into the Earth below, thereby infusing our lives with holiness and spiritual merits.[88] Each individual meditation presented in this chapter is intended to generate a new spiritual reality. Like the rungs of a ladder, each one of these realities ascends in an orderly fashion, deriving from those that preceded it, whilst paralleling the stages of physical consumption. In other words, these meditations spiritually prepare the teeth, the jaws, the mechanisms of chewing, swallowing, digesting, and eliminating — all with the aim of drawing life-force down from Above.

In the Ari's teachings from *Shaar HaMitzvot* (*Parashat Ekev*), it is written:

> When you eat, you should have this intention, in accordance with what I have taught you: All created things are called *manin tevirin*, "broken vessels." With the emergence of [the World of] *Tikkun*, a portion of those vessels were repaired and a portion not. Hence, we need to isolate, clarify, and elevate the sparks concealed in our food from amidst the harmful refuse. This is the secret of supernal "eating," which is also

a process of isolating the palatable from the unpalatable, with the latter being shunted below into the *klipot*.

When eating in conjunction with these special meditations aimed at repairing the "broken vessels," a parallel process of "sifting and clarifying" is generated in the upper worlds.

EVERYTHING STARTS WITH *ALEPH* - א

Most of the Ari's eating meditations involve varying forms of the letter *aleph* (א), the first letter in the Hebrew alphabet, therefore I will preface a few words about the Hebrew alphabet in general. In the Kabbalistic works *Etz Chayim* and *Otzrot Chayim*, there appears a chapter entitled *Shaar TaNT"A*, which are initials for *taamim* (cantillation signs), *nekudot* (punctuation signs), *tagim* (crowns), and *otiyot* (letters). These are the four components of Hebrew script as used in the writing of holy texts, such as Torah scrolls, *tefillin*, and *mezuzot*.

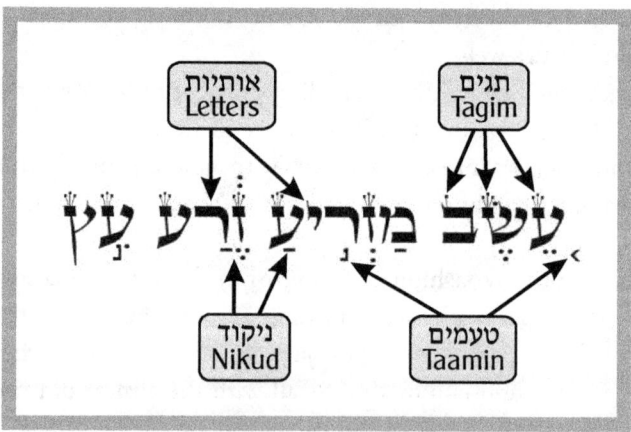

Figure 4: The different components of Hebrew

According to Kabbalah, the Hebrew letters are vessels for containing the lights of *Ein-sof* and are responsible for fashioning reality, as it is written:[89] "All the letters descended into the [World of] *Beriah* together with the *kelim*, in the form of the *nitzotzot* (sparks)." In broad terms, the twenty-two letters of the Hebrew alphabet have their source in *sod*, "mystical interpretation lofty spiritual realms. Their appearance in our world suggests a kind of "Divine instantiation" of spiritual forces that have their source in the World of *Atzilut*. Through the various shapes and permutations of these letters, the Holy One creates and sustains all created things.[90] The shape and construction of each letter indicates a unique pathway for God's creative energy and bears many spiritual significances.

The letter *aleph*, as the first letter of the alphabet, occupies a central place in the early Kabbalistic tradition, both in the Zohar and in the writings of the Ari. It is composed of a small *yod* on its upper right, a small *yod* on its lower left, and a diagonal *vav* in the middle connected to both. In addition, there is a small spike on the tip of the upper *yod*.

The following is a diagram depicting the letter *aleph* with the Kabbalistic significances of its component parts:

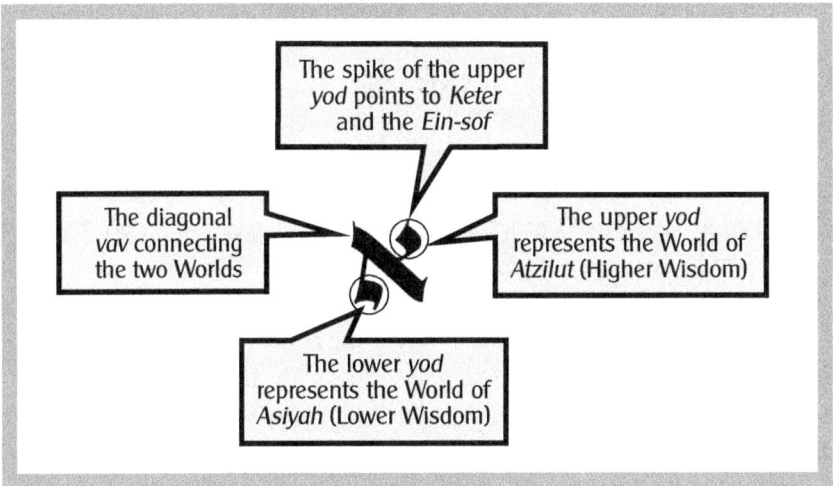

Figure 5: The components of the letter Aleph

The small *yod* on its upper right represents the World of *Atzilut*, with its spike pointing upwards to the hidden realm of *Ein-sof*.

The diagonal *vav* below it represents the power to draw down the *Or Ein-sof* and render it accessible through the *tzimtzum*.

The small *yod* on the lower left represents subsequent contractions of the *Or Ein-sof* to the extent that it can be revealed in the lowest World of *Asiyah*.

The name *aleph* itself contains various allusions as well:

- *Aleph* as in **Alupho shel Olam**, the "Master of the World," a moniker applied to God as the One Who generates and sustains all created things through the power of His word.

- *Aleph* as in the verse (Job 33:33), **alephcha chochma**: "I will teach you wisdom."

- The three letters of the name *aleph* —*aleph*, *lamed*, and *peh* — permute into the word *pele*, "wonder," whose significance we will soon see.

In the second part of this chapter, we will see how, for the purposes of meditation, the letter *aleph* is sometimes visualized as having a small *dalet* on its lower left rather than a small *yod*, or a diagonal *vav* that is split lengthwise.

THE MEDITATIONS OF MANOACH

Kabbalistic interpretation of Scripture reveals a dimension of meaning far removed from the literal narrative. This is the realm of Biblical interpretation referred to as *sod*, "mystical interpretation."[91] Whoever aspires to grasp the mysteries of Kabbalah must first reconcile themselves to this non-intuitive interpretive approach, often radically different from the standard Biblical exegesis. The Scriptural basis for understanding the connection between the letter *aleph* and the meditations for eating is surprisingly, the Biblical account of a man whose name was Manoach, the father of mighty Samson. In this account, Manoach's wife encounters an angel who informs her of Samson's impending birth, instructing her to raise him as a Nazirite (one who abstains from drinking wine or contact with the dead and does not cut his hair). Not knowing that the bearer of this news was an angel, Manoach, in reciprocation for his good tidings, invited him to dine with them. The following conversation then ensued:

> Manoach said to the angel of God: "Please stay with us and we will prepare you a delicious goat meal." The angel of God said to Manoach: "If you detain me, I will not eat your food. If you wish to serve up an offering, serve it up to God" — for Manoach did not know that he was an angel of God. Manoach asked the angel of God: "What is your name, so that when your words come true, we could honor you?" The angel of

God answered him: "Why is it that you ask my name? It is unfathomable ('*peli*')!" (Judges 13:15-18)

The Ari, in *Shaar HaMitzvot*, transforms this straightforward biblical story into a major source of his doctrine on eating:

> Before one eats, one should meditate upon isolating and clarifying the good that is in the food from the bad which is mixed in with it. Know that there are other meditations greater than this regarding the *birur* of eating. Manoach, however, would eat employing the basic meditation just mentioned… that which revolves around the letter *aleph* deriving from the *sephirah* of *Chochmah* (Wisdom). That is why the angel was revealed to him as a *pele* [for the letters of *pele* permute into *aleph* → פלא אלף]. However, Manoach's meditation was far from being the most sublime and refined. Hence, our Sages teach us that Manoach was a boor, for the wise man employs greater meditations than this. Hence, the angel said to him, "Even if you detain me, I still will not eat your food" - as your meditations are not so great. In the case of Abraham, however, it is stated that the angels who visited him ate with him — literally — as our Sages have described (Gen. Rabbah 86). With our above explanation, one can now understand the name Manoach, for its letters divide into *mem-vav* (numerically = 46) and *nun-chet* (numerically = 58). These numbers form the basis of the meditations that we are about to describe. Being as Manoach practiced these meditations all the days of his life, that is why he was given this name.[92]

Through the prism of Kabbalah, the story of Manoach in the Book of Judges is transformed into the basis of a specific sequence of eating meditations referred to as "Manoach meditations."[93] According to the Ari's explanation, Manoach would base his eating meditations on the letter *aleph*, which is associated with the *sephirah* of *Chochmah* as alluded to by the verse (Job 33:33), **aleph**cha *chochma*: "I will teach you wisdom."[94] The angel refused his invitation to join him in eating — "I will not eat your food" — being as Manoach was not on a sufficiently high spiritual level to free the holy sparks from the *klipot* in his food.

The majority of Manoach's meditations are based upon the four ways one could inscribe the letter *aleph*. The use and application of these four letter-forms will be expanded upon in the coming pages.

MANOACH VERSUS ABRAHAM

As mentioned earlier, even though Manoach was privileged to converse with an angel, in comparison to our forefather Abraham he was an ignorant boor and that is why the angel refused to share a meal with him.[95] In contrast, this is the conversation Abraham has with his visiting angels:

> And [Abraham] said: "My Lord, if I find favor in Your eyes, please do not pass before Your servant. Some water will be brought … and I will fetch a portion of bread so that you may sate your hearts" … And they said: "Do so, just as you said."

The Torah relates that the angels sat themselves down to a meal of meat and bread together with Abraham. This was because Abraham was supremely righteous and capable of freeing the holy sparks from the impure *klipot*. Accordingly, there is another more-exalted sequence of meditations referred to as "Our Forefather Abraham's Meditations," which are beyond the scope of this book.

THE STAGES OF EATING

1. Declaration before eating.
2. Preparing one's utensils.
3. Viewing the food.
4. Placing the food in one's mouth.
5. Chewing the food.
6. Swallowing the food.
7. Digesting the food.
8. Prayer after eating.

It is not easy in practice to correlate each meditation to its corresponding stage of eating. However, the "appetizer approach" that we described earlier allows us to execute meditations over the course of an entire meal as befits the circumstances and our abilities.[96]

Declaration Before Eating

The Kabbalistic custom before undertaking any significant spiritual activity is to preface it with a declaration of intent. This declaration, in varying forms, appears hundreds of times in the Ari's meditations. Sometimes it begins with the words "Let it be my intent to draw down life-force... Yehi ratzon milfane-cha..." and at other times, "I hereby fulfill the positive commandment of... Herini mekayeim mitzvat..." This prefatory statement is intended to help us focus our thoughts and enter into the appropriate frame of mind. It is not part of the Ari's actual meditations but rather a means of establishing one's objectives. When one eats, one must have in mind that one is elevating the food from its material source, be it animal or vegetable, to the human plane or even higher.

Here is the short prayer that serves as such a declaration, followed by a concise explanation of its wording:

> "Let it be my intent to draw down life-force (*Shefa*) and nourishment from the outer dimension of *Abba* and *Ima* into *Ze'ir Anpin*; and to entice life-force and nourishment from the World of *Yetzirah* into the World of *Asiyah*; and to clarify the good in the food and to clarify the holy sparks that are mixed therein."[97]

Let it be my intent to draw down life-force and nourishment: to allure and attract the life-force that nourishes and sustains the universe from God's hidden reserves into the lower realms.

From the outer dimension: The physical food that delights the body derives from the outer dimension of the supernal realms, whereas those religious commandments that do not involve physical pleasure derive from the inner dimension of those realms. Hence, prayer has its source in the inner dimension while eating, an act of physical gratification, has its source in the outer dimension.

Of *Abba* and *Ima*: The act of bestowing nourishment is identified with the male persona of *Abba* (Father), while the act of receiving and absorbing that nourishment is identified with the female persona of *Ima* (Mother).[98]

Into Ze'ir Anpin: The male persona of *Ze'ir Anpin* (The Small Countenance), the "son" of *Abba* and *Ima* and the central persona of the World of *Yetzirah*, is the closest interface between the esoteric partzufim (Abba and Ima) and the spiritual influence within our own world, as well as being the persona that we can influence in return. *Ze'ir Anpin* is the medium through which God outwardly manifests Himself in Creation, unlike *Abba* and *Ima* who radiate His Divinity in the hidden realms of *Atzilut* and *Beriah*.[99] *Ze'ir Anpin* is also called *Adam* (Man) or *Olam Katan* (Microcosm), insofar as it is comprised of all the spiritual antecedents of our own world.

And to entice life-force and nourishment from the World of *Yetzirah* into the World of *Asiyah*: The nourishment that we receive in the World of *Asiyah* has its immediate source is in the preceding World, that of *Yetzirah*. That World represents the male provider, whereas the World of *Asiyah* represents the female recipient.

And to clarify the good in the food and to clarify the holy sparks that are mixed therein: Freeing the holy spark that is hidden in the food constitutes the actual *tikkun*, or **restoration**, prescribed by Kabbalah, as explained earlier. Executing this *tikkun* triggers the physiological process associated with it.

CUSTOMS OF BEST PRACTICE

During the different stage of one's meal, one should ponder and meditate on various forms of the letter *aleph* and on various Holy Names, and thereby understand how the Divine life-force permeates through every stage of eating. The meditations are carried out **in thought alone** by picturing the letters in one's imagination — with eyes shut or open. For one who is seasoned in the practice of these meditations, they should take no more than a minute or two at the beginning of one's meal. It is highly recommended for beginners to use a printed sheet, and to point with their fingers at every letter and Name (my teacher, Rabbi Attiah, considers a beginner to be someone who has "only" been practicing these meditations for thirty years!).

The above instruction to "meditate" involves picturing the letters and Names in one's mind, a kind of guided imagery. As an exercise, one can shut one's eyes and try to imagine the letter in all its details. This exercise is valid for all meditations. In principle, there is nothing wrong with meditating on a graphic image of the letter if that will improve one's concentration.[100] Like a multi-storied building, each level of meditation in the series stands upon the levels below it, accruing strength and power as they progress upward.

I will first present a chart with the letters and Names for meditation listed according to the stages of eating described earlier, and will then elaborate somewhat on each meditation. In order not to overwhelm the reader, I have placed much of the more detailed and deeper explanations, sources and supplemental material in the appendix at the end of the book.

PART 2

ARI'S MEDITATIONS – A PRACTICAL GUIDE

DECLARATION OF PURPOSE

The main source for most of the Ari's eating meditations is the section of *Shaar HaMitzvot* on the Torah portion of *Eikev*, the exact version of which appears in the prayer book of the Rashash.[101] The custom of the Ari is to connect the letters and their shape to the *gematria* (numerical value) of the holy Names, as well as to the *gematria* characterizing each stage in the eating process.

In the previous section, we cited a short prayer that serves as a declaration of intent before commencing with one's meal. There is also a prayer that is said at the completion of these meditations which clearly summarizes their purpose:

> May it be Your Will, Our Lord God and God of our Forefathers, that all the sparks of holiness that exist in this food be properly extracted and rectified; and that You O Lord, in Your great Mercy, perform a kindness by completing the extraction and restoration of those sparks which we have not properly extracted and rectified so that no mishap results from my actions. May You unify together all the sparks of holiness that have been scattered among the *klipot* as a result of my actions and restore them to holiness, cleansed of all evil, as they were at the outset; and may You purify our souls.

In the above prayer we see how the purpose of these meditations is to extract and free the sparks of holiness that are trapped in the *klipot* while at the same time asking God to complete the work that we have missed and so purify us and prevent any possible mishap resulting from our efforts.[102]

THE ACTUAL MEDITATIONS ACCORDING TO THE STAGE OF EATING

The following is a chart summarizing the meditations that correspond to the various stages of eating, followed by a detailed explanation of each stage and its attendant practice.

Figure 6: Full Meditative Overview

STAGE	PICTURED LETTERS	MEDITATIVE THOUGHTS
1. Preparing one's teeth ל״ב Lev (32)		Yod (10) + Vav (6) + Vav (6) + Yod (10) = 32
2. Viewing the food מ״ו Mooh (46)		Yod (10) + Vav (6) + Yod (10) = **26** (Upper jaw) Yod (10) + Vav (6) + Dalet (4) = **20** (Lower jaw) **46**
3. Placing the food in one's mouth נ״ח Nach (58)		Yod (10) + Vav (6) + Vav (6) + Yod (10) = 32 Yod (10) + Vav (6) + Vav (6) + Dalet (4) = **26** **58** = *ochel* (food)
4. Contemplating the food לח״ם Lechem (78)		Yod (10) + Vav (6) + Vav (6) + Yod (10) = 32 Yod (10) + Vav (6) + Vav (6) + Dalet (4) = 26 Yod (10) + Vav (6) + Dalet (4) = **20** **78** = *lechem* (repast)
5. Chewing the food ד״ק Dak (104)		Yod (10) + Vav (6) + Yod (10) = 26 Yod (10) + Vav (6) + Dalet (4) = 20 Yod (10) + Vav (6) + Vav (6) + Yod (10) = 32 Yod (10) + Vav (6) + Vav (6) + Dalet (4) = **26** **104** = *dak* (finely ground) Meditate on chewing the food finely so that the sparks of holiness may be released from the *klipot*.
6. Swallowing the food פ״ד Pad (84)		Yod (10) + Vav (6) + Vav (6) + Yod (10) = 32 Yod (10) + Vav (6) + Vav (6) + Dalet (4) = 26 Yod (10) + Vav (6) + Yod (10) = **26** **84** = Meditate on the guttural letters of the Hebrew alphabet: א, ח, ה, ע *aleph* (=1), *heh* (=5), *chet* (=8), and *yin* (=70) = 84
7. Digesting the food שי״ע Shah (370)	מ״ו נ״ח לח״ם ד״ק פ״ד	Reconjure the previous five meditations in their stated order. Their respective *gematrias* — 46, 58, 78, 104, 84 — add up to 370, the number of "lights" radiating from the face of *Arich Anpin* and which fill the Four Worlds, advancing their restoration.

84

As noted earlier, while meditating, the lower leg of the letter *aleph* is sometimes pictured as a *yod* and at other times as a small *dalet*. In order to help distinguish one from the other in the above chart, the *aleph* with a lower *yod* is pictured in blue while the *aleph* with a lower *dalet* is pictured in red:

One will also notice in the above chart that the letter *aleph* is sometimes pictured with the diagonal *vav* split along its length. As we will see, this is meant to suggest the passage from one World to the next:

STAGE 1: PREPARING ONE'S SPIRITUAL TEETH

This first meditation in the series, centers around preparing the utensils used in the process of eating, chief of which are one's teeth. Hence, the Ari instructs us as follows:

One should meditate on this form of the letter *aleph*: ✖ , whose *gematria* is 32, alluding to the 32 teeth in one's mouth, which correspond to the 32 "pathways of *Chochmah* (Wisdom)" by which the *birur* (extraction) takes place.

The 32 teeth in one's mouth are the first anatomical parts to be engaged in the process of breaking down food into its various components. This serves to crystallize in our mind, by way of visual imagery, the essence of our meditation.

Figure 7: Preparing One's Spiritual Teeth

$$\text{✖} = 10 + 10 + 6 + 6 = 32$$

For an expanded version of this meditation See Appendix A.

STAGE 2: VIEWING THE FOOD

The next two meditations revolve around the letters of the name Manoach, the Biblical figure, who the Ari sees as the source for his eating meditations. The objects of preparation at this stage are our two jaws that power our teeth as they begin to clarify the sparks within our food.

In the first step, one should gaze upon the food and imagine the letter *aleph* in its common form, as two *yods* (10+10) connected by a single diagonal *vav* (6): א. This produces the standard *gematria* of the Name *Havayah*, 26, corresponding to the upper jaw. Immediately following, one should imagine the letter *aleph* with the lower *yod* replaced by a small *dalet*, ד, resulting in a *gematria* of 20 (10+4+6), corresponding to the lower jaw. The upper and lower jaws correspond as well to male and female. That is why the *aleph* associated with lower jaw has a *dalet*, the letter that Kabbalah associates with the female.[103]

The combined value of these two *gematrias* (26+20) is 46, which is the value of the first and third letters of the name Manoach: *mem* (40) and *vav* (6).

Figure 8: Viewing the Food

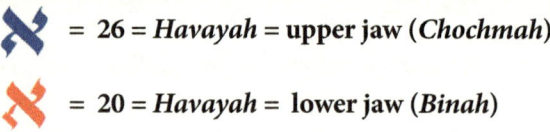

= 26 = *Havayah* = **upper jaw (*Chochmah*)**

= 20 = *Havayah* = **lower jaw (*Binah*)**

For an expanded version of this meditation See Appendix B.

STAGE 3: PLACING THE FOOD IN ONE'S MOUTH

In this meditation we also commence by imagining the two *alephs*, one with a lower *yod* and the other with a lower *dalet*. However, instead of the singular diagonal *vav*, we imagine these *alephs* with their *vav* split lengthwise.

With this meditation, we complete the association between the extraction of the sparks in our food and the Biblical figure of Manoach, Samson's father, who lived in 1450 BCE.

Figure 9: Placing the Food in One's Mouth

$$\aleph \quad = 32$$
$$\aleph \quad = 26$$
$$\overline{}$$

58 = *ochel* (food), as well as *Kel* + *Havayah*

For an expanded version of this meditation See Appendix C.

STAGE 4: CONTEMPLATING THE ACTUAL FOOD IN ONE'S MOUTH

At this stage, we shift our focus from ourselves and how we are about to execute the *tikkun*, to the food that is the object of the *tikkun*.

This meditation is associated with the word *lechem*. Although *lechem* is commonly translated as "bread," in Biblical sources it can refer by association to any major source of nourishment or satiation[104]. Hence, the Psalmist praises God for the "*lechem* that nourishes the heart of man" (Ps. 104:15), echoing Abraham's words to the angels: "I will fetch a portion of *lechem* so that you may sate your hearts." Sating or nourishing the heart requires more than just a portion of bread.

Hence, it appears logical to apply the term *lechem*, which is the focus of this stage of meditation, to any significant source of nourishment and not just bread.

Figure 10: Contemplating the Food in One's Mouth

$$\aleph \quad = 32$$
$$= 26$$
$$\underline{= 20}$$

78 = lechem = Havayah (26) X 3

For an expanded version of this meditation See Appendix D.

STAGE 5: CHEWING THE FOOD

This meditation is performed while chewing our food and grinding it finely with our 32 teeth. In this stage, we begin the process of breaking down the food and rectifying it both physically and spiritually. The Ari instructs us as follows:

> One should meditate on grinding the *lechem* very finely with the 32 teeth so that the [sparks of] holiness may be released from the *klipot*, thereby refining the food in accordance with the *gematria* of Manoach which equals 104, spelling *dak*, "fine" [as in finely ground].

We have waited hungrily for this point in our book where finally it is possible to taste some food, referred to broadly as *lechem*. A careful reading of the Ari's above instruction provides a revolutionary answer to the question, "Why do we eat?" On the face of it, the question appears strange; certainly, we eat because we are hungry and want to live and accrue strength (and of course, because the food is tasty). Kabbalah, however, offers an altogether different reason: We eat in order to release the sparks of holiness from the *klipot*, as well as to spiritually restore ourselves and the food we are eating! The sensations of hunger and thirst exist so as to drive us toward this work of restoration.

Figure 11: Chewing the Food

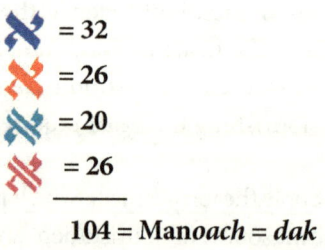

$$= 32$$
$$= 26$$
$$= 20$$
$$= 26$$
_____
104 = Man*oach* = *dak*

For an expanded version of this meditation See Appendix E.

STAGE 6: SWALLOWING THE FOOD

Upon swallowing the food, the Ari instructs us as follows: "One should have in mind that this is the completion of the extraction process that takes place in the stomach as the beneficial part of the food is absorbed into the blood and the waste is expelled."

The food in our mouths descends into the stomach by way of the esophagus, which is a muscular tube connecting the throat to the stomach and which forces the food down by way of peristaltic contractions. The Kabbalists ascribed a great deal of importance to the dual function of the throat, which is responsible not only for facilitating speech but also for facilitating the breakdown and digestion of our food.

The chewing and swallowing of food calls for the involvement of one's mouth, teeth, tongue, palate, and throat. Kabbalah links these five anatomical components to the five phonetic classes of the Hebrew language, which are essentially the five different sounds produced by the mouth.

At this stage of meditation, the images to be pictured are three of the four *aleph* forms pictured in the last stage: the two variants of the *aleph* with a split *vav*, א and א, whose *gematrias* are 32 and 26, respectively; and the standard *aleph*, א, whose *gematria* is 26. Together they produce a *gematria* of 84, which is the combined value of the guttural letters formed by the throat: *aleph* (1), *heh* (5), *chet* (8), and *ayin* (70), reflecting the centrality of the throat in this stage of *tikkun*.

Figure 12: Swallowing the Food

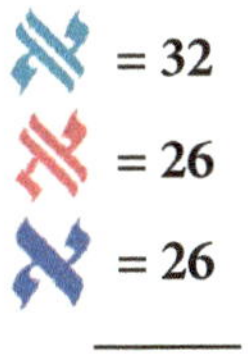

א = 32

א = 26

א = 26

---

84 = *aleph* (1), *heh* (5), *chet* (8), and *ayin* (70), the gutturals

For an expanded version of this meditation See Appendix F.

STAGE 7: DIGESTING THE FOOD

This, the final stage of our meditation, combines all the stages that preceded it into a single unified meditation. Unlike the previous stages, the physical aspect — digestion — is automatic and requires no effort on our part. The mental aspect, however, requires us to reconjure the previous five meditations, beginning with the stage of viewing our food. All in all, that entails visualizing five sets of *aleph* sequences and their corresponding *gematrias* in the following order:

Figure 13: Digesting the Food

א א		46	מ"ו	Mooh
א א		58	נ"ח	Nach
א א א		78	לח"ם	Lechem
א א א א	104	ד"ק	Dak
א א א		84	פ"ד	Pad

Pursuant to the order of the stages, the *gematrias* that we have meditated upon are 46, 58, 78, 104, and 84, producing a combined value of 370. This is a very significant number in the Ari's Kabbalah. In many of his works,[105] the Ari discusses the Divine countenance of *Atik Yomin* (the Ancient Days), the most exalted of the *partzufim*, or "personae," that we have mentioned in the course of this work.

For an expanded version of this meditation See Appendix G.

A Post-Meal Prayer

This prayer is NOT a generic grace after meals, but a supplication that our mode of mindful, Kabbalistic eating will achieve the goal for which it was intended. It also expresses our gratitude for having been privileged to rectify the foods with which we have been blessed:

> May it be Your Will, our Lord God and God of our forefathers, that by dint of the five *gematrias* — 46, 58, 78, 104, and 84, whose sum alludes to the 370 "lights" that is equal to twice 185, which itself is the *gematria* of the holy name *Kel* when spelled out in full (*aleph lamed*) — may my eating serve as an offering whose purpose is to elevate the supernatural powers [the sparks of holiness trapped in our food] , each realm successively higher, from the lowest World of *Asiyah* to the World of *Yetzirah* and from there to the World of *Beriah*, and from there to the World of *Atzilut* until they ultimately reach the Infinite Creator. From this lofty sanctuary, may a new measure of Divine life-force *Shefa* descend via the same order of Worlds until it reaches me, and may every one of my physical limbs strengthen its corresponding spiritual limb above.

> May it be Your Will, our Lord God and God of our forefathers, that all the sparks of holiness in this food be fittingly extracted and rectified; and whatever is not appropriately extracted and rectified, I pray that You Lord (*Kel*) Who in Your abundant mercies acts with kindness, will complete the task of extracting and rectifying them. And may You guard me and save me from eating any forbidden thing and combine all the sparks of holiness as decreed at the very beginning of creation, cleansed of all evil; and may You purify our souls. Amen!

Chapter Summary

In this chapter we have learned that the most powerful acts of *tikkun* are surprisingly those involving routine worldly pleasures, such as eating, and not just the ritual commandments of the Torah (as one might expect). I have demonstrated this *Tikkun* in brief a series of meditations that may be practiced during the various stages of eating. Any level of executing these meditations is praiseworthy — no matter how little one understands regarding the significance of the imagined letters and Names. Every effort we make in this world triggers massive developments in the upper realms that ultimately manifest in the descent of Divine life-force into our World of *Asiyah*.

All the Ari's meditations revolve around various forms of the letter *aleph* (א). Through the various stages of one's meal, one ponders, meditates, and engraves these letter-forms in one's mind. If one has enough time and presence of mind, one can also ponder the significance of the *gematrias* and holy names associated with these letter-forms. These meditative acts, according to Kabbalah, generate both spiritual and material life-force for the benefit of both the individual and the environment. The more one practices these exercises, the easier they will become. One will also notice that he or she is eating less, with greater patience and serenity, proper meditation on the holy names transmitted through Kabbalah brings about great healing and repair to the shattered realms of Creation.

Practical Implications

- One should pause before starting one's meal and take several breaths. It is best to say a short personal prayer for the success of the task at hand.

- One should not eat while reading a book or newspaper or while listening to or watching screens.

- While chewing, one should refrain from speaking even with friends or family.

- One should try and use the meditation chart in picturing the various forms of the letter *aleph* and considering their significance, while trying to apply each meditation to its relevant stage of eating — each in accordance with the time available and one's presence of mind.

Chapter 7

BLESSING — NOT JUST AN EXPRESSION OF GRATITUDE

The purpose of this chapter is to explain the Kabbalistic significance of the traditional blessings recited before eating and other occasions.

BACKGROUND

The meditations that we have dealt with up till now are those practiced **during** the actual act of eating. In this chapter I will elaborate on the Kabbalistic meaning for those who recite the blessings that **precede** eating and the role that these blessings play in the task of rectifying our food and elevating the sparks. This topic is referred to by the Ari as *Matbeia Nrachah*, the "format of blessing."

For thousands of years Jews have recited blessings both before and after eating; every category of food has its own unique, proscribed blessing. These blessings are referred to as "blessings of enjoyment," (*birkat hahanaa*), which our Sages instituted that they be recited prior to enjoying gastronomical pleasures. For instance, prior to eating foods cooked or baked from grains we bless the One Who "creates varieties of foods;" over vegetables, the One Who "creates the fruit of the earth;" over fruit, the One Who "creates the fruit of the tree;" over wine, the One Who "creates the fruit of the vine;" and over all other foods, the One "by whose word everything came into being." To underscore the stipulation that pleasure is the essential requirement, it should be noted that no blessing is made over fare that is nutritious but foul tasting (such as fish oil or bitter medicine) whereas unhealthy, tasty food (such as potato chips and coca cola) do require a blessing before the first mouthful.

CATEGORIES OF BLESSINGS

Jewish practice involves the performance of ritual acts, such as keeping the sabbath and the blowing of the *shofar*, as well as engaging in pleasurable acts such as eating. The Kabbalistic work *Nehar Shalom* (see RaSHaSH) explains the kabbalistic difference between a ritual act and a pleasurable act:

> The higher *partzufim* (personae) of *Abba* (Father) and *Ima* (Mother) correspond to *Olam Haba* (the World to Come), representing the inner dimension of the created realm where there is no eating or drinking, corresponding in the human body to the windpipe and the lungs ... the lower *partzufim* of *Abba* and *Ima* correspond to our own physical world, representing the outer dimension of the created realm where there is food for the body. From these latter *partzufim* derive the *mochin* (spiritual intellect) of the Chayot ("living" angels) as well as the physical sustenance provided by eating and drinking. In the human body, they correspond to the gullet, intestines, and other organs ... Hence, the blessing over a ritual act, or *mitzvah*, influences the hidden world, which is the inner dimension of the created realm, whereas the blessing over a pleasurable act affects the outer dimension of the created realm.[106]

Ritual commandments, or *mitzvot*, provide an interface between the commanding Creator (the source) and those who are commanded (the target). That is why *mitzvot* are compared to *Olam Haba* and are identified with the "inner dimension," corresponding to man's respiratory tract. Conversely, our physical pleasures, which in general are not the subject of a command, occupy a lower plane than the God-given *mitzvot*. They are identified with this world and the "outer dimension" of the created realm and correspond to the human digestive tract. Based on this explanation, one can understand why Kabbalah identifies the source of nutritional life-force as flowing from the lower *partzufim* of *Abba* and *Ima*.

THE WORK OF MAN VERSUS THE WORK OF HEAVEN

Our Sages instituted three categories of blessings:

> Blessings over mitzvot - "Blessed are you, Lord our God, King of the Universe, who sanctified us by his commandments, and has commanded us to light the sabbath candles".

Blessings of praise and awe, such as upon hearing thunder — "Blessed are You, Lord our God, King of the universe whose power and might fill the world".

Blessings of physical enjoyment, such as when eating an apple — "Blessed are You, Lord our God, King of the universe, Who created the fruit of the tree".

Action and activity constitute signs of life, as opposed to stagnancy and inertia, which are symptoms of cessation and death. This principle is especially obvious in regard to human action, as expressed by the statement in the Jerusalem Talmud (*Berachot* 68a):

"There isn't a single Jew who doesn't perform (at least) one hundred *mitzvot* every day."

In order to increase the possibility that man's daily activity should transpire within a spiritual framework, our Sages decreed that one should recite one hundred blessings every day in correspondence to the many active deeds that he routinely carries out.

Why did the Sages invest so much significance on the institution of blessings? A partial answer can be found in the following Midrashic legend:

It once happened that the evil Turnus Rufus [the Roman governor of Judea in 100 AD] mockingly asked the great sage Rabbi Akiva: "Which works are more becoming, the works of God or the works of man?" … Rabbi Akiva brought him some ears of grain and some loaves of bread and said, "These are the work of God and these are the work of man. Aren't these loaves more becoming than the ears of grain?"[107]

Rabbi Akiva's message is crystal clear: without man's participation, the work of creation remains sorely lacking. In Chapter 5 we spoke of the "extraction of the holy sparks," explaining that the descent of God's Infinite Light into the finite realm led to a "shattering of the vessels." This event caused **most** of these Divine lights to retreat back into their infinite source, while isolated sparks *nitzotzot* trapped within the shards of the shattered vessels became the foundation for the formation of the three lower Worlds: the World of *Beriah* (Creation), the World of *Yetzirah* (Formation), and the World of *Asiyah* (Action). It is man's job to improve upon God's imperfect Creation and thereby restore its intended Divine character, as expressed in God's mandate to Adam and Eve: "Fill the earth and gain mastery over it" (Gen. 1:28). In a certain sense, then, the works of man surpass the initial works of Heaven by elevating them to a higher plane.

The "blessings of enjoyment" are not of biblical origin, but, rather, were instituted by the Sages of the *Mishnah*. The only blessing related to food that appears in the Torah is the blessing to be recited after the completion of a meal, as it states (Deut. 8:10), "You shall eat and be satisfied and bless the Lord your God." That is, the blessing follows one's having sated oneself through eating. What then, is the source for making a blessing **prior** to partaking of a physical pleasure such as eating? The Talmud suggests an answer based upon the reconciliation of two conflicting verses:

> It is forbidden to derive pleasure from this world without first making a blessing, and whoever does so is guilty, as it were, of pilfering Heavenly property, for it is written (Psa. 24:1), "To God is the earth and all its fullness." A contradiction is raised because another verse states (ibid. 115:16), "As for the heavens, the heavens are God's, but the earth He gave to mankind"! In truth, it is not difficult: ["To God is the earth and all its fullness"] applies prior to making a blessing, whereas ["the earth He gave to mankind"] applies after having made a blessing.[108]

Clarification of this Talmudic passage can be summarized by the following Q&A:

Question: To whom does the earth belong, to God or to man?

Answer: Prior to our acknowledgement of God as Creator via our blessing, the produce of the earth belongs to Him. However, subsequent to our blessing and acknowledgment, He transfers ownership to us, so that we may derive pleasure from it.

Essentially, the blessing is a form of obtaining permission from the Creator to somewhat diminish the earth's fullness, thereby affecting not only the material balance of Creation, but the spiritual balance as well. It is through the blessing that we restore the Divine life-force that we have diminished.

This is how the 17th century Kabbalist, Rabbi Moses Luzzatto, describes the process:

> The Exalted One desired that all worldly things become sanctified by man's using them for his needs and his pleasure ... This is the mysti-

cal significance of the verse, "As for the heavens, the heavens are God's, but the earth He gave to mankind." The power was given to man's soul to draw down God's Divine Presence and light. God permitted man all worldly things for his personal use **in order that** that they may be restored by the holiness which man draws down and confers upon these objects as well as himself and the environment.[109]

WHAT'S MORE IMPORTANT — BLESSINGS OF ENJOYMENT OR OF *MITZVOT*?

Our Sages go on to address another category of blessing: Blessings prior to the performance of a *mitzvah*, which begin "Blessed are You, O Lord our God, King of the universe, Who has sanctified us with His *mitzvot* and commanded us …." Is one category of blessing more important than the other? Logic would seem to dictate the importance of *mitzvah* blessings, which derive from God directly addressing us with a command, over and above the importance of blessings that simply attend the partaking of a physical pleasure. To our great surprise, that is not the opinion of the Ari:

> My teacher also taught me that the attainment of *ruach hakodesh* (Divine Enlightenment) is chiefly dependent upon one's intention and exactitude in reciting the blessings over enjoyment — for it is through them that the power of those *klipot* that inhere in our food is neutralized.[110]

This passage has far-reaching implications and therefore warrants special attention. It suggests that one can attain the highest levels of Divine inspiration by focusing properly on the blessings over enjoyment before eating — not by donning *tefillin* or affixing a *mezuzah*, but, paradoxically, by making a blessing prior to eating a steak or drinking a cup of coffee!

The rationale behind this counter intuitive doctrine is quite straightforward: Sanctifying something that is in the realm of the mundane, food being the classic example, basic to both man and animal, effects a greater spiritual restoration than performing a *mitzvah*, which already originates in the realm of the sacred. We have previously encountered this surprising message in Chapter 2, where I suggested that eating was the primary incentive in God's creating the universe and was responsible for the dramatic shift that occurred after man partook of the Tree of Knowledge.

THE ESSENCE OF A BLESSING[111]

When one blesses another human being, one is in essentially extending him a gift — in word or deed. This is clearly not the case when one blesses the Creator Who lacks nothing and cannot be given anything and therefore does not benefit at all from our blessing. Hence, when we refer to God as *baruch* (Blessed) at the start of our blessings, the meaning is that He is the "Source of all blessing," just as the adjective *rachum* (Merciful) describes Him as the font of all mercy. Through our blessing God, we are declaring that the source of all goodness in the world is found in Him and not in the work of our own hands. We are just facilitators of God's blessing, who, like the farmer working his land and tending his crops, simply creates the right conditions for God to bless his produce.

There is even a philological connection between the word *brachah*, "blessing," and the word *havrachah*, the "bending" of a branch into the ground for the purpose of generating new growth. Another word from the same root — *breichah* — refers to a reservoir of water. Both words imply God's conferring blessing upon His Creation through the propagation of new life.

In summary, our blessing summons forth Divine bounty from the Source of all life, thereby enhancing and increasing the goodness in the world. Imagine massive storehouses in Heaven containing all manner of material resources necessary for the preservation of the universe. These storehouses await the blessings of man, uttered with proper intention, in order that they may release their bounty. This idea is hinted at in the words of the prophet (Malachi 3:10): "I will open for you the skylights of the heavens and pour out upon you blessing without limit."

IMMATURE ABUNDANCE (*MOCHIN* DE'KATNUT) VERSUS MATURE ABUNDANCE (*MOCHIN* DE'GADLUT)

The Kabbalah of the Ari posits an established three stage process that repeats itself every time one acts to draw down Divine life-force. The following "format of blessing" offers a distilled prototype of this pattern of action:

- **Blessed are You, O Lord our God** initiates the blessing format and draws forth a reduced measure of Divine life-force referred to as *mochin d'katnut*, "immature *mochin*."[112]

- **King of the universe** represents the core of the blessing format, through which two actions occur:

  » The "immature *mochin*" soar upward through the spiritual realms until they reach the pinnacle of their potential, referred to Kabbalistically as the *Abba* and *Ima* of *Adam Kadmon*, the male and female aspects of Primordial man, the earliest and most exalted *partzuf* of Creation.

  » As a result of the "immature *mochin*" reaching this pinnacle, a central event occurs which is referred to in Kabbalah as *yichud*, "unification," specifically the union of male life-force and female life-force. This event gives birth to a new spiritual force, *mochin d'gadlut*, "mature *mochin*."

- **Who creates the fruit of the tree** (or other such endings) concludes the blessing and causes "mature *mochin*" to descend and spread throughout the realms of Creation until it reaches our own material realm. This stage is that of *chalukat hashefa*, the distribution of Divine life-force.

This series of events occurs every time a person initiates a process of "cosmic repair" - *Tikun* in the Kabbalistic sense. The intensity and quality of the Divine life-force *Shefa* generated by the blessing accompanying such an act, depends on several variables:

- Whether the initiated action constitutes a *mitzvah*; whether that *mitzvah* is Biblical in origin, Rabbinic, or purely optional.[113]

- The nature of the day when performed e.g. on a Sabbath, a Festival day, or a regular weekday.

- The degree of intent accompanying the act and the level of knowledge possessed by the doer.

The degree of life-force drawn down into the world through the blessing is determined by these variable circumstances as well as by the Creator's 'desire' to assist in the process.

A Deeper Look into the Format of Blessing

This picture of a waterfall is meant to illustrate the devolution of Divine life-force through the various *partzufim* that takes place when one recites a blessing. The source of Divine life-force is in the *partzuf* of *Keter Elyon* (the Supernal Crown), from where it proceeds through various stations before arriving in our own material realm, the World of *Asiyah*.

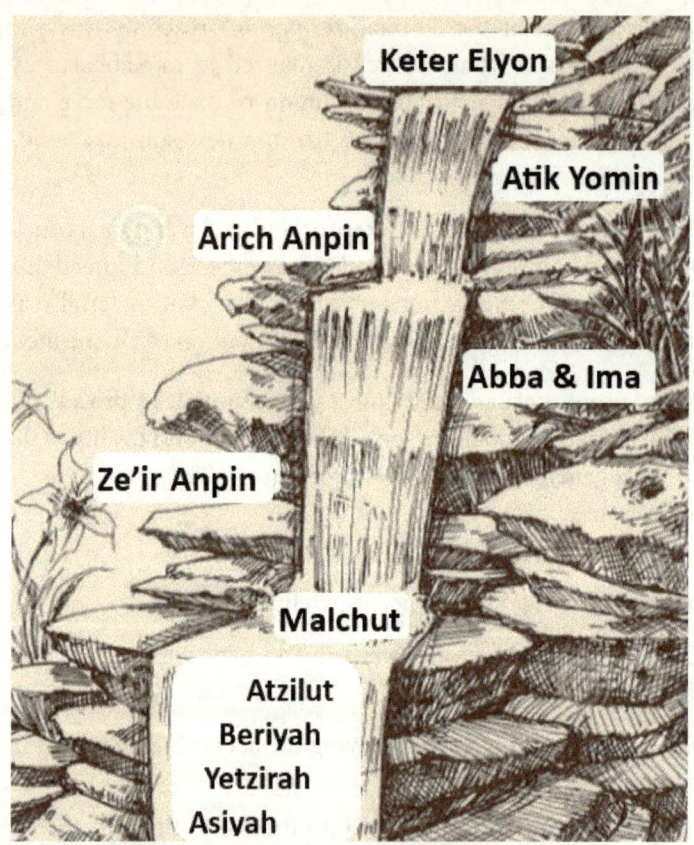

Figure 14: The Waterfall of Descending Life-force

The format of a standard blessing over food is as follows:

Baruch[1] ata[2] Adonai, Elokeinu[3] Melech ha'olam[4], borei pri ha'eitz[5]

"Blessed[1] are You[2], O Lord our God[3], King of the universe[4], Who creates the fruit of the tree[5]."

We will now delve into the spiritual significance of each word in this blessing, which should inform our consciousness whenever we recite it.

1. Baruch (Blessed)

One should imagine the formation of a conduit or channel from the *partzuf* of *Keter Elyon* that will convey a small initial measure of Divine life-force from the highest point in the World of *Atzilut*. Uttering the word *Baruch* declares that *Keter Elyon* is the source of all blessings, analogous to a boundless reservoir (*breichah*) of sweet water. Creating the conduit is analogous to inserting a small straw into the base of the reservoir, thereby allowing a thin stream of water to begin trickling down. This stream attracts a variety of life-giving forces, such as the lights *(Orot)* and abundance *(Mochin)* of the male and female persona *(Partzufim)*, the five forces of *Gevurah* (Might) and the five forces of *Chesed* (Kindness). This burgeoning stream continues to surge past the *partzufim* of *Atik Yomin* (Ancient Days) and *Arich Anpin* (The Long Countenance) until it finally arrives at the *Yesod* (Foundation) of *Abba* (Father) and *Ima* (Mother). At this point the stream strengthens into a flowing river which, as it flows and swirls past various stations, accrues additional spiritual force, as if absorbing various minerals and other beneficial elements.

2. Ata (are You)

We address the Infinite One using the second-person pronoun *ata* (You), implying familiarity, even intimacy. At this stage, the male and female life-forces that have flowed down from *Keter Elyon* to the *partzufim* of *Abba* and *Ima* **unite**. The Ari analogizes this to the passing of paternal seed into the maternal womb, requiring us to mentally draw forth a *tipah*, or drop, from the *Yesod* of *Abba* into the *Yesod* of *Ima*.[114] The union of *Abba* and *Ima* constitutes a bond whose purpose is to generate a new life-force in Creation, one which forms the basis of the World of *Tikkun* (Restoration).[115]

3. *Adonai, Elokeinu* (O Lord our God)

At this point in the blessing, the narrow 'stream' that originated in *Keter Elyon* that began as a drop in the ocean has substantially grown, but it is still hidden away and out of reach in the womb of *Ima* — like a treasure locked in a safe. In order for this new life-force — *Shefa* to emerge into the open and cause benefit to its surroundings, we need to take it to the next level of its evolution and to actualize its immense potential. This is achieved by way of these two Divine Names, *Adonai* and *Elokeinu*. Uttering these words combined with the right intention extracts the nascent life-force from the womb of *Ima* into the open, depositing it on the "head," that is, the "cognitive" *sephirot*, of the next *partzuf*, *Ze'ir Anpin* (The Small Countenance), from where it launches into activity.

One may wonder why the dissemination of this new life-force into the *partzuf* of *Ze'ir Anpin* serves a precondition in generating significant spiritual activity. The explanation is as follows:

The *partzuf* of *Ze'ir Anpin* serves as the metaphysical interface that directs all the affairs of Creation, since the more esoteric *partzufim* that precede it actually have no direct influence upon our physical existence. The *partzuf* of *Ze'ir Anpin* is the sole spiritual gateway and the only metaphysical entity that directly interfaces and binds spiritual man and earthly man to each other.

The chief influence of *Ze'ir Anpin* on Creation is achieved through the six "emotive" *sephirot* from *Chesed* (Kindness), *Gevurah* (Might), *Tiferet* (Beauty), *Netzach* (Victory), *Hod* (Splendor) to *Yesod* (Foundation). The Zohar explains that when the Torah states that "God fashioned the heavens and the earth in six days," it is alluding to the role that the six *sephirot* from *Chesed* to *Yesod* played in mediating that creation. Hence, they are referred to in Kabbalah as the "six extremities" defining the very space of Creation, or as the "constructive *sephirot*."

The three "cognitive" *sephirot* of *Ze'ir Anpin* — its *Chochmah*, *Binah*, and *Daat* — constitute its *mochin* (spiritual intellect), composed of the "lights" that it received from *Abba* and *Ima*. It is there that the spiritual force originating in *Keter Elyon* resides, fully equipped and prepared for its next role. The *mochin* of *Ze'ir Anpin* are nevertheless referred to in Kabbalah as *mochin d'katnut*, immature *mochin*, insofar as they have yet to achieve their full potential for advancing Creation.

4. *Melech ha'olam* (King of the universe)

This phrase introduces the most dramatic and significant stage of the process we have been exploring, made up of the following steps:

- The **elevation** of all the accrued forces alluded to in the previous four words — *Baruch ata Adonai, Elokeinu* — including the 288 sparks of holiness trapped in the *klipot*. [116]

- This **ascent**, leading in the opposite direction of the flow that we have tracked until now, carries these forces upward, *partzuf* after *partzuf* and step after step,[117] until they return to their source in *Keter Elyon*. The ascent, however, does not stop there, as these forces continue upward, exiting the World of *Atzilut* and continuing toward the most exalted *partzuf* spoken of by the Ari. *Adam Kadmon* (Primordial man) — specifically, its male and female aspects.

- At this point another unification takes place between these two aspects of *Adam Kadmon*, a much loftier unification than the one described above between the *partzufim* of *Abba* and *Ima*. The spiritual power, that is engendered by this union, is referred to in Kabbalah as *mochin d'gadlut*, mature *mochin*. Its purpose, like that of *Ze'ir Anpin*'s *mochin d'katnut*, is to generate new life-force, in this case, the ten *sephirot* operating in the Worlds of *Yetzirah* and *Asiyah*. These are the raw material from which all forces of *mochin* are constructed, as was briefly explained in Chapter 5.

5. *Borei pri ha'eitz* (Who creates the fruit of the tree)

With the conclusion of the blessing, the intended purpose of the entire process is realized: the distribution of Divine life-force — the mature *mochin* that were just generated — among the lower Worlds of *Beriah*, *Yetzirah*, and *Asiyah*, culminating in the four material realms of *Domem* (Inanimate), *Tzomeach* (Vegetable), *Chai* (Animal), and especially, *Medaber* (Human). The extent of life-force that is distributed as a result of the properly pondered blessing depends, as indicated earlier, on several factors, the most important one being the level of knowledge and righteousness possessed by the one making the blessing.

The mechanism implied by the blessing format, described above, applies irrespective of the blessing's conclusion, which depends on the particular food being consumed or the mitzvah being performed.

This brief review of Kabbalah's teachings regarding the blessing format hardly scratches the surface of what the mystical tradition has to say about the topic. Indeed, one of our greatest contemporary Kabbalists — my teacher, Rabbi Mordechai Attiah — has written a 300-page treatise just on the word *Baruch* without coming close to exhausting the subject.

Chapter Summary

We have learned, in a somewhat abridged format, that the recitation of a blessing, prior to enjoying one's food, is a form of requesting permission from the Creator to benefit from His Creation. After permission is given, the food passes into our possession so that we may enjoy it. Still, eating the food causes a diminution in Creation that is our obligation and privilege to compensate for by way of the Kabbalistic intentions, alluded to in the format of the blessing. The following is a summary of those intentions:

Baruch (Blessed) — The source of all blessing releases a flow of Divine life-force referred to as *mochin d'katnut,* immature *mochin.*

Ata (are You) — the intimate union between male and female life-forces.

Adonai, Elokeinu (O Lord our God) — the generation of a new life-force that is conveyed to the *partzuf* of *Ze'ir Anpin.*

Melech ha'olam (King of the universe) — the upward propulsion of immature *mochin* to the highest *partzuf, Adam Kadmon,* where a more sublime source of Divine life-force, mature *mochin,* is created.

Borei (Who creates) etc... — the drawing down of mature *mochin* into the lower realms, culminating in our own material plane of existence.

Practical Consequences

- One should recite blessings slowly and pleasantly, and not rattle off the words as if tearing down the obstacles preventing one's enjoyment.

Chapter 8

THE DIFFERENCES BETWEEN KABBALISTIC MEDITATION AND CLASSIC MINDFULNESS

The purpose of this chapter is to present the commonalities and the differences between Kabbalistic meditation and the modern practice of mindfulness.

MINDFULNESS — A MODERN PERSPECTIVE

The terms mindfulness, awareness, and meditative consciousness are similar both in meaning and objective. In the course of this chapter, I will demonstrate that Kabbalistic meditation commences from the point where secular, meditative states conclude. Nevertheless, they collectively represent a psycho-spiritual process aimed at increasing our awareness of events occurring in the here-and-now. For thousands of years, people have aspired to achieve such states of consciousness, as is apparent from the ancient writings of the East. According to the late scholar, Rabbi Dr. Aryeh Kaplan, such practices were already in wide use by the ancient prophets of Israel.[118] Focused, concentrated thinking constitutes the foundation of Jewish service overall, but particularly of the Ari's meditations, as is evident from the term used to describe them: *kavanah*, which means an exclusively focused thought.[119]

The antithesis of mindfulness is referred to by various terms such as stupor, distraction, obliviousness, and apathy. many believe that such lack of concentration is one of the defining characteristics of our generation, especially in Western culture.[120] Let us illustrate this by way of a common scenario: A person hurriedly rushes to a meeting. Were we to ask him upon his arrival what details he remembers from his route: how many people he passed, what they were wearing, if he locked the car and where he left the keys — chances are he would be unable to answer any of those questions with any degree of certainty. This common phenomenon is often called "inattentiveness" and it occurs due to a defense mechanism in the brain that filters out (for our own good) most stimuli deemed not vital to our actions at present. Just as too many peripherals connected to a computer reduce its performance, so too many stimuli demanding our attention harm our focus.

We are indeed incapable of absorbing more than a very small percentage of what is occurring around us. We are constantly being assaulted by sensory stimuli, most of which are irrelevant to our routine daily functioning. That is how a Harvard-educated neuropsychologist formulated it.[121]

THE BIOCHEMICAL BASIS OF INATTENTIVENESS

The brain defends itself from overload just like an electrical circuit. It filters from direct consciousness, through complex neurological processes, any activity that does not require special skill, rendering it autonomic. Over the last decades, this function has been amplified, because of a sharp rise in the quantity and quality of rapid stimuli constantly assaulting our senses. In this digital era, we are asked to operate along multiple channels, quickly and simultaneously. One prominent indication of this new reality is the research showing that the present generation of children and youth are prone to attention deficit disorder due to their increased exposure to smartphones and computers.[122]

Just as certain factors can lead to increased inattentiveness, so too can other factors serve to focus one's attention; particularly, the concerted, self-initiated mental activity of meditation and mindfulness. One can measure the neurobiological effects of meditation by way of functional and structural changes in the grey-white matter of the brain, especially in those areas associated with concentration and memory, facial recognition and sensory processing or self-regulation. At the molecular level, it has been discovered that as dopamine and melatonin increase, serotonin activity is regulated, and levels of cortisol and norepinephrine decrease. These findings are supported by functional and structural changes that show up through imaging techniques such as fMRI or EEG.[123] Serotonin, norepinephrine, and dopamine are very powerful neuro-chemical transmitters that fulfill a central function in regulating mood. In several studies done on participants subsequent to their having meditated, a dramatic increase was seen in the levels of these neuro-chemical transmitters.[124]

SELF-AWARENESS

In contrast to animals, we, as human beings, are not only aware of our surroundings but also of our own internal state — our thoughts and our feelings. This special distinction allows us to supervise ourselves.[125] The 17th-centuury philosopher, Rene Descartes, was among the first to identify self-awareness as unique to human beings, emphasizing the kind of knowledge that one ascertains through thought alone and without the support of sensual stimuli. He coined the famous Latin saying: Cogito, ergo sum, "I think, therefore I am."[126] In short, both science and philosophy confirm the thesis that man has the capacity to ponder his spiritual/psychological state and, hence, to adapt and shape himself.

MINDFULNESS — NOT JUST FOR KABBALISTS

Attachment to God, loving Him and fearing Him — these are central goals according to the view of Torah, as evident from the following verses:

> Now, O Israel, what does the Lord your God ask of you? Only to fear the Lord your God, to walk in all His ways and to love Him, and to serve the Lord your God with **all** your heart and all your soul. (Deut. 10:12)

> You shall love the Lord your God with **all** your heart and **all** your soul and **all** your might. (Ibid. 6:5)

These verses demand of man *all* of his heart and *all* of his soul, that is, 100% of his attention. Such a demand obligates man to maintain a heightened psycho-spiritual awareness through which to channel and harness his thoughts, his feelings, and his actions toward this end. Essentially, this means being aware and in control of both overall and particular experience. This is an absolute obligation for every Jew who is faithful to his tradition.

An Ancient Meditative Prayer

In order to illustrate how deeply ingrained the meditative element is in the spiritual DNA of the Jewish people, let us ponder the ultimate *mitzvah* that demands for an intentioned focusing of one's thoughts — the *mitzvah* of prayer. There are a limited number of *mitzvot* that are performed solely with one's mind and heart — absent any physical action. A good example would be the six constant *mitzvot*: To know there is a God; not to believe in other gods; to know that God is One; to love Him; to fear Him; and not to be led astray by one's desires. As for the *mitzvah* of prayer, this is what the Talmud states:

> The prayers were instituted by our forefathers. Abraham instituted the morning prayer, as it states (Gen. 19:27): "Abraham rose early in the morning to the place where he had stood before God" — where he had stood in prayer … Isaac instituted the afternoon prayer, as it states (ibid. 24:63): "Isaac went out to commune in the field toward evening" — to meditate in prayer … and Jacob instituted the evening prayer, as it states (ibid. 28:11): "He encountered (*paga*) the place and stayed overnight" — the word *paga* alluding as well to entreaty and prayer.[127]

These are the ancient roots of the thrice-daily routine of Jewish prayer. Let us look closer at the distinct language used to describe the act of prayer associated with each of the three forefathers and try to understand its relevance to the topic of mindfulness:

- **Abraham** *stood* in prayer — The Torah refers to the founder of monotheism as "Abraham the Hebrew" (ibid. 14:13). The Midrash explains that the word for Hebrew, *ivri*, teaches us that Abraham stood on one "side," or *ever*, while the rest of the world, which was steeped in idolatry, stood on the other. He stubbornly resisted the current of his time and stood firm in his beliefs, leading the Talmud to identify him with the psalmist Eitan the Ezrachite, whose name Eitan means "steadfast."[128] How appropriate for the first prayer in history, the morning prayer instituted by the spiritual revolutionary Abraham, to be described in terms of standing firm.

- **Isaac** went out *to commune* in the field —Our forefather Isaac, representing the succeeding generation, no longer needs to stand fast; instead, he ventures forward toward a new goal. The word *la'suach*, "to commune," implies a pouring out of one's heart.[129] The setting of the field suggests a connection to nature and naturalness, which abets truthful communication. Indeed, the verb *l'hitpallel*, "to pray," is a reflexive one, implying that the act of prayer is one of acting on oneself, not unlike the act of meditation.

- He (**Jacob**) *encountered* (*paga*) the place — Jacob takes the encounter with God to a new level. The Hebrew root *paga* can also mean to "entreat" or to "strike." Hence Jacob incorporated into his entreaty of God a laser-like focus of thought and spiritual insight. This kind of focused thought serves to neutralize any external stimuli, honing and guiding one's prayer, like an arrow, so that it may "strike" its intended target.

This understanding of the Talmudic account teaches us that the forefathers introduced into the world a wholly new human activity: meditative prayer combining moral steadfastness, emotional forthrightness, and heightened concentration of the mind. This form of prayer is deeply rooted in the Jewish people, having been passed on by our biological and spiritual forebears.

These initial guidelines informed the *Mishnah*'s later articulation of how one should comport oneself in prayer:

One should only get up to pray in a **deliberate frame of mind**. The early pietists would **wait an hour** before praying so that they could properly direct their hearts to our **Father in Heaven**. Even were a king to enquire as to one's welfare, **one is not allowed to reply** [while in the midst of praying]. Even if a snake were to wind itself around one's heel, one should not stop.[130]

From this *Mishnah* we can clearly see that our Sages in the 2nd century CE established several meditative principles regarding prayer:

- **A serious frame of mind**— a solemn frame of mind.

- **Wait an hour** — Pausing for some time, so as to direct one's heart — the need for quiet preparation.

- **To our Father in Heaven** — placing the presence of God in the center of our awareness.

- **One is not allowed to reply … one should not stop** — fixating on one's objective: entering so deeply into a meditative state that one remains oblivious to outside distractions regardless of their content.

The principles appearing in this *Mishnah* were later codified into law as follows:

> The one praying needs **to focus his heart**…that is, focus upon the meaning of the words that his lips are uttering; and he should **imagine that the Shechinah, God's Divine Presence, is there opposite him**, as it states, "I shall place God opposite me always;" and he should summon his concentration and **remove any distracting thoughts** from his mind until his thinking and focus on his prayer is completely untainted… Such was the practice among the pious and righteous of old: they would seclude themselves and concentrate on their prayers until they were **stripped of their physicality, their Divine consciousness heightened** almost to the level of prophecy. If an outside thought should enter while praying, one should remain quiet until the thought is nullified… Upon achieving all this, one may be assured that his prayer will be accepted.[131]

"Stripped of their physicality, their Divine consciousness heightened" is an extremely ambitious and very lofty aim, especially considering that it is addressed to every Jew, not just the spiritually elite.

The first Lubavitcher Rebbe wrote in one of his discourses[132] that one must pass through three stages on the way to authentic prayer: *Yishuv hada'at*, a settled mind; *hitbonenut*, deep concentration; and *hitbodedut*, thought isolation. *Yishuv hada'at* is required to silence background noise and calm one's mind. *Hitbonenut* seeks to exclusively focus one's thoughts on the words of prayer. The purpose of *hitbodedut* is to achieve a state whereby one's level of *hitbonenut* is so profound that no extraneous thought is able to penetrate and so achieving a mental state where only the words of prayer exist. This can be also described as a meditative trance

MISSION IMPOSSIBLE?

Even though this state of mind appears almost unrealistic, nevertheless such is the ideal that one should aspire to. In an expression of amazing candor, the Sages of the Jerusalem Talmud share some of their (unsuccessful) experiences while attempting to pray:

"R. Chiya said:[133] In all my life, I have only had proper intention once ...
Shmuel said:[134] I would find myself counting chicks. R. Boon bar Hiyya
said: I would count the bricks of a building. R. Matanya said: I am thankful to my head for having bowed on its own when I reached the *Modim*
blessing [where one must bow the head]."[135]

These brave confessions are especially impressive considering the stature of
these great Sages, 2nd-century Talmudic figures. The message to be taken from
these personal testimonies is one of hope and not of despair, as even these
great men experienced occasional failure in their spiritual endeavors, yet still
persevered.

An opposite example of accomplished prayer may be found in the testimony of Rabbi Akiva, another great Sage, who stated that when praying on
his own, he would start in one corner of the room and, upon concluding, find
himself in another corner altogether, having been physically displaced by the
ecstasy and fervor of his praying.[136]

The human capacity for self-awareness is a Heavenly gift associated
with our having been created in God's image, thereby allowing us to take our
spiritual pulse and act intentionally rather than instinctively. When faced with
a dilemma demanding principled action rather than base impulse, we are obligated to look inward; this ability is called "introspection," intro=inward and
spection=looking. man resembles God in his capacity to distinguish between
good and evil, as indicated by the words of the serpent as it enticed Eve into
eating from the Tree of Knowledge (Gen. 3:5): "For God knows that on the
day you eat from it, your eyes will be opened and you will be like God, know-
ers of good and evil."

Man is obligated by his very nature to distinguish between good and
evil. Should he wish to do good, he needs to channel his thoughts and desires
— to amplify some thoughts and suppress others, in accordance with his will.
This human characteristic is not to be found among plants or animals; with
them, everything occurs through instinct or innate nature — a simple fact
that needs no proof.

It was explained previously that the brain shunts to the back of our
consciousness our awareness of routine actions that we continually repeat.
Actions such as walking, eating, even praying, are thrust into our subcon-
scious and occur without thought — what is called in a Biblical verse, "rote
human dictate."[137] Still, we have just learned that if one truly wills it, one can

restore to consciousness our awareness of those routine actions. Practice and stubborn effort are required to undo negative habits acquired over the years.

THE DIFFERENCE BETWEEN THE ARI'S MEDITATIONS AND CLASSICAL MEDITATION

As we have already seen, the Ari refers to his Kabbalistic exercises of the mind as *kavanot*. Perhaps the contemporary term best suited to translate *kavanah* is "meditation." The classic act of meditation aims to free the spirit from its physical confines by way of mental concentration, enabling one to be lifted into a spiritually transcendent domain. Meditation is an exercise which employs specific techniques — such as concentrating on an object or word — to train one's consciousness and achieve a pristine, calm, and emotionally stable spiritual state.[138] Other examples of meditative technique include yoga, deep breathing, and guided imagery.[139] Most meditative approaches, both ancient and modern, make use of mantras — a single word or image that is repeatedly summoned over a set length of time. Focusing on a mantra or a candle flame for the purpose of neutralizing external stimuli clears the brain of foreign, unprompted thoughts. Clearing one's brain and settling one's mind are exactly what the meditative act aims to achieve.

The nature of Kabbalistic meditation is quite different. Kabbalistic meditations involve a variety of thoughts and mental images which are intended to lead one to profound insights regarding the ebb and flow of Divine life-force along the continuum of Worlds described in Kabbalistic teachings. Whereas classic meditation seeks to clear the brain, Kabbalistic meditation seeks to fill it. One could, however, formulate their relationship as follows:

The point at which classic meditation ends is the point at which Kabbalistic meditation begins.

In Kabbalistic meditation, it is not sufficient to concentrate on a single word or breath. Much mental effort is required, including a series of spiritual maneuvers that are characteristic of all the Ari's *kavanot*. Albeit at the end of this process we are meant to achieve the same serene spiritual state as in classic meditation, it comes with a significant bonus: aligning our consciousness with a higher plane of consciousness and drawing down upon us and the world Divine blessing and life-force, to the benefit of our souls.

In the Ari's meditations, the Holy Names of God are the standard focus of thought — especially the Names *Havayah*, *Ekyeh*, and *Elokim* — together with their more complex permuted forms.[140] It is important to note that according to many great Kabbalists, there is no benefit to meditating on these Names without understanding their role in the broader Divine picture. Meditation is not some kind of occult activity, like uttering inexplicable incantations for magical effect; it is a finely honed mental discipline that invites Divine goodness and influence to suffuse our world.[141]

THE STAGES OF KABBALISTIC MEDITATION

As indicated above, the mind must first be cleared before it could be filled with Divine thoughts. Thus, Kabbalists use ancient techniques, resembling those of classic meditation, to calm themselves and prepare their consciousness for focusing on these Divine subjects. There are several authentic and delicate stages in preparation for meditation. I will deal with those cited earlier in the name of the first Lubavitcher Rebbe which, although discussed there in relation to prayer, are applicable to all types of meditation as well:

1. *YISHUV HADA'AT* — A TRANQUIL MIND

In works of Jewish law, it is stated that one should not initiate prayer while in a state of sadness, lethargy, frivolousness, or idle activity; but only from a serious frame of mind. That is why the early pietists would wait an hour before beginning to pray, so as to achieve a stable spiritual state allowing proper concentration.[142] One also needs to symbolically cleanse oneself before prayer by ritually washing one's hands, even if they are already clean. Our Sages have also taught us that if one needs to use the toilet, he should do so before commencing with prayer.[143] The purpose of settling the mind is to neutralize any peripheral demands for our attention and suppress any competing thoughts relating to our "outside" lives (family, work, finances, security etc.)

2. *HITBONENUT* — DEEP CONCENTRATION

One needs to concentrate before praying on being in awe of the Infinite Creator and on being joyful at being allowed to approach Him in prayer. Such preparation should express itself in one's attire as well, attire that should project respect for the King before Whom one is about to stand. One should not hold anything that one is afraid of dropping, lest it distract him from his prayers. One should concentrate on the words issuing from his lips.[144] It is best to pray from a prayer book, as this will enhance one's concentration.[145]

3. *HITBODEDUT* — SELF ISOLATION

One needs to arrive at a state of concentration where even if a king were to inquire as to his welfare, he would not reply; where even if a snake were to curl itself around his heel, he would not stop. His entire reality must be reduced to the act of praying — to the point of his being totally *boded*, "isolated."[146] The founder of Chasidism, known as the Baal Shem Tov (Master of the Good Name), famously reinterpreted God's words to Noah, "Enter the ark (*teivah*)," as a general invitation to all who are about to pray to enter "the word" (also *teivah* in Hebrew) in a total state of absorption.[147]

4. DIRECTED & FOCUSED IMAGINATION

The implication of "directed and focused meditation" is actually all the Kabbalistic Kavavnot described in this book - and much more ! Upon completing the three previous stages, one inevitably arrives at a serene state of mind, calm and optimally focused. From this base one can proceed toward realizing one's spiritual objective, be it the service of prayer or the practice of Kabbalistic meditation.

The following story illustrates the power of concentration that can be achieved during prayer: Rabbi Chaim Greineman was once faced with an urgent life-or-death question that he needed to address to his uncle, the Chazon Ish.[148] It was Yom Kippur and the latter was deep in prayer. Rabbi Greineman first tried calling him by his name. Upon getting no response, he pulled on the sleeve of his uncle's jacket. Once again, no response. Finally, he was forced to place his two hands on his uncle's shoulders and forcibly shake him. Only then did the Chazon Ish open his eyes and break his concentration, listening to the question and rendering his opinion. The Chazon Ish succeeded in achieving such heights of concentration only after years of work and practice.

Silence is Golden

According to our Sages, the prototype of prayer in the Bible is that of the barren woman Hannah, future mother of the prophet Samuel (see Sam. 1). Scripture describes her heartfelt prayer as follows (ibid. 1:13): "Only her lips moved; her voice was not heard." The Talmud[149] learns from this that when praying, one's voice should not be audible, adding that "those who raise their voice in prayer are of little faith,"[150] insofar as they appear to believe that God cannot hear a prayer that is whispered. Later Talmudists[151] understood this to mean that one's voice should not be audible to others, but that one should be able to hear his own words of prayer and not just imagine the words in his head. When it comes to the Ari's meditations, the situation is different: Then, one is obligated to silently reflect and refrain from uttering anything, since the value of silent kabbalistic meditation far surpasses that of whispered, audible prayer.

Returning to our topic, a distinction is to be made between the act of eating, which certainly does not need to be conducted in silence, and its accompanying meditations which are carried out in one's mind and heart alone — and which under no circumstances are to be voiced out loud. Doing so would constitute a desecration of the holy realms being contemplated by improperly conferring upon them tangible expression in this, the lowest of realm of Creation, the World of *Asiyah*.

Chapter Summary

One of the brain's defense mechanisms in this frenzied world of ours is to ignore any stimuli that are unrelated to the task at hand, thereby causing a loss of attentiveness to what is occurring around us. But mindfulness and concentration are important for a person's psycho-spiritual health — not to mention for one's service of God. Mindfulness, despite the difficulty in attaining it, is necessary for a Jew to succeed in Torah study and prayer. There is a difference between classic meditation, whose purpose is to clear the head, and Kabbalistic meditation, whose purpose is to constructively fill the head.

Practical Implications

- Before any activity requiring concentration (such as prayer or eating meditations), one should try to traverse the following stages:

  » *Yishuv hadaʿat* (Calming one's mind) — by ignoring extraneous background noise.

  » *Hitbonenut* (Deep concentration) — by setting your sight on the plate or meditation sheet, and not on what is happening around you.

  » *Kavanah* (Active intent) — by concentrating your attention on the details of the eating meditations.

- While praying or reciting blessings, the words should be audible to one's own ears. While carrying out the Ari's meditations, one should mentally reflect without vocalizing.

Chapter 9

WHAT TO EAT AND TABLE ETIQUETTE

The purpose of this chapter is to explore what kind of table conduct is recommended and whether there is a preferred dietary regimen according to Kabbalah.

THE KABBALISTIC OBLIGATION TO EAT HEALTHY

We have demonstrated that Kabbalah has a detailed plan of action and a coherent vision regarding **what to think about** while eating, but the message is far less clear regarding **what to eat**. Nevertheless, we can say with absolute certainty that one is obligated to consume healthy, natural food and avoid processed or engineered food. This obligation stems not only from the explicit commandment to "safeguard oneself extremely well" (Deut. 4:15), but also from the underlying spiritual advantages that it confers.

According to the Ari's teachings, as we have seen, sparks, or *nitzotzot*, of the *Or Ein-sof* (Infinite Light) sustain every created element — inanimate, vegetable, animal, and human — having been pressed into nature at the time of *shevirat hakelim*, the "shattering of the vessels" (see Chapter 3). Those sparks are waiting patiently to be released from their *klipot* by way of Kabbalistically informed eating as described in this book. The more that the elements of nature remain preserved in their original pristine form, the greater is their potential for achieving restoration (*tikkun*) when consumed in the prescribed manner. Conversely, the more that these natural elements are broken down and reconstituted through artificial and unnatural processes, the more their innate spiritual power weakens and the less effectual their restoration. This hypothesis explains why there is a Kabbalistic obligation to eat healthily and to avoid junk food (see Chapter 2 on "The Spiritual Harm of Junk Food").

Proper Eating manners

The standard Jewish codes lays down a set of instructions for how to eat which Kabbalah agrees with and adopts. Our Sages formulated a certain table etiquette for reasons not directly related to Kabbalistic meditation. However, since employing Kabbalistic meditations whilst ignoring basic table manners would render one "a Torah-sanctioned barbarian,"[152] I have seen fit to mention some of the Halachic guidelines for proper dining: One should not engage in conversation while chewing one's food, as our Sages have stated:

- "One should not converse while eating, lest the food enter one's windpipe instead of the gullet and lead to choking"[153]

- one should not ingest too much food at once in the manner of gluttons

- one should not down an entire glass of wine or alcoholic beverage all at once; nor eat quickly or loudly chomping on his food, but rather should chew slowly with his mouth closed, taking care not to dirty his clothing, his hands, or his beard.[154]

What is Kosher?

Kashrut (noun of the adjective kosher), the ritual "suitability" of various foods, has forever been a trademark of the Jewish people. This dietary regimen was never subject to interpretation or relegated to mere custom; it was universally accepted by all factions of Jews from ancient times on. It is to a great degree responsible for having shielded Jews over the millennia from the twin threats of antisemitism and assimilation.

What are the criteria for food to be considered kosher? Despite its ubiquitous use, the term *kosher*, in relation to food, appears nowhere in the Bible. The proper term in Scripture for kosher is *tahor*, "pure" — a word that implies a more value-oriented connotation. The distinction between pure and impure animals already appears in Genesis, where we are told that God commanded Noah, "Of every pure animal take for you seven pairs … and of the animal that is not pure, two" (Gen. 7:2). Upon exiting the ark, we are told, "Noah built an altar to God and took from every pure animal and every pure bird, and offered burnt-offerings up on the altar" (ibid. 8:20).

Jewish law contains an extensive body of rules and laws defining the *kashrut* of plant and animal-based foodstuff, including the prohibition of mixing certain foods together, such as dairy and meat. Kosher mammals are identified by two characteristics: cleft hooves and the regurgitation (chewing) of their cud.[155] Nevertheless, they may be disqualified by suffering from a physical defect that is normally fatal within the space of a year — a status referred to as *treifah*; or by having died without a proper ritual slaughter — a status referred to as *neveilah*.[156] Even after having properly slaughtered a kosher animal, one is forbidden to consume its blood, certain of its organ fats and the sciatic nerve. In addition, one is not allowed to consume a limb or flesh that has been severed from a living animal.

Kosher fowl also have identifying characteristics. For instance, birds of prey are prohibited. Kosher fish must possess fins and scales. There are even rules of *kashrut* that apply to plants, such as forbidding the mixed cultivation of certain distinct species[157] and the ban of produce that consecrated for use by the priests or produce that has been cultivated during the Sabbatical year.

THE RATIONALE FOR *KASHRUT*

In general, Scripture avoids offering rationales for the *mitzvot*. Hence, we cannot presume to truly know the reasons for the laws of kashrut or why God commanded them. Still, one can discern in these laws there are several clear motifs: The common feature of all pure animals is that they are docile and are herbivorous, only consuming vegetation — in contrast to impure animals that are for the most part predatory and possess a vicious side. The impermissibility of un-slaughtered carcasses, which for the most part are victims of predatory violence, also distances us from the cruel side of nature. Some identify the basis for prohibiting swine as that animal's predilection for wallowing in and consuming garbage. Despite possessing cleft hooves, the swine's inability to regurgitate its cud is seen as an internal character defect.[158] Fish scales, a typical sign of fish that are non-predatory, also serve as a passive defense against sea prowlers, while their fins enable them to quickly escape danger.

PRESERVING THE ORDER OF THE SPECIES

The account of creation found in Genesis employs the term *l'mino*, "according to its kind," no less than sixteen times, such as in the verse (Gen. 1:12), "The earth brought forth vegetation: herbage yielding seed *according to its kind*; and trees producing fruit, each containing its seed *according to its kind.*" The implication is that the Creator brought forth a variety of species, in the animal kingdom as well, with the intention that they propagate among themselves so as to preserve the initial pristine order of Creation. This principle forms the conceptual basis of various prohibitions, such as *kilayim*, the planting together of different seeds; *shaatnez*, the mixing of wool and linen in garments; and the crossbreeding of different animals or species of trees. By preserving Creation's initial order, one affirms the work of the Creator.[159]

The Talmud states: "It was taught in the Academy of Rabbi Yishmael: Sin clogs a person's heart, as it is stated (Lev. 11:43), "Do not render yourselves unclean through them [the eight impure creepy crawlers] lest they render you impure (*nitmeitem*)." Do not read the word as *nitmeitem* [impure], but rather as *nitamtem*, 'lest they clog your heart.'"[160] Rashi explains this to mean that sin insulates and seals off the heart from the influence of wisdom.

Maimonides writes: "Know that whatever foods are prohibited by the Torah —their nutritional effect is deplorable … They [the Torah's prohibitions] are the indicators by which we know the praiseworthy kind of food from the deplorable kind"[161] — that is, the unhealthy kind. Furthermore: "It was known to the Sages that impurity weakens natural human intellect and confounds it, disassociating it from Divine intellect until it be purified. The wellsprings of the intellect are stopped up by impurity."[162]

The preceding quotations indicate that non-kosher food is spiritually harmful to the one who consumes it.

THE CHARACTER BENEFITS OF EATING KOSHER

The principle behind the above rationales for eating kosher can be summed up by the popular aphorism, "You are what you eat." Consuming the meat of docile animals confers serenity; kosher slaughter, which is done with a minimum of pain to the animal, instills compassion; and avoiding the mixture of different species preserves the integrity of Creation and confers faithfulness.[163]

We saw in Chapter 3 that the Kabbalistic notion of a soul inhering in each of the four created domains (inanimate, vegetable, animal, and human) lays down the spiritual foundation for conveying these traits. In *Shaar HaMitzvot* (*Eikev*), the Ari explains the essential difference between pure and impure animals:

Know that regarding impure animals, man has no power whatsoever to extract their holiness and that is why they are forbidden to eat. The holiness of pure animals, on the other hand, can be extracted [through proper consumption]. Conversely, one who consumes an impure animal or fowl absorbs the impurity himself and loses whatever holiness he himself possesses.

This passage establishes on extremely fundamental principle: extracting the holy sparks that exist in pure (kosher) meat and releasing them from their *klipot*, spiritually elevates the person who is eating. In stark contrast, a person who consumes impure meat, such as pork or carcass meat, the holy sparks are buried so deep that they cannot be redeemed by human activity. Rather than serve to edify and purify the eater, consuming such meat will only impart greater impurity. Such is the metaphysical reality as posited by Kabbalah.

VEGETARIAN OR CARNIVORE — IS THERE A KABALISTIC PREFERENCE?

The debate surrounding this topic is as ancient as it is pendulous. There is a dispute between the earliest bible commentators whether Adam and Eve were permitted to eat meat, and amongst those who held that it was forbidden to then, there is a lack of consensus at what point in history was meat allowed. Halachic authorities similarly argue whether the consumption of meat is a) forbidden, b) permissible or c) obligatory and the entire range of opinions can be found.

Originally in the garden of Eden, God commanded Adam and Eve as follows (Gen. 1:29): " And God said: "Behold I have given you every plant that propagates seed on the face of the earth, and every tree with fruit that propagates seed; it shall be yours for food. And to every beast of the earth, and to every bird of the sky, and to everything that crawls on the earth, which possesses a living soul — every green vegetation shall be for food." This verse does seem to indicate that man had no right to kill animals for food, so that both mankind and animals alike were only permitted to consume vegetation (ibid. 1:30),[164] despite the seemingly contradictory verse "Rule over the fish of the sea and the birds of the sky and over every living thing that crawls on the earth".

Animals were not to be eaten because they were spiritually unblemished and did not require a *Tikun*. This apparent prohibition against eating meat reflected the sublime moral character possessed by the first man and woman, which precluded the possibility of their inflicting pain upon any living creature. Additionally, the Ari (*Shaar Hamitzvot* 79) expounds the verse (Gen. 2:20), "Man assigned names to all the livestock and to the birds of the sky and to all the beasts of the field." – By dint of Adam naming all the animal species in the world, they become spiritually whole and did not require restoration via eating and therefore become forbidden. In contrast, "every plant ... and every tree with fruit" still required *tikkun* and therefore man was commanded to eat them.

As a result of the sin of eating from the Tree of Knowledge, as well as the sins of the ensuing generations leading up to the Noachide deluge, the natural order was compromised to the extent that vegetation could no longer serve as the mainstay of human survival. When the Flood subsided and Noah exited the ark with his family, God introduced a new dietary standard (ibid. 9:3): "Every moving thing that lives shall serve for you as food; like the green vegetation, I have given you everything." man's moral decline led to a new ecological balance, whereby people were virtually forced to eat meat, without opprobrium, in order to survive.

The elevated spiritual state attained by the Israelites during their sojourn in the Wilderness dictated that meat only be consumed within the framework of offerings brought in the Tabernacle.[165] Upon entering and settling the Land of Israel, the impracticality of bringing one's animals to Jerusalem led to the following dispensation (Deut. 12:20), "When God your Lord will expand your borders ... and you say, 'I will eat meat,' for you will have a craving to eat meat, you shall eat meat with all your heart's desire." Although this does not constitute an obligation, later authorities do mandate the eating of meat on Festival days, "for there is no joy without meat and wine."[166]

The conclusion we can draw from this oscillating account is that vegetarianism is the fitting choice for humanity in a perfectly moral world. However, a world that still requires massive *tikkun* is not 'ready' for such a level of indulgent pampering on a massive scale and the choice is up to the individual. It is interesting to note the idea of Rabbi Avraham Yitzchak Hacohen Kook (1865 — 1935, the first Chief Rabbi of the Land of Israel), that global vegetarians is a futuristic, messianic vision, and that carnivorism is a necessary 'evil' designed to minimize man's violent nature by satiating his bloodthirsty tendencies.[167]

The Kabbalistic Rationale for *Kashrut*

The Ari in *Shaar HaMitzvot* goes on to say:

> After the sin of the first man, eating no longer effects a total edification [of our food], and even the inferior edification that can be achieved is limited to those pure animals whose holiness exceeds the strength of their *klipot*. As regards impure animals, however, they cannot be edified whatsoever and so they are forbidden to eat.

As elaborated upon earlier,[168] elevating the domains of *Domem* (Inanimate), *Tzomeach* (Vegetable), *Chai* (Animal), and *Medaber* (Human) is identified with the work of *birur*, "extracting" the holy sparks from their captivity in the material world. In the previous segment from the Ari, he posits that extracting holy sparks from their *klipot* is only possible with kosher animals. We do not have the wherewithal to restore an impure animal for its *kelipah* is too coarse. Not only can't we restore it, but even the attempt to do so by eating it puts us at great spiritual risk:

> Not only will one be unable to extract its holiness by way of eating it, but just the opposite: the *kelipah* of impurity which is comingled in these animals shall seize and cling to the one who partakes of them, so that whatever holiness inheres within him shall be withdrawn.

The Ari explains that consuming non-kosher meat is devastating for one's soul for it absorbs and assimilates the soul of the non-kosher animal together with its forces of impurity. The preferred and healthy course is for the soul of the vegetative *tzomeach* to absorb and elevate the soul of the inanimate *domem*, and then for the living animal to consume the *tzomeach* so that it could elevate both together. Finally, the human, in absorbing the soul of the animal, elevates all three domains and sanctifies all the worlds. Were he or she to consume an impure animal, its soul would debase their own. That, in the view of Kabbalah, is the reason for the Torah forbidding certain foods.

A further passage addresses the issue of vegetarianism versus the eating of meat:

> Furthermore, even the inferior edification achieved by eating pure animals is only optimal when the eater is a God-fearing Torah scholar employing the proper meditations. That is why our Sages taught that

an unlearned person (ignoramus) **should not eat meat**, for when the lesser sanctity of his soul mixes with the soul of the animal, so the little sanctity he possesses will be depleted for he hasn't the ability to refine the animal's impurities. From this, one may understand the extent to which one should refrain from eating too much meat.

MEAT - FOR THE SPIRITUALLY ENLIGHTENED ONLY

The Ari cites here as law the opinion that an "unlearned person" (*am haa'retz*) should not eat meat; only a God-fearing Torah scholar is permitted to eat kosher meat. Since edifying the vegetative domain requires less in the way of spiritual caliber, that is where the unlearned person should concentrate his efforts. The Ari mentions as well that the Torah scholar's qualification for edifying the animal domain includes his familiarity with the proper meditations necessary for elevating the soul of the *chai* to the level of the human *medaber*. The same conclusion appears in *Machberet HaKodesh* (*Shaar HaShabbat* p. 37):

> Only a Torah scholar can refine and elevate a pure animal. Hence, the unlearned one is forbidden to eat meat, for if he does, the little holiness that he possesses will disappear and he will gravitate toward the animal that he is incapable of edifying.

Man's entire purpose in life is to sanctify his existence and restore the world. Hence, if there's a fear that one's actions may do more harm than good: then it is best to invoke the Talmudic precept *Passivity is Preferable* (Nida 59b) and refrain from eating meat.[169] From Kabbalah's vantage point, that is the reason that eating meat is sometimes forbidden, sometimes permitted, and sometimes obligatory — all in accordance with the spiritual caliber of the one eating. One unsuited to eating meat will cause the animal's soul to contaminate his own, as opposed to the righteous person who can purify the animal's soul. Obviously, we are incapable of deciding who is worthy of eating meat and who is not, so each should act according to his own understanding.

The Sages of the Talmud concurred with the Kabbalists, recommending as well that one limit the consumption of meat to only as much as necessary for one's health. Thus, the Talmud states (*Chullin* 84a): "Our Sages taught: It is written (Deut. 12:20), 'When God your Lord will expand your borders ... and you say, "I will eat meat," for you will have a craving to eat meat, you shall eat meat with all your heart's desire.' The Torah is teaching us etiquette: One should only eat meat out of craving, when one's body and soul require it — but not in gluttonous fashion … 'You shall slaughter one of your cattle or sheep' (ibid. 21) — one of your own and not meat bought in the market.[170] May one perhaps slaughter the only cow he owns, or the only sheep? Thus, the verse teaches us: '…one of your cattle,' and not all of your cattle; 'one of your sheep,' and not all of your sheep."

BACK TO THE MAN I SAW EATING

This brings us back to that memorable dinner that I described in this book's foreword, where I saw a very dignified gentleman, a Torah scholar and a Kabbalist, taking part in a festive meal (at a circumcision). I asked him why there was no meat on his plate — after all, it was a festive meal where the custom is to eat meat. He answered me that meat was only for the Sabbath. Now I understand the reason.

One should note that according to Kabbalah milk and eggs are of animal origin, just as meat is. Only according to its contemporary definition can one be a vegetarian while eating milk and eggs; according to Kabbalah, only a vegan would qualify as a vegetarian.

THE ASTONISHING REVERSAL OF THE PIG !

The future will usher in many far-reaching changes in the realm of Jewish law, including the annulment of some animal impurity. Even the pig, the animal most identified as non-kosher, is slated to reclaim the permissible status that it enjoyed prior to the giving of the Torah. This is alluded to by the Hebrew word for pig, *chazir*, from a root meaning "to reverse" — for in the future its kosher status will be reversed. In the meantime, the pig has the distinction of being the most reviled of impure animals. But once all the *klipot* become re-fined in the future to come, it will be possible to enjoy the good trapped within them, including the pig which will then be considered a pure animal.[171] The Kabbalistic work, *Ben Yehoyada*, elaborates:

> This does not mean that the laws of the Torah will change - for the *mitz-vot* are eternal. Rather, the pig will somehow anatomically change and begin to chew the cud (ruminate) and together with its cleft hooves thus

will be rendered pure and permissible as a result of being born with the two accepted signs of *kashrut*. The 'earlier' version of pig without these signs will die off leaving the new breed of kosher pig with these signs.[172]

The Talmud describes a great feast to be enjoyed in Messianic times by the righteous, with its main course being the leviathan, a mythical sea creature.[173] Some identify the Leviathan with a whale, which, lacking scales, is a non-kosher fish. According to this opinion, one would have to say that the whale, too, is destined to grow scales and thereby qualify as kosher in Messianic times.

This anatomical upgrade is an expression of what is to be the spiritual elevation of the animal kingdom. Paradoxically, it also sets the stage for the next global transformation regarding man's source of nutrition — a return to the original and authentic veganism. As shown in Chapter 2, animals were forbidden to Adam in the Garden of Eden, since God's initial intention was that man's food should derive solely from plants. Subsequent to Adam's sin and the Flood, marking a catastrophic moral decline, mankind was permitted to consume animals and fish in an attempt, according to some, to sublimate his violent nature.

The growing popularity of vegetarianism and veganism in recent times perhaps indicates an escalation of the Messianic process to which the Jewish people and indeed much of mankind aspire.

THE COMMANDMENT TO EAT HEALTHILY

Just as there are no specific guidelines regarding vegetarianism versus meat-eating, similarly Kabbalah provides no specific dietary instructions what should feature on one's plate — and this situation is certainly for the best. In Chapter 2 we explained why eating has the distinction of being the reason for creation and why according to Kabbalah one must eat healthily. The definition of what constitutes healthy food seems to change every few years in accordance with newly revealed scientific data. When I was a teenager in England of the seventies, the medical establishment recommended eating quantities of red meat, cheese, and eggs — protein, fat, and calcium having been viewed as the guarantors of good health. However, by the nineties, cholesterol had become Public Enemy No. 1 and meat, cheese, and eggs were all discouraged in favor of low-fat and vegetarian fare. With the coming of the new millennium, the tables turned once again and the new enemy was carbohydrates.

Diets, such as Atkin's, containing a lot of fat but a minimum of carbs captured the market. All that the Torah prescribes is to eat healthy — in whatever way that is understood in context of the contemporary scientific data.

The following are a few guidelines offered by Maimonides which would appear to hold today as well:[174]

- One should only eat when one is hungry and drink when one is thirsty.

- One should eliminate bodily waste as soon as one feels the urge.

- One should never eat to satiation, but only to three-quarters full.

- Once digestion begins, one should only drink what is necessary and not more, even after one's food has been digested.

- Before commencing to eat, one should walk or perform some other physical activity that will warm one's body.

- As a rule, one should exercise every morning until one's body warms up and then rest until one regains one's strength before eating breakfast.

HEALTH AND HYGIENE

Caring for one's health and personal hygiene are as paramount as any other *mitzvah* in the Torah. Evidence of this can be found in the account of how the Talmudic sage, Hillel the Elder,[175] was once walking along when he encountered his students who asked him where he was going:

Hillel: I am going to perform a *mitzvah*.

His students: What *mitzvah* is that?

Hillel: I am going to bathe in the bathhouse.

His students: Is that indeed a *mitzvah*?

Hillel: Certainly! If a statue of the king needs to be cleaned and washed down, I, who was created in the image of God, all the more so![176]

Man was created in the image of God and according to His likeness. His physical actions, and even his physical form, reflect the state of higher spiritual worlds, as alluded to by the verse, "From my flesh I shall envision God."[177] Therefore, each and every one of us is obligated to preserve his or her health and body as if it were a gold medal deposited with us by the King for safekeeping, to be returned to Him in the future as we received it.

WHEN TO EAT

There is an adage, whose origins are as obscure as its credibility: "Eat breakfast as if you are a king, lunch as if you are a prince, and supper as if you are a pauper." It would appear that our Sages agreed with at least the first part of that saying, for they ascribed much importance to the morning meal, which they referred to as "the morning bread:"

> After praying, one may eat the morning bread - if that is one's custom, and if not, he should make it his custom.

Note the wording, "if that is one's custom" — this is not an obligatory rule but simply advisable in the event one normally has the morning meal. Still, the source ends by stating that "it is best that one makes it his custom." Anyone who has ever enjoyed a continental breakfast as served in Israeli hotels can testify that this is one law that Israelis are very careful to observe!

Thankfully, our Sages saw fit not to impose their medical opinions upon later generations of Jews. They knew that these things are not a matter of tradition or Divinely inspired, and hence were subject to change in accordance with evolving scientific knowledge. For instance, a study conducted at the University of Melbourne, Australia, and published in the British Medical Journal (BMJ), revealed that skipping breakfast helps people to lose weight and to remain healthier.[178] The fact that our Sages instituted three meals over the Sabbath as a means of taking special delight in that day suggests that they viewed two meals as being sufficient during the rest of the week, or at least regular snacks.

ABSTINENCE VERSUS INDULGENCE

Is it appropriate to invest in preparing extravagant gourmet meals or is it preferable to stick to standard simple fare? Being as there is no definitive answer to this question in the sources, I will briefly present the two opposing authentic approaches, thereby enabling the reader to choose between them.

On one hand, the Torah commands us to fast on Yom Kippur, emphasizing that afflicting oneself brings atonement and purification from sin:

In the seventh month, on the tenth of the month, you shall afflict yourselves … for on this day He shall atone for you by purifying you; from all
your sins before God you shall be purified. (Lev. 16:29-30)

On the other hand, this special day occurs only once a year. Its rarity proves
that the Torah does not wish to encourage fasting and self-affliction. This
can be further proved by the fact that the Torah mandates the eating of one's
Temple offerings in a state of joy, as it states (Deut. 12:7), "You shall eat there
before the Lord your God and you shall rejoice with all your resources." Our
Sages later extended this obligation of joyful eating to the Sabbath, basing
themselves on the words of the prophet (Isa. 58:13), "Proclaim the Sabbath
a delight."

The topic of the Nazirite vows perhaps underscores more than anything else the tension in the Torah between the value of abstinence over
that of indulgence. In Christianity, the monk forswears the most physical of
natural pleasures — sexual relations. In Judaism, the Nazirite is only commanded to abstain from drinking wine, coming in contact with the dead,
and cutting his hair. It is permissible, and even a *mitzvah*, for a Jew to take
upon himself certain social proscriptions or abstinent behaviors only for a
temporary period — the standard Nazirite vow is limited to thirty days.[179] At
the end of that period, he must bring a sin-offering, the reason for which is
debated by the Rabbis. Nachmanides is of the opinion that the sin-offering
atones for the Nazirite's terminating his period of abstinence and returning to the hedonistic pleasures of existence, for he believed that moderat-
ing one's enjoyment of physical pleasures is commendable and advisable for
whoever can.[180]

These considerations aside, it should be emphasized that one is never
allowed to overindulge our physical desires. Nachmanides states that this was
the Torah's intent in commanding us, "You shall be holy" (Lev. 19:2). Had
the Torah not commanded us thus, one could have allowed himself to be a
"Torah-sanctioned boor" — wolfing down meat and guzzling wine, while
claiming to be free of sin providing the meat and wine are certified kosher.
That is why we were commanded to "be holy," so as not to engage in gluttony.
Still, the Torah refrained from defining the measure of gluttony, being as people's needs are different depending on their size and metabolism. Some people
have fast metabolisms, allowing them to eat more, while others have slow metabolisms, calling for a lesser intake. Two people with the same metabolism

may have different nutritional needs depending on the degree of physical exercise they get on a regular basis.[181] That is why the instruction is simply to "be holy" — that is, allow yourself as much food as you need to have the strength and contentment to do good deeds.

THE OBLIGATION TO ENJOY FOOD

In contrast to the previous approach that supports abstinence, there is an opposing opinion that forbids afflicting oneself and abstaining from enjoying good food. As stated in the Talmud, "whosoever regularly fasts is called a sinner."[182] Indeed, as opposed to the opinion cited earlier, there is another opinion of the Sages regarding the reason for the Nazirite being called a sinner:

> "Rabbi Elazar HaKapar said: Who did the Nazirite sin against? [Against himself,] for he denied himself wine. One can extrapolate from this: If one who denies himself wine alone is called a sinner, all the more so one who denies himself food altogether."[183]

Our Sages have also said: "In the future one will have to give an accounting for everything he laid his eyes upon but did not eat![184] From this source we learn that one should partake of all the delightful and varied foods that God has created in the world, and thank Him for them. Thus, His Name will be sanctified in the world, both through the blessings proffered to Him and through the contentment derived from His goodly Creation, allowing one to properly apprehend His Torah — as testified to by Rava: "The wine [that I drank] and the fragrances [that I smelled] opened my eyes [in Torah]."[185]

From Maimonides' following words, we see that he, too, disapproved of abstinence:

> If one should perhaps say, "I am not going to eat meat or drink wine" — this, too, is a bad path not to be followed. One who follows this path is called a **sinner** ... That is why our Sages have taught us to only refrain from those things that the Torah has proscribed and not from those things that are permissible. Thus, have they stated: **"Is what the Torah has forbidden insufficient for you that you need to forbid additional things for yourself!"**[186]

A Suggested Bridge Between Abstinence and Indulgence

The opinions we have brought on this subject appear to be in opposition to each other. I would like to suggest a middle path that might epitomize the position of the Torah which exploits a small but highly significant ancient 'typo'. It states in the Talmud:

> Three things **broaden** (*marchiv*) a person's mind: A beautiful dwelling, a beautiful wife, and beautiful clothes.[187]

An alternative version of this statement is found in manuscripts, interchanges two letters in the Hebrew verb, thus turning the statement on its head:

> Three things **destroy** (*machriv*) a person's mind: A beautiful dwelling, a beautiful wife, and beautiful clothes.

The Torah certainly does not condemn the comforts and pleasures of this world. That is why we are commanded, "You shall rejoice in all the good that the Lord your God has given you" (Deut. 26:11). However, the Torah wants us to know who is serving whom. Do worldly delights broaden and settle our mind so that we can be free to develop our spiritual side and perform kindnesses, or are they our masters, impelling us to tirelessly pursue the attainment of more and more pleasure and comfort? If the first case is true, then it is possibly a *mitzvah* to invest in delicious food and a beautiful home so that one's heart might be open to serving God expansively as well. However, if the second case is true, it is best that one restrain his indulgences and assume a lifestyle of simplicity until the fire of his desires subsides. In the words of Maimonides: "One needs to direct his heart and all his actions toward knowing God alone … as Solomon said in his wisdom, 'In all your ways, know Him.'"[188]

Chapter Summary

Nowhere in Jewish sources is there clear guidance as to what, when, and how to eat in the course of a normal day. Apparently, the answer depends upon the person's own makeup and character. If one tends to overeat, being drawn to gastronomic pleasures beyond what is necessary, he should, like the Nazirite, willingly assume a regimen of abstinence until he finds that his appetite has been substantially reduced. The main message is that one should eat healthily and enjoy what one is eating, but not eat to satiation. One may certainly partake of worldly pleasures, providing they serve to enhance one's awareness of the true purpose in life: to praise God and grow spiritually. But if the pursuit of food overpowers you and renders you a slave to your appetites — a boorish connoisseur —then it is best to adopt a spartan lifestyle until you are cured of your self-indulgent habits. The laws of *kashrut* are intended to prevent us from eating foods that are spiritually harmful. One can see that the Torah only permitted animals with a gentle and docile character. At the same time, it forbade us from corrupting the order of Creation by crossbreeding different species.

In general, meat is permitted and even required on the Sabbath and Festivals. It is also recommended at religious celebrations, especially for people of great stature. On a regular weekday, however, it is best to avoid meat or at least minimize its consumption.

PRACTICAL IMPLICATIONS

- One should engage in light exercise, as well as eliminate any bodily waste, before commencing to eat.
- One should eat healthy, tasty food in a quantity that satisfies but does not leave one "stuffed."
- It is recommended to limit oneself to two meals a day during the week, with preference given to the morning meal (be it a full meal or a light one), but there is no obligation in this regard.
- There is no religious preference accorded to vegetarianism over a diet of meat so long as one is able to control himself and elevate his food in accordance with the meditations described in Chapter 6.
- The noble purpose of appetizing, delicious food is to promote a tranquil, content physical state so enabling us to concentrate on the primary task - our spiritual growth . In the event one is overpowered by gastronomic desires, it is best to adopt a simpler diet so as not to turn the means into the end.

Chapter 10

BETWEEN SCIENCE AND FAITH

This chapter aims to highlight the complementary and symbiotic relationship that exists between science and faith[189] and to show how the mysteries of nature resonate with the language of Kabbalah. This rapprochement between science and faith as facilitated through Kabbalah constitutes a kind of tango dance and calls for a fresh look at some of the latest discoveries in science.

In this chapter, I will discuss a variety of topics, such as the age of the universe, the identities of Adam vs Homo Sapiens, and will relate to apparent contradictions between science and faith. Since the existence of a 'soul' lies at the heart of the Ari's meditations, special emphasis will be given to the scientific debate surrounding this topic. Despite the importance of this chapter, it has been placed at the end of the book so as not to disrupt the discourse surrounding the primary subject of eating.

NATURE — STATISTICAL RANDOMNESS OR THE FINGERPRINTS OF THE CREATOR

More powerful than any philosophical argument, it is the wonders of Nature that fuel the vigorous debate between those who support the statistical randomness of the universe in contrast to those who argue for intelligent design (Creator). The following are a few characteristic examples of the arguments often given in favor of intelligent design: A newborn's brain is composed of some 100 billion neurons. In order to arrive at that immense number, 4,286 interconnected neurons are formed every second of the nine-month-long gestation period! Another oft-cited wonder is the cosmological computation of the weakest electromagnetic force responsible for the repulsion of like-charged atomic particles: 10^{36} stronger than their gravitational attraction, or in long form, the incredible value of 1,000,000,000,000,000,000,000,000,000,000,000,0 00.[190] A deviation of even **one** zero would have rendered the universe as we know it unsustainable and precluded the development of life. Professor Roger Penrose, a British physicist and mathematician,[191] has calculated that the statistical chance of the universe having evolved randomly is 1 in $10^{10^{23}}$ (referred to as the Penrose Number), an unfathomable number that is greater than the number of atoms in the entire universe.[192] Does this figure have the power to demolish the argument for statistical randomness?

The Atheists' Claims

Atheist and agnostic scientists offer a narrative that can be summarized like this: The cosmos contains 10^{24} (1 followed by 24 zeros) stars that evolved over 13 billion years. The combination of such an immeasurable number of planets with varying climates with a life span of 13 billion years, greatly enhances the statistical probability of at least one such planet existing able to host the exact conditions required for the development of intelligent life.[193]

The following are some of the opinions of leading scientists, both modern and classical, championing the atheistic thesis, whose arguments are still totally relevant:

- The cosmologist Stephen Hawking has written that subatomic particles such as protons and electrons emerge spontaneously out of nowhere, remain for a time, and then disappear. Insofar as the universe itself was once the size of a subatomic particle, known in physics as *baryogenesis* according to the Uncertainty Principle the Big Bang could have occurred spontaneously out of nowhere, with no necessity for a Creator to trigger it.

- The astronomer Pierre Laplace (c. 1800) showed that one could explain planetary orbits by the laws of motion alone, thereby convincing himself that there was no need for a "higher intelligence." Anecdotally, Napoleon rebuked Laplace for not mentioning the Creator in his book

Celestial Mechanics, whereupon Laplace bluntly replied 'I had no need of that hypothesis.'

- Charles Darwin (also in 1800's) showed that the evolutionary principles of natural selection and survival of the fittest render obsolete the need for a Creator to explain the formation of the species.

Based on these arguments, and many others like them, it is a fact that most scientists of the past century believe that there exists sufficient evidence to confirm the randomness of the universe without having to resort to an intelligent Creator.

To deal with Penrose's computation regarding the statistical impossibility of a randomly-evolved universe, many cosmologists proposed the theory of a "multiverse," arguing that an infinite number of parallel universes exist simultaneously. This thesis explains the delicate and unexpected fine-tuning of our universe, promising that at least one of these parallel universes would succeed at producing such conditions. The main problem with this theory is that it is destined to remain hypothetical since it suggests that each universe is analogous to a black hole that is unobservable to those outside its perimeters; hence, the theory cannot be empirically confirmed. This is what Stephen Hawking himself said in one of his last interviews:

> "I was never a fan of the multiverse theory insofar as it is impossible to measure the size or nature of different universes."

Astonishingly, the fact that the scientific establishment, in the main, prefers to adopt a theory that is most atypical in the history of science simply to avoid the alternative of an intelligent Creator — should really invite a much broader discussion as to the role that intellectual honesty should play in the enterprise of scientific inquiry.

THE SHIFT IN RELATIONS

Starting in the 19th century, the natural and historic partnership between science and faith (and between scientists and believers) began to crumble and part ways. many factors were responsible for this, chiefly the discoveries of cosmology and the publication of Darwin's *Origin of the Species*. These two developments led much of the scientific community to view the attempt at mixing science and faith as an inappropriate incursion into territory outside their purview. The alienation between science and belief only deepened with the advent of the 21st century. A poll taken in 1990 among 1,646 professors of the natural and social sciences from 21 American universities revealed that more than 70% of them identified as agnostic, denying the possibility of ascertaining the existence of God or anything else that is non-material.[194] There is no doubt that an abyss has opened that divides and separates the spiritual and scientific domains, and for many it is unbridgeable.

MATERIALISM — MATTER IS ALL THAT MATTERS

The philosophical doctrine known as "Materialism" claims that nothing exists beyond the basic matter of nature and that every cosmic or biological phenomenon is the sole result of material interactions. Accordingly, it is not appropriate to attribute spirituality or Godliness to phenomena that we are currently unable to understand (the proverbial "God of the gaps"), for with time and scientific advancement all will become clear; even spiritual, psychological, and cognitive states will be proven to have a neurobiological basis in the brain. In the 19th century, materialism, as a philosophical approach, prevailed in the Western world and is still popular amongst most scientists today. One of its most prominent proponents today is the philosopher, John Searle.[195] He believes that even the hard challenge of 'consciousness' is simply a consequence of neurological interactions in the brain that may be described purely in scientific terms alone and that supernatural qualities need not be attributed to it.

In his book *The God Delusion*, the 'high priest' of atheism, Professor Richard Dawkins, summarizes his argument as to why the existence of a Creator is untenable:

> The temptation to attribute a reason why there is something rather than nothing is a false one, because the designer hypothesis immediately raises the larger problem of who designed the designer. The whole problem we started out with was the problem of explaining statistical improbability. It is obviously no solution to postulate something even more improbable.[196]

Friedrich Nietzsche put it starkly when he asked "Is man merely a mistake of God's? Or God merely a mistake of man?". It should go without saying that that there is not a religious person in the world who believes in a Creator Who Himself was created. Despite the claim being theologically shallow to the point of ridiculous, Dawkins suggests that Darwin's theory is a better alternative. Dawkins does not presume to prove with absolute certainty that there is no God. In his eyes, however, the existence of God must be something infinitely more complex than any natural theory of the universe; hence, it is best to do without Him, even if it invites a despairing outlook on life:

> We have simply evolved from bacteria; we are nothing more than glorified monkeys. There are no gods, no goals, and no goal-oriented superpowers of any kind. There is also no life after death. No ethics, no meaning to life, and no human free will.[197]

ARGUMENTS FOR INTELLIGENT DESIGN

On the other hand, many have arrived at the conclusion that there is indeed a reasonable scientific basis for supporting the idea that the universe was brought into being by an intelligent Creator Who Himself exists **outside** the laws of physics. The main scientific argument for this position is the virtually non-existent statistical probability of the universe having emerged randomly, as computed by Roger Penrose (The Penrose Number - see above). This principle of mathematical improbability applies to virtually all the core phenomena explored by cosmology and evolutionary biology and is totally unrelated to any personal or religious/theological considerations.

One example of the argument for design: Scientists were amazed to discover a long and detailed list of cosmic coincidences that suggest that the universe is inexplicably fine-tuned as if destined to facilitate the development of complex molecular structures and life forms.[198] Similarly, many serious mathematicians have cast doubt on the credibility of Darwin's theory of evolution. Large gaps in the fossil record contradict the idea of "transitional forms" linking one form of a species to that which evolved later.[199]

In recent years there have been some indications that appear to show that this trend among scientists is shifting back to the pre-Darwinian era. A comprehensive study performed in 2016, which included a poll of 22,525 scientists and intensive interviews with 609 others, revealed that 65% of scientists in India, Italy, and Turkey identify as religious, while 30% of those in France, Britain, and the United States subscribe to some kind of religious or spiritual belief.[200] With the advent of the new millennium, there has been a steady increase in the number of academic studies focused on abstract and non-empirical subjects such as the nature of reality, consciousness, and near-death experiences. Many of these studies have succeeded in generating reproducible results and in arriving at consistent conclusions. This new interest has led many to believe that the disconnect between the realms of science and faith is patently unjustifiable and narrowing at an accelerated pace.[201] The following are just some of the leading scientists in their field who represent the vanguard of this new trend in academic thinking:

- Professor Peter Fenwick of Cambridge is a neurophysiologist and president of an international research center specializing in near-death experiences. Fenwick has documented more than 300 cases of people who have survived clinical death, arguing that human consciousness extends beyond mere brain function.

- Professor John Polkinghorne (1930-2021)[202] was a theoretical physicist and professor of mathematical physics at Cambridge. His work in quantum physics strengthened his belief in spiritual metaphysics and even led him to become an ordained priest.

- Professor Francis Collins is an American geneticist who discovered the genes associated with a number of diseases, as well as being a former director of America's National Human Genome Research Institute. Once a confirmed atheist, he turned into a devout believer after discovering the wondrous harmony between science and faith. He has written: "The God of Scripture is also the God of the genome. One may find Him in the cathedral or in the laboratory. Through the study of God's amazing Creation, science actually becomes a means of worship."

- Freeman Dyson (1923-2020), a physicist and British-American mathematician, was a professor at the Institute for Advanced Study at Princeton. He was a believing Christian who argued that religion and science complement each other. Richard Dawkins was appalled that one of the world's greatest scientists was a religious man, sharply condemning him for having accepted the prestigious Templeton prize for the study of science's relationship to spirituality. This maybe his most famous quotation "Science and religion are two windows that people look through, trying to understand the big universe outside, trying to understand why we are here. The two windows give different views, but they look out at the same universe. Both views are one-sided, neither is complete. Both leave out essential features of the real world. And both are worthy of respect."

According to a famous anecdote, a horseshoe — superstitiously considered to be a good luck charm — hung above the door of the renowned theoretical physicist Niels Bohr. A senior physicist who visited him once was surprised to see this talisman prominently displayed above the scientist's door. When he asked Bohr if he really believes that the horseshoe brings luck, Bohr answered him: "Of course not, but the amazing thing is that it works — even if you don't believe in it!"

This short review of countervailing opinions in the scientific community regarding science and faith indicates that a growing and esteemed cadre of scientists now believes that science lacks a rational explanation for how the cosmos came into being and how life formed on the planet. In the next paragraph, I would like to demonstrate how the inexplicable is actually integrally woven into the fabric of the universe.

QUANTUM PHYSICS AS A MODEL OF THE INEXPLICABLE

There is one field of modern science where the counter-intuitive reigns supreme, and it just happens to be the field that deals with the foundation of all that exists — quantum physics. Here we will encounter phenomena that contradict the principles of classical physics as well as common sense. It is not for naught that quantum thought has been dubbed quite unscientifically as "quantum strangeness."[203] Here are several of its most unreasonable and surprising characteristics:

- **The observer effect** — claiming that quantum particles behave differently when not observed than they do when subject to observation (somewhat similar to the behavior of children!).[204]

- **Quantum entanglement** — whereby pairs of particles exert a direct effect upon each other despite being light years apart, famously called by Einstein as "spooky action at a distance". This empirically proven phenomenon contradicts the well-known rule that information cannot travel faster than the speed of light.[205]

- **The uncertainty principle** — claims that it is impossible to know with exactness both the position and the speed of a photon insofar as it behaves simultaneously as both as a particle and a wave (duality).[206]

Based on these principles, two independent observers may simultaneously perform the same experiment but measure different results — whilst both being correct! According to this, our best theory for understanding the building blocks of nature, scientific facts are subjective. This situation has understandably robbed many a physicist of his sleep, for quantum systems occupying several states at the same time simply do not operate according to the rules that they are accustomed to.[207]

Max Planck was a German theoretical physicist whose discovery of energy quanta won him the Nobel Prize said in 1944, "As a man who has devoted his whole life to the most clear-headed science, to the study of matter, I can tell you as a result of my research about atoms this much: There is no matter as such. All matter originates and exists only by virtue of a force which brings the particle of an atom to vibration and holds this most minute solar system of the atom together. We must assume behind this force the existence of a conscious and intelligent spirit. This spirit is the matrix of all matter."[208]

Erwin Schrodinger, a leading formulator of quantum physics, published his classic work, *What is Life?* in 1944, wherein he proposed that genetic mutations of molecular structure are determined by the laws of quantum mechanics. The simple basis of this thesis is the fact that individual organic cells are also composed of subatomic particles and electromagnetic waves, sharing certain qualities of both simultaneously. This contradicted simple logic as well as the laws of classical physics, leading the physicist Richard Feynman to once say: "If you think you understand quantum mechanics, you don't understand quantum mechanics."[209] To quote Werner Heisenberg, proponent of the Uncertainty Principle "Not only is the universe stranger than we think, it is stranger than we can think !"

HUMANS ARE ALSO MADE OF STARDUST

Every atom in our DNA, blood, skin, and bones is composed of the same elements that can be found in the stars — carbon, hydrogen, nitrogen, oxygen, sulphur and phosphorus. One must therefore conclude that the same "strange" laws of physics that apply to the stars apply to humans as well. This is what Lawrence Krauss, the physicist and cosmologist, had to say in his book:

> Every atom in your body came from a star that exploded. The atoms in your left hand probably came from a different star than your right hand.

It really is the most poetic thing I know about physics: You are all star-dust. You couldn't be here if stars hadn't exploded.[210]

There is a developing field in the real sciences called quantum biology that seeks to identify quantum phenomena in plants and animals and even inside the living cell itself![211] The significance and implications of quantum biology are tremendous: those strange and illogical characteristics enumerated above (and many more like them) form the basic fabric of all living organisms and occur in humans all the time. The organic living world behaves with a quantum strangeness that has no logical explanation. The inability to measure physical phenomena with certainty or to explain them logically does not turn physical science into science fiction or impair its standing whatsoever. Just the opposite — it impels other scientists to regard quantum physicists with awe and respect.

The thesis that the illogical nature of quantum mechanics hints at the possibility of a divine power outside of the cosmic framework is supported by several distinguished scientists, including Professor John Polkinghorne, a theoretical physicist at Cambridge (mentioned earlier) and John Lennox, a professor of mathematics at Oxford. The following is a passage from Polkinghorne's book, *Quantum Physics and Theology*:

> Because atomic behavior is so unlike ordinary experience, it is very diffi-cult to get used to, and it appears peculiar and mysterious to everyone… we shall tackle immediately the basic element of the mysterious behavior in its most strange form. We choose to examine a phenomenon which is impossible, absolutely impossible, to explain in any classical way, and which has in it the heart of quantum mechanics. In reality, it contains the only mystery. We cannot make the mystery go away by "explaining" how it works. We will just tell you how it works.[212]

Later in his book, he compares one-to-one those phenomena that contradict the laws of classical physics to certain spiritual/mystical precepts and as a result has his belief in a Creator strengthened.

THE NECESSITY FOR FREE WILL

I have presented in this chapter various positions on the relationship between science and faith, citing some of the leading figures in the field. I would like to suggest that the choice to believe in the randomness of the universe or conversely, the belief in a guiding hand, is a philosophical choice of faith and not at all a statistical or scientific one. There is no escaping the conclusion that the common denominator between the position of the believer and that of the atheist is still "faith," and not any kind of objective or scientific proof.

This conclusion is fully supported by classic Torah principles. It is an iron-clad rule according to Jewish thought that every individual is able to decide what to believe and how to act. Every intelligent thinker is required to galvanize his free will, along with his other unique talents, in deciding which narrative he will tell himself and pass on to the next generation. The absurd notion that one could unambiguously prove or disprove the existence of God is doomed to failure, for it negates human free will, an untenable proposition as stated in no uncertain terms by Maimonides:

> One should not entertain the thought proposed by various fools and ignorant people that God decrees at a person's conception whether he will be righteous or evil. It is not so …. It is a central tenet and foundation of the Torah … that the Creator does not compel or decree upon people that they must act good or bad; There is no one who compels him, sentences him, or leads him towards either of these two paths. Rather, he, on his own initiative and decision, tends to the path he chooses.[213]

The free-willed choice between good and evil that Maimonides speaks of is contingent upon resolving the question of whether there exists a God Who demands of us moral behavior. Were we able to solve the riddle of God's existence empirically, it would mean divesting us of free choice and ceding our will to the results of scientific inquiry. In his introduction to *A Guide for the Perplexed*, Maimonides formulates the implications even more sharply when he states that the perplexed individual would be forced to either choose his intellect and dispose of his faith or choose his faith and turn his back on his intellect!

The necessity for the existence of free-will enables, in the most legitimate way, both the skeptical scientist and the man of faith to simultaneously ponder **the same facts** and to arrive at fateful and **opposite** conclusions. The atheist sees in the *Homo sapiens* ("thinking man") an anomaly pointing to the randomness and purposelessness of life. The believer, on the other hand, sees in him a unique creation, directed and purposeful.

The principle of free will is anchored in an additional principle — Heisenberg's Uncertainty Principle, which claims that it is impossible to predict the momentum of subatomic particles for their behavior is unantici-pated. This freedom of action is built into the fabric of the entire cosmos.

If neither the scientist nor the believer could prove his position, one may ask what is to be gained from bringing evidence supporting a possible rapprochement between the two, this being my aim both in this chapter and in this book. I can offer three answers: a) The parallels between science and spirituality are fascinating and thought-provoking, and do not lose their value even if they remain speculative and not empirically provable. b) They provide a counterweight to the opinions of those scientists who claim to have scientif-ic proof that God does not exist. c) For people of faith, it fulfills the Psalmist's dictum (Psa. 19:1): "The heavens declare the glory of God and the firmament proclaims the work of His hands."

CONTRADICTIONS BETWEEN SCIENCE AND FAITH

The issue of apparent contradictions between science and faith preoccupies groups on both sides of the divide, leading to greatly diverging answers. For those who exclusively adhere to science, no contradictions exist since as far as they are concerned God does not exist. As for those who put their faith exclusively in God, no contradictions exist since science is untrustworthy. For the majority of people in between these extremes, who believe in a God and science in various measures,[214] there are two possible approaches when faced with these contradictions:

- Science and faith occupy two completely different domains; hence, it is illogical to speak of a contradiction between them.[215]

- Science and faith complement each other, such that any apparent contra-diction between them must derive from a faulty understanding of one or both together.[216]

The Oxford dictionary defines science as "knowledge about the structure and behavior of the natural and physical world, based on facts that you can prove, for example by experiments." The role of science is to identify observable phe-nomena and then interpret them by way of a theory that accords with the empirical data. The scientist is not asked, nor will he **ever** be asked, to explain **why** proteins form spontaneously and then randomly develop into chains of DNA but will simply explain **how** and in what sequence it happens. The cor-ollary is also true: a person of faith should never be asked to explain **how** life develops spontaneously from proteins, that's the purview of the scientist, but can legitimately offer an explanation as to **why,** or more accurately for what purpose, it all happens — this is the scope of a belief system. Ultimately for a person of faith, all the wondrous, natural processes that the scientist is able to describe occur due to the will of a Creator, Who is exclusively responsible for having formed the universe and Whose Will is the engine that continues to guide and sustain it.

As indicated above, there are those who argue that a head-on collision between science and faith is impossible for the simple reason that each operates in a completely different sphere with no points of friction between them. The mandate of science is to ponder, describe, and explain observable reality. Science, however, will never be able to (nor will it be asked to) answer why particles behave in a certain way or why gravity acts as it does. Such questions are not legitimate in the framework of scientific inquiry, for science deals with one question alone: how? — and not "for what reason?"[217] Allow me to cite the golden words of the late Rabbi Lord Jonathan Sacks:

Science is concerned with explanation:

Religion is concerned with meaning.

Science takes things apart to see how they work:

Religion puts things together to see what they mean.

Science analyses:

Religion integrates.

Science breaks things down into their component parts:

Religion binds people together in relationships of trust.

Science tells us what is:

Religion tells us what ought to be. [218]

THE EXISTENCE OF THE SOUL

In the wake of our discussion regarding the source of Creation, I would like to move on to a new topic which is at the heart of the Ari's system of Kabbalah: the existence of the soul. We saw in Chapter 5 (The Foundational Principles of the *Shevirah* and *Tikkun*) that the Ari takes a "radical" position, positing that the material and spiritual realms are **interwoven, entangled, and**

linked together to the extent that one confirms the existence of the other, like Siamese twins.

The modern philosophical view called dualism argues that alongside physical matter, yet extrinsic to it, there exists an entirely independent realm of mind and spirit. According to this view, ultimate existence is beyond the grasp of understanding and hence cannot be truly described in any way.[219] The primary proponents of dualism were Plato and the philosopher Rene Descartes. After dualism, there arose a school of thought referred to as panpsychism that argues for an essential and constant linkage between physical matter and its spiritual counterpart. This linkage is what confers "being" and existence to the thing itself.[220] Among the philosophers supporting this school of thought were Spinoza, Liebnitz, Schopenhauer, and William James.[221]

Recently, both approaches have gained popularity, especially in light of new revelations regarding self[222] that focus the discussion on subjective, first-person experience. An angry person is capable of simultaneously experiencing his anger and contemplating it like an outside observer, even sensing that he is contemplating his anger! Inanimate objects, such as a thermostat, a toaster, a computer, or even the most sophisticated AI bot, are incapable of such experiences. One fervent modern-day proponent of this dualist approach is Professor David Chalmers, a philosopher and scientist specializing in the psychology of mind and of language.

Kabbalah has a well-ordered response to the challenge posed by consciousness, explaining it in terms of the varying layers of the human soul, of which there are five: *nefesh,* the awareness of one's physicality; *ruach,* the awareness of one's emotions; *neshamah,* the awareness of one's intellect; *chayah,* the awareness of God's transcendence; and *yechidah,* the experience of one's own nullity and absolute unification with the Divine. The Kabbalistic thesis is that these five levels of consciousness communicate with each other, each from its respective province of responsibility, and together they confer one with a sense of subjective self-consciousness.

THE ATOM — THE INTERFACE BETWEEN MATTER AND SOUL

Is it possible to identify the point at which the body "interfaces" with the soul? The soul that sustains the four domains of *domem, tzomeach, chai,* and *medaber*, according to the teachings of the Ari, is reminiscent in some aspects of the basic forces of energy that hold together particles of matter, such as the nuclear forces that bond protons and neutrons to atoms and thereby sustain all the matter in the universe. Subatomic energy is not the soul spoken of in Kabbalah; rather it is the physical "effect" resulting from the prime "cause," God's creative force. Divine energy is the prime cause generating subatomic motion, constituting the underlying fabric of all that exists in the universe, from the smallest of particles to the vastest of galaxies. The physical expression of this Divine energy is the elliptical-circuitous path of electrons orbiting the protons inside the nucleus of the spiritual atom that supplies them with their orbital force. Every scientific discovery peels off another layer of the enigma that inheres in nature, but science will never reach a discovery that precludes the **why** question. This limitation is what John Polkinghorne terms 'epistemological reductionism' that simply replaces facts involved in one type of discourse with other facts from another type. (Reductionism — Interdisciplinary Encyclopedia of Religion and Science 2002)

THE SOUL OF THE FOUR CREATED DOMAINS

We are accustomed to a natural world in which the vegetative, animal, and human domains each live off their own unique sources of nutrition, thus growing and developing. Grass draws its nutrients from the inanimate earth and grows; cows eat the vegetative grass and grow; and humans eat the meat of animals and grow.

The Kabbalistic explanation for the development and growth of these created domains is based on an understanding of matter's spiritual makeup.[223] The Ari presents an orderly treatise identifying the spiritual components of the various created realms. We will now present his basic approach which posits that behind each of the four created domains there exists a creative spiritual force sustaining it and responsible for the changes that occur in it. In his work *Etz Chaim* (Shaar 50:2), he writes:

> *Domem* (the inanimate domain) possesses a physical aspect as well as a soul that sustains it. Above it is *tzomeach* (the vegetative domain) whose physical aspect also contains within it a vegetative soul. Above it is *chai* (the animal domain) whose physical aspect also contains an animal soul. **And it is certainly the case that the higher domain subsumes**

within it the lower domain. Hence, *domem*, being the lowest domain, possesses nothing more than its own physical and spiritual aspects. *Tzomeach*, the subsequent domain, includes the physical and spiritual aspects of *domem* in addition to its own physical and spiritual aspects. Being as *tzomeach* occupies a higher rung, the *domem* elements are incorporated into the *tzomeach*. Next, *chai* (the animal domain) consumes the *tzomeach* and thereby incorporates the physical and spiritual aspects of both the *tzomeach* and *domem* into its own physical and spiritual makeup. In the same way, *medaber* (the human domain) incorporates within it the physical and spiritual aspects of all three domains that lie beneath it — the inanimate, the vegetative, and the animal — in addition to its own unique physical and spiritual aspect.

Every domain of Creation has a unique soul that characterizes it. For example, a stone possesses an inanimate soul unique to stone, whereas a diamond possesses an inanimate soul unique to diamond. Likewise, wheat possesses a vegetative soul unique to wheat, and so on regarding the constituents of all four domains. The character of every natural element within the universe is determined by the type and quality of the unique soul that it possesses. In the next section, I will attempt to translate this last sentence into scientific terms, suggesting that the uniqueness of every element's soul is determined by its **atomic number**, which is the number of protons in the element as depicted in the periodic table.

A similar chord is struck in the Ari's work, *Shaarei Kedushah*:

The element of earth is called *domem*, and everything inside it is called the soul of *domem*. Similarly, the element of water, which promotes vegetative growth, is called *tzomeach*, and everything inside it is called the soul of *tzomeach*. The other elements follow in suit. This is what one finds the philosophers referring to as "powers," as when they say that the vegetative soul has the power to nourish, the power to attract, the power to digest and the power to repel. They also say that the animal soul is known as the source of movement and of feeling, for it has the power of arousal, the power of imagination, the power to mentally picture, and so forth with all the other elements.[224]

In this passage, the Ari repeatedly refers to the terms "soul" and "power," in accordance with his claim that each of the four created domains is composed of a physical aspect and a spiritual aspect. The spiritual aspect is what enlivens the physical aspect. According to the Ari, it is the constant presence of a spiritual "engine", breathing life into all of material reality.

The existence of the human soul is unsurprisingly frequently mentioned in the writings of the ancient Greeks who used the term "ensoulment" to describe the moment when the body is endowed with a soul, thus granting it life.[225] The soul was thought of as the spiritual breath that animates **all** living organisms, **not** just human beings. The anthropological concept of "animism" (from the Latin *anima*) ascribes a soul to Nature in general, including both its animate and inanimate elements, such that there is no categorical distinction between matter and the soul or spirit that sustains it. Apparently, this implies a strong resemblance to the Kabbalistic view. The 19th century anthropologist Sir Edward Tylor developed the idea of animism, defining it as "the general doctrine of souls and other spiritual beings in general."[226] Animism established the belief that all natural elements (including non-human) possess souls.

A SCIENTIFIC INTERPRETATION OF THE SOUL THAT RESIDES WITHIN MATTER

The Ari broadens the definition of "the soul within matter" and details exactly how it is that the soul forms the elements of the universe and what the engine is that shapes and sustains them. As discussed in Chapter 3 under the section heading "Defining The Elements and Domains of Creation," the Ari identified four **elements** and four **domains** which account for all of material reality:

- Fire, Air, Water, and Earth are the four basic **elements** that support life, but which exist as **static** components.

- Inanimate, Vegetative, Animal, and Human are the four domains into which all created things fall, but which are **dynamic** and variable.

The purpose of the created domains is to combine differing measures of the static elements into a myriad of newly constructed products, as the Ari writes (*Mevo Shaarim* 6:2:10):

The realm of the *domem* includes metals and precious stones whose material composition and form are composed from all the four created realms [*Domem* (Inanimate), *Tzomeach* (Vegetative), *Chai* (Animal), and

Medaber (Human)], just that **the element of earth dominates them**. Hence, the soul within them is only there **to mix and compound** the four [static] elements [Fire, Air, Water and Earth] with the four created realms … Hence it is called the composite soul that **establishes and sustains them in place, without changing them** from their original state.

In order to make sense of these Kabbalistic ideas, I would like to suggest a novel translation of the Ari's words into scientific terms which, in my opinion, serve as fitting metaphors:

> **The element of earth dominates them** — Each of the four elements represents a different type of physical matter and, as such, possesses a unique number of protons in its atoms (its atomic number). The number of protons and neutrons together determine the element's mass number; the more protons, the more mass (and vice versa).

> **To mix and compound** — a mixture is something formed from a combination of two or more materials; a compound is made of two or more elements that bond chemically. (An element is a material whose atoms all possess an identical number of protons.)

> **Establishes and sustains them in place** — refers to the single-value identification of every chemical element, namely, its atomic number as it appears in the periodic table. The atomic number is the number that defines the element's unique status — as to whether it is carbon, oxygen, helium, gold or lead.

> **Without changing them** — In nature, the number of protons in a particular element is fixed forever. It can only be changed through the aggressive intervention of scientists under laboratory conditions or naturally as in proton fusion within the sun.

In brief, each of the four basic elements is sustained by a soul that renders it eternally immutable. The plethora of created entities in the cosmos is the result of these souls mixing and intertwining in infinitely varying proportions. This understanding of creation lends itself naturally to the above association with the periodic table and atomic numbers.

My interpretation has found support from a contemporary Kabbalist, Rabbi Shabtai Sabato,[227] who has proposed that the spiritual component of every created element determines its physical character. A famous passage of the Zohar — known by its opening words, *Patach Eliyahu* ("Elijah opened") — states:

> The scales of righteousness are the two pillars of truth; the measure of righteousness is the sign of the covenant.[228]

Rabbi Sabato in his commentary to *Tikkunei HaZohar* also suggested that the "measure of righteousness" alludes to the atomic number identified with every element, which reflects the unique soul that inheres within every element of Creation. Thus, within the immense tapestry of the physical universe resides an immense complex of souls sustaining its existence.

Many point to the existence of evil as an argument against a beneficent Creator Who is the source of immortal souls, however the very ability to support the opposing forces is woven into the very fabric of nature. There exist many forms of visible energy, such as chemical, electrical, mechanical, nuclear and gravitational alongside the much vaunted dark energy, whose exact nature remains a mystery and can only be indirectly inferred. This energy reminds of the Zohar's concept of butzina d'kardunita, "the candle of darkness" which alludes to the concealment of His Infinite Light so that Creation could reveal itself in the *tzimtzum*. Just as one can only contemplate the sun when its light is obscured, so does the concealment of God's Light (darkness) enable the revelation of Creation. The parallel between the nature of evil and dark energy, both of which are an integral and paradoxical part of creation is very intuitive and appealing.

SOME THOUGHTS ON RELATIVITY AND THE AGE OF THE UNIVERSE

The account of how Creation evolved, as related in the Ari's writings, describes a series of events that occurred **prior** to the formation of physical matter. In keeping with the accepted theory of relativity, it is impossible to interpret those stages described by the Ari in a literal sense, for the dimension of time, which is necessary for events to occur in sequence, had not yet been created. Rather than describe a sequence of time, the Ari's account implies a sequence of importance in the eyes of the Creator. One can apply this same insight to the account in Genesis of the six days of Creation. We are told there that the heavenly bodies — the sun, the moon, and the stars — were created on the fourth day, thereby precluding the existence of a 24-hour day prior to that time. We must therefore assume that the "days" of Creation were not meant to be interpreted literally, but rather as qualitative stages in the flowering of Creation.

In accordance with the same approach, it is perfectly logical for one who adheres to the Torah to subscribe to the accepted scientific theory that the Big Bang occurred 14 billion years ago and not 6,000 years ago, as well as to the assumption that billions of years — and not six days — passed before the first man appeared on the scene. There is even a very elegant mathematical hypothesis that aims to reconcile the Biblical chronology with current scientific understanding. Here it is in brief: According to the accepted scientific theory, at its inception, the universe was concentrated in a single homogenous point — an infinitely dense aggregation of energy — called a "singularity." The explosion of that singularity caused a rapid expansion referred to as "cosmic inflation," whereby in a fraction of a second the universe grew exponentially, continuing that expansion to this day. The electromagnetic radiation, that we refer to as light, travels at a speed of 300 million meters a second, that being the distance that separates two pulses of light emitted one second apart. These two pulses traveling in space over billions of years should be expected to reach the earth one second apart, but since the universe is constantly expanding, the distance between them is expanding as well. Due to these conditions, the two pulses will actually reach earth much more than one second apart. In fact, the ratio between our time and time at the inception of the universe is 1,000,000,000,00 (a trillion) to 1. That means that if one were hypothetically to have sent out a series of signals one second apart at the time of the Big Bang, from our vantage point today they would reach us a trillion seconds apart, almost 37,000 years apart ! The observational basis for this expansion of time is referred to by astronomers as "cosmological redshift," the effect upon light's wavelength (toward the red end of the spectrum) by its being stretched with the expansion of the universe.

When the Torah speaks of Creation occurring in the space of six days, it is speaking from the vantage point of the universe's inception, looking forward. That means that from our vantage point, it would take six trillion days for that information to reach us. Hence the world should appear to us as being around 14 billion years old, amazingly close to the estimate of modern science! This is the argument made by Dr. Gerald Schroeder,[229] which appears in his books where he backs up this hypothesis with mathematical computation.

WHO WAS ADAM

We have already pointed out that the work of spiritually rectifying Creation was assigned exclusively to man. But which man are we exactly talking about? There are at least 15 biological species of man over the various epochs of human history, starting with *Homo habilis* who roamed the earth three million years ago and culminating with *Homo sapiens* who first appeared 300,00 years ago. What is the difference between them and the man, whom we speak of as being created in the image of God? The following thesis accepts as perfectly harmonious scientists' prevalent position regarding the evolution of man and all the elements of Jewish tradition, without having to distort either one.

According to prevailing theories, the most recent living form, from which all surviving life on earth has descended, was a bacteria-like single-cell organism, dubbed by scientists as LUCA (Last Universal Common Ancestor). Evolutionary theory suggests that this organism evolved into a single-cell organism capable of replicating itself and undergoing mutations. After the passage of eons and an immense number of mutations, LUCA eventually evolved into man. The statistical probability of this occurring is estimated to be 1 in $10^{2.680}$, that is 1 followed by 2,680 zeros![230] Regardless, according to most scientists that is exactly how *Homo sapiens* came into being.

In the Torah's view, the cosmos also formed gradually until a single planet among billions emerged as capable of sustaining life. From that pre-historical moment, the first bacteria-like organism underwent various mutations and versions until it achieved the perfection necessary for it to become a human body with a destiny of its own. Currently, this is the scientific position accepted and taught in most of the world's higher institutions of learning. In its view, it is perfectly reasonable to conclude that humans are descended from the monkey, as Darwin concluded in his major work. What might surprise many is that the Ari concluded this as well in his work, *Adam Yashar*:

> Between the *chai* (animal domain) and the *medaber* (human domain) is the monkey, just as there is an intermediate realm between the Creator and His Creation.[231]

It is nevertheless clear that the Torah sees an essential and fundamental distinction between man and monkey. The verse in Psalms (8:6) testifies, "You have rendered him slightly less than the angels, and You have crowned him with esteem and majesty." King David would not have written this relating to a glorified chimpanzee. A careful reading of Genesis' first chapters brings us to the conclusion that the reason we celebrate the Jewish New Year on the first of Tishrei is because that was the day, approximately 6,000 years ago, when man first appeared on the scene — a man with no predecessor or ancestor. He merited the name *Adam*, which shares the same root as *adameh*, "I liken myself," as in the verse (Isa. 14:14), "I liken myself to the One on high." Adam perceives His Creator, while aware of himself and capable of distinguishing between good and evil. This is the description in the Torah that defines the unique and special status of the first man, created in God's image and likeness:

> And God said: Let us make man in our image and according to our likeness … And God created man in His image; in the image of God, He created him; male and female He created them. (Gen. 1:26-27)

> And the Lord God formed man out of the dust of the earth, **and He blew the breath of life into his nostrils, and man became a living soul.** (ibid. 2:7)

At a certain time in prehistory, the world and its inhabitants matured to the point of preparedness necessary for advancing to the next stage. The Hebrew year in which this book was written was 5782, meaning that 5,782 years earlier God blew the breath of life into the body of the creature *Homo sapiens* — an extraordinary compelling act that rendered him an altogether new creature, not merely version 2.0 of *sapiens* 1.0. Prior to receiving the Divine breath of life and becoming a living soul, he was simply a creature with the identical morphology of a *Homo sapiens*, but certainly not human. A split second after receiving his soul, his nature changed altogether and it was then that he was called **Adam**, created **in the image of God**; the crown of Creation, for whom the entire process was undertaken. This revolution, as opposed to evolution (for it did not occur gradually) was concluded the moment that God first addressed man (ibid. 1:28): "And God said to them: Be fruitful and multiply, fill the earth and master it …" At that point, the clock of history began ticking and will continue until its end. For 6,000 years mankind has been charged with the duty to perfect the world to the best of its ability. Starkly contrasting with this view, Richard Dawkins states "There never was a last Homo Erectus who gave birth to the first Homo Sapiens". (see YouTube debate with Cardinal Pell, April 16, 2012)

ARCHEOLOGICAL SUPPORT FOR THE TRANSFORMATION OF *HOMO SAPIENS* INTO MAN

Scripture describes a qualitative leap in the emergence of man occurring approximately 6,000 years ago and archeology provides us with an impressive indication of this change. Although the soul does not leave behind material traces, its sociological footprints are recorded loud and clear within the relics of ancient Mesopotamia (modern-day Iraq), where our forefather Abraham was born 4,000 years ago. Scholars agree that the earliest script, which they call protowriting, appeared around 6,000 years ago. This was a symbol system intended to convey information in the form of signs and pictographs, which gradually developed into a sophisticated stick-form of writing called cuneiform.[232]

The correlation between the timing of this early script and Scripture's account of man's being endowed with a soul is not coincidental. The trigger that led to the creation of writing was the transition in human dwelling from caves and small villages to urban centers where the recording of commercial transactions and other information necessitated a system of documentation. Neolithic man's move into large and permanent settlement is dated back to between 5,000 to 9,000 years ago, without scholarly consensus as to its reason. Theories abound as to the reason for this major leap forward, such as the domestication of plants and animals, the advantages of cooperative agriculture,[233] or the desire for comfortable living conditions,[234] all of which contributed to a population explosion. As to the ultimate reason for this move, one might assume, in accordance with the testimony of Scripture, that the investment of man with a soul engendered self-awareness, not just in the individual but in the collective as well. This would have generated a collective desire to improve man's physical conditions and cultivate social relations beyond what was necessary simply for survival.

HARMONY BETWEEN SCRIPTURE AND SCIENCE

As we have seen, Scripture's understanding of man's origins, and those of the universe at large, predated scientific theory by around 3,000 years, but with one essential difference: Cosmology and evolutionary science attribute the Big Bang and the development of the species to **random** chemical processes without a guiding hand or purpose, whereas the working assumption of Scripture is that there is a grand **Architect** responsible for Creation Who has a master plan and a purpose for our existence. In the six "days" between the 25th of Elul and the 1st of Tishrei, Rosh HaShanah, there emerged the inanimate realm, the vegetive realm, the animal realm, and eventually the human realm — all in accordance with the order of the simple (pshat) understanding of Torah's verses. Every physical detail in nature exists in its unique and intricate way according to the Divine instructions inherent within the first spark of God's creative light — from the subatomic properties of inanimate matter to the genetic code required to generate the myriad varieties of life-forms populating the universe to this day. This is also the view of Dr. Gerald Schroeder as presented in his various writings.[235]

THE DIFFERENCE BETWEEN THE SCIENTIST AND THE KABBALIST

The physicist Lawrence Krauss has suggested that empty space is actually filled with virtual particles (matter and antimatter pairs) coming into existence and then annihilating each other instantly in a process called quantum fluctuation. By redefining nothing as something, he posits that the universe could very well have formed *ex nihilo* as a result of the Big Bang which produced matter with the qualities of both mass and space. The universe continues to exist thanks to these subatomic particles orbiting around themselves at the speed of light (the standard model).[236]

The Kabbalist would obviously agree that the universe was formed out of nothing, but rather than define "nothing" as "no thing," he would define it as the ultimate "Thing," the Infinite One.[237] He would add to the scientist's explanation the words of the Ari, that the universe was formed and continues to exist as a result of it having "risen in the Will of the Creator."[238] Hence, the statement that opens Genesis — "In the beginning of God's creating the heavens and the earth" — was followed one nanosecond later by the Big Bang. That is the story of creation *ex nihilo* in contemporary terms. Creation, in the sense of "something emerging from something," continues to occur every second through the constant force of attraction between subatomic particles causing matter to persist without stop.

A restatement of the biblical verse describing how light was created might appear like this:

> "And God said: Let there be light" … and then the electromagnetic force proportional to the electrical charge, the magnetic field, and the speed

of the particle divided by the deviation of the magnetic field's strength
— Maxwell's four differential equations — combined, "**and there was
light.**"

Arno Penzias, a physicist and religious Jew, was awarded the 1978 Nobel Prize
in physics for discovering the cosmic microwave background radiation (CMB)
that helped confirm the theory of the Big Bang. The mysterious background
hum that he detected is an echo of the Big Bang, allowing us a view of the universe as it existed 400,000 years after that initial cataclysm. It was at that point
that the universe went from being entirely opaque to transparent due to the
emergence of light. [239] Thus, stated Penzias:

> This is how I view God. By contemplating the order that exists in the
> world, we can conclude that there is a purpose, and from that purpose
> we can receive some knowledge as to the Creator Who planned all of
> this. I view God through His handiwork, and these works of His hint
> at His intentions. Out of these intentions, I get an impression as to His
> character.[240]

In keeping with this approach, it is possible to assert that science joined the
ranks of Aristotle and Kabbalah in conferring some non-physical life-force or
energy even upon the inanimate realm of Creation — even more so upon the
vegetative, animal, and human realms. The Ari describes the soul of *domem*
(the inanimate realm) in Divine rather than scientific terms as "the capacity in
the earth to differentiate between and sprout an assortment of seeds, thirsting
for the rains like a wife for her husband,"[241] Thus we see two schools of thought
arguing for the same principle: That there exists a mysterious and invisible life-
force sustaining the inanimate realm. There is no contradiction in believing that
the Torah is God-given and at the same time welcoming with open arms the
truth of those scientific laws for which there is a consensus. Belief in the Torah
and Kabbalah is not irrational or in opposition to logic; it is simply outside the
bounds of rationalism and logic, that is *A*rational.

A FINAL WORD

In this chapter I tried to show a reasonable scientific possibility for the existence of a soul informing every material element, an idea that is the foundation
of the Ari's meditations. The belief that there is a dedicated power of soul that

sustains every component in the universe radically influences our relationship to reality. Whoever believes in the existence of such powers of the soul is, in essence, declaring that spiritual forces are in control of the protons and atoms that shape reality and are responsible for the physiological processes that sustain every living thing.

Chapter Summary

Every aspect of the laws of nature reflects the splendor and greatness of the Creator and contributes immensely to the understanding of inner spiritual processes. That is why it is a *mitzvah* to invest time and effort to study sciences.

I have presented four standard approaches for explaining the relationship between science and Torah:[242]

- The Torah is perfectly precise and where there is a contradiction between it and science, science is wrong.

- Science is perfectly precise and in the event of such contradictions, the Torah is wrong.

- Torah and science occupy entirely separate domains and, hence, no significance can be ascribed to either contradiction or agreement between them.

- There is a harmonious connection between Torah and science, and hence contradictions between them can be resolved by attempting a renewed interpretation of one or the other.

Aside from these approaches, I have shown that the Ari's Kabbalah affords an additional, more novel, approach: The Ari argues that there exists a continuous and intimate reciprocal connection between Torah and science — or, more exactly, between the supernal spiritual realms and our own physical world. Spirit and matter are so interwoven together that every physical structure can be said to mirror a spiritual state. Consequently, every physical act accompanied by a Kabbalistic meditation and vice versa, activates a spiritual process that draws down a bounty of life-force from the Divine source of that act.

The Ari's approach is based on Kabbalah's understanding of how the universe is descended from God's Infinite Light, which through a series of gradual contractions (*tzimtzumim*) allowed an increasingly material reality to evolve, culminating in the World of *Asiyah* (Action), the metaphysical substrate of our own material world. With each successive *tzimtzum*, a new realm emerged whose root lay in the realm above it, just like a tree branch that exactly clones its features from the trunk. In light of this, it is reasonable to expect that the laws of physics and physiology, in all their details, would reflect the spiritual processes that brought them into being. The example that has been highlighted in this book is obviously the tight connection between extracting the holy sparks from our food and the overall mechanism of eating and digestion.

Chapter 11

Social Implications of the Metaphysical Structure of the Universe

The purpose of this chapter is to highlight several social implications that derive from the Kabbalistic structure of the universe and the "elevation of worlds" discussed above. Although this topic does not directly bear on the central topic of eating, I saw fit to include it due to its innovative sociological insights.

Social rigidity Versus the "Elevation of Worlds"

In Chapter 3 (The Structure of the Universe and the Food Chain) I introduced the classification of the natural world into four hierarchical categories: *domem* (inanimate), *tzomeach* (vegetative), *chai* (animal), and *medaber* (human). I demonstrated that according to the Ari this classification is not immutable but dynamic, since each level could be incorporated into those above it and hence "elevated." This ascension is ultimately achieved by the human act of eating whereby the inanimate, vegetive, and animal realms of nature are all elevated and edified through human consumption, especially when accompanied by the Ari's meditations on eating.

It is both instructive and illuminating to compare the dynamic stratification described above with the fixed social stratification of the Middle Ages. Social classes back then were seen as religiously axiomatic: The king occupied the highest rung, followed by the nobility and clergy, with the farmers and peasants at the bottom of the ladder.[243] Richard I, King of England, proclaimed already in 1193: "I was born into a class that does not allow me to recognize any authority above me — other than God." King Richard is the one who coined the adage, *Dieu et mon droit*, "God and my right [hand]," which is still the motto of the monarchy in the United Kingdom.[244] The absolute impossibility of breaking out of one's ascribed status and climbing the social ladder was even affirmed theologically, generating the people's bitter resentment towards the monarchy and the Church.

Many historians see in this social immutability one of the chief causes leading eventually to Europe's two great revolutions: the French Revolution and the Russian October Revolution.[245] A growing number of French citizens refused to make peace with the nobility's authority, instead absorbing the ideas of equality and freedom of the individual as presented by Voltaire, Jean-Jacques Rousseau, and Denis Diderot, who strove to establish a new society based on equality and reason.

A similar situation reigned in Russia at the end of the 19th century. The traditional thinking of Tsar Nicholas II and his dynasty was that he was "the ruler, the holy father, and the benefactor of his people." In line with this conception, he expected that the people would show understanding and accept the given social hierarchy despite the harsh conditions that reigned at the time. This social immobility, with its roots in the divinely decreed "Great Chain of Being,"[246] left Tsar Nicholas totally out of touch with the mood in his land. His blind faith in the divine right granted him to rule led to one of the most violent revolutions in the annals of mankind and changed the face of history.[247]

Vestiges of such hegemony and social immobility are even evident in the not-so-distant past. For example, in 1947, when Queen Elizabeth of England wished to marry a Greek citizen, the prospective groom was forced to undergo a series of actions that progressively stripped his original identity. It began by surrendering his Greek citizenship and changing his original Greek name, Phillipos Glucksburg, to Phillip Mountbatten, his mother's maiden name. Subsequently, he had to receive British citizenship and abandon the Greek Orthodox Church and convert to the Anglican Church, Britain's official religion. Only after erasing his national and religious identity was he allowed to ascend the ladder and join the ranks of the British royal family. On the day before his wedding, King George VI granted him the title of "His Royal Highness," and only **on the very morning** of the wedding (June 20, 1947) did citizen Phillip become the Duke of Edenborough in the district of London — perhaps out of fear that the fresh prince might, at the last minute, be a no-show at his own wedding. "Such shall be done for the man whom the king wishes to honor!" (Esther 6:9)

In total contrast to the inflexible "Chain of Being" that led to the European class wars, the social stratification of the Jewish world, particularly amongst its scholars is totally fluid, reflecting the dynamic mobility associated with the Kabbalistic "elevation of worlds." In Judaism, there were two classes that defined themselves based on ancestral lineage: the priesthood and the monarchy. The most esteemed class within the community — the scholarly and learned class, was never limited by pedigree, only ability counts.

We are taught that there are three "crowns" in Judaism: the crown of Torah; the crown of priesthood, which belongs to the descendants of Aaron, the first High Priest; and the crown of kingship, which King David merited and is the inheritance of his descendants. The crown of Torah, however, may rest on the head of whoever aspires to adorn himself with it.[248] A priest must be born to a father who is a priest; a young king must ascend the throne by virtue of being descended from a king, but in the most prestigious sphere of Torah scholarship — there are no established privileges or entitlements; let whoever wishes to claim the crown of Torah, come and take it.

This impartiality is best demonstrated by the way in which the 71 justices of Judaism's highest court, the Sanhedrin, were chosen. Maimonides writes as follows:

> One should only appoint to the Sanhedrin, both the higher and the lower courts, wise and insightful men, outstanding in their Torah wisdom, and who possess broad knowledge, being somewhat familiar with other disciplines, such as medicine …[249]

The necessary qualifications for Torah leadership are wisdom, intelligence, integrity, and good character traits — no mention of family pedigree or proximity to power. Additionally, the deliberations of the Sanhedrin are conducted democratically with only one purpose in mind: getting to the truth:

> In cases concerning matters of ritual purity or impurity, deliberations commence with the senior judge [offering his opinion]. In capital cases, deliberations commence with junior judges.[250]

The above *Mishnah* teaches us that when it comes to purely religious or ritual matters, the senior judge should be the first to offer an opinion as to whether

the decision is permissible or impermissible, pure or impure — for the proto-
col amongst Torah scholars is to hear the more acknowledged scholar before
those of lesser distinction. In criminal cases involving capital punishment,
however, the practice is to first hear the junior judges who are generally
younger and less wise, and then only afterwards to solicit the senior judge's
opinion. The reason for this simple: if the senior judge were to state his opinion first, the fear is that the junior judges would be embarrassed to contradict
them, thereby reducing the scope of perspectives and possibly leading to an
unwarranted conviction culminating in the defendant's death.

In this same spirit, we find the Talmud stating that in deciding the list
of people deserving special respect, "a Torah scholar of illegitimate birth
(mamzer) takes precedence over a High Priest who is an ignoramus."[251] Even
though there is no higher status than that of the High Priest, and no lower
status than that of one born illegitimately, it is one's **level of wisdom** that
confers respect and prominence, overriding even the highest appointment
in the land.

THE MISSION OF THE TALMUD — UNCOVERING THE TRUTH

The Talmud is the magnum opus of the Jewish people, containing 2,711 pages
in 37 tractates compiled between the 3rd century BCE to the 5th century CE.
Whoever has imbibed even a sip of its waters knows that there is no obstacle
to, or fear of, challenging the words of the great Sages. On the contrary, the
sage's prime obligation is to seek out the truth by demanding a source and an
explanation for every opinion rendered, regardless of the status or pedigree of
the one rendering it. This would include even Rabbi Judah the Prince, head
of the Sanhedrin and redactor of the *Mishnah*, who was a scion of Hillel the
Elder's family. Even in his case, there was no fear in asking, "Rabbi! How do
you know this?" Indeed, it was even encouraged. It is not for naught that the
highest rung of Creation, the domain of man, is referred to as *medaber*, "the
verbal" domain. The account in Genesis states (Gen. 2:7), "and He blew the
breath of life into his nostrils, and man became a living soul." The Aramaic
translation of this verse renders it as follows: "He blew the breath of life into
his nostrils and man became **an uttering spirit**." The implication is that the
Divine breath with which man was imbued transmuted into **a verbalizing**

spirit. Conversely, that verbalizing spirit can transmute back into a Divine breath when man uses his mouth to speak words of truth and meaning. Not only does he realize his destiny in doing so, but he merits occupying the highest rung in the heavenly scale of values.

"Accept the truth from whoever speaks it"[252] is one of Maimonides' most famous sayings, emphasizing the importance of substance spoken over the person speaking. many historians attribute the success of Jewish scientists over the centuries to their healthy sense of skepticism. Twenty percent of all Nobel prizes have been awarded to Jews, although they comprise only 0.2% of the world's population. Anecdotally, Walter Isaacson in his biography of Albert Einstein suggests that Einstein's tendency to challenge hierarchical authority was the source of his great creativity and as he himself testified that as a child he received instruction both in the Bible and in the Talmud."[253]

The ability to speak truth is what enables upward mobility on the ladder of wisdom. The following is one example among many of how high one can ascend: Rabbi Akiva was a shepherd, a descendant of converts, who was illiterate until age 40 — and still he became one of the greatest Sages of Israel. The Talmud relates that his ability to derive "piles upon piles" of laws from the tiny crowns that adorn the letters of the Torah moved Moses in Heaven to ask God, "Such a person exists in Your world and You gave the Torah through me?"[254]

This upward mobility in the realm of wisdom, which is so evident from the history of Jewish scholarship, derives from the very hierarchy of Creation, otherwise known in the Ari's Kabbalah as the "Elevation of Worlds."

CHAPTER SUMMARY

The division of the universe into a hierarchy of realms is not limited to its physical aspect alone, but pervades its metaphysical, spiritual aspects to the extent that indicators can be discerned in various patterns of social organization. Classical philosophy viewed the social hierarchy as divinely ordained and fixed, with no possibility of rising in social rank, which generated great frustration and social inequality, eventually sparking the great revolutions of the 19th century.

In direct contrast to this approach, the Ari's conception of the "elevation of worlds," allowing every element of Creation to ascend to a higher level, led the Jewish intelligentsia to understand that birth and pedigree are secondary, insofar as the individual is measured by his personal value alone.

The ancient kabalistic concept of the "elevation of worlds" preceded by two millennia the fundamental right accorded to each individual to advance and strive upward in every field of pursuit, taken for granted in modern society.

GLOSSARY OF HEBREW TERMS

א	*Aleph*. According to Kabbalah, the shape of the first letter of the Hebrew alphabet illustrates the way in which Divine life-force is drawn down into the world: the tip of the upper *yod* points to the Infinite One Himself; the upper *yod* represents His expanding Wisdom; the diagonal *vav* in the middle represents the dividing line between the upper and lower realms of Creation, while also serving as a bridge between them; the lower *yod* represents the lower realms that receive God's life-force and then channel it into our own material world through its 'foot' pointing downward.
Abba* and *Ima	"Father" and "Mother." Two supernal *partzufim*, or "personae," that generate new Divine life-force when unified through Kabbalistic meditation.
ABY"A	Initials for the four Worlds of ***Atzilut*** (Emanation), ***Beriyah*** (Creation). ***Yetzirah*** (Formation), and ***Asiyah*** (Action) that make up the World of *Tikkun* that came into being after *Shevirat HaKelim* [in the World of *Tohu* (Chaos)]. The shards of the broken vessels together with their captive *nitzotzot* descended into these four Worlds, arranging themselves in accordance with the configuration of *sephirot* in each World.
Achorayim	Literally, "rearward." A reiterative way of spelling out a word. For example, the word *olam* would be spelled *o-ol-ola-olam*. Its use indicates that the word is associated with a weak life-force whose expansive force diminishes as it propagates, thereby requiring it to constantly draw upon its source in order to advance its revelation. Also referred to as *ribu'a*, "square."
Adam Kadmon (A"K)	"Primordial man," the first *partzuf* that God created subsequent to the *tzimtzum* that concealed His Infinite Light. *A"K* is the most inclusive framework prefiguring all of Creation. There is no connection **whatsoever** between this Kabbalistic term and prehistoric man in anthropology.

Adonai	One of God's seven holy names that are forbidden to erase when written in context in Hebrew. This Name represents God's mastery over the world. It corresponds to the last of the ten *sephirot*, *Malchut*. It is the name that we pronounce in place of God's ineffable Name, *Havayah*.
Aliyat HaOlamot	"The Elevation of Worlds." The Kabbalistic mechanism by which Creation is rectified; a centerpiece of the Ari's Kabbalah. This process is predicated on the dynamic aspect of the Four Worlds, which can be upgraded or downgraded in accordance with the meditative acts of man or the will of the Creator.
Arich Anpin	The "Long Countenance." One of the five main *partzufim* that occupy each of the Four Worlds. Identified with the "supernal Crown" from which it derives. The Ari's Kabbalah refers to it as "complete Divinity."
Atik Yomin	The "Ancient Days." The most exalted *partzuf*, also identified with the supernal Crown. An exclusive agent of unification and kindness, whose main role is to "sweeten" the harsh judgments that derive from the lower *partzufim*.
Av Sag D'AK	Denotes the highest level of reality following the initial *tzimtzum* of the *Ein-sof*. Paradoxically, this most sublime level of reality is regularly drawn upon when practicing the humblest meditations, such as those associated with the blessings over food.
Av (72), Sag (63), Mah (45), Ban (52)	Four gematrias corresponding to four different ways of fully spelling out the holy Name of God, *Havayah*. Their order corresponds to the four letters of the Name *Havayah* itself: *Av* (72) corresponds to the letter *yod* and the *partzuf* of *Abba*; *Sag* (63) corresponds to the first *heh* and the *partzuf* of *Ima*; *Mah* (45) corresponds to the letter *vav* and the *partzuf* of *Zeir Anpin*; and *Ban* (52) corresponds to the final *heh* and the *partzuf* of *Nukva*.
Berachah	"Blessing." A formula instituted by the Sages for praising God on various occasions. The three main types of blessing: Those recited over the performance of a *mitzvah* (e.g., upon donning tefillin); those recited on experiencing God's majesty and greatness (e.g., upon hearing thunder or seeing lightning); those recited upon deriving enjoyment from His Creation (e.g., before and after eating).

Birur

"Extraction" or "refinement." The process of extracting holy sparks from the *klipot* and elevating them back to their supernal source, thereby refining reality. The central process of *tikkun* in the Kabbalah of the Ari.

Chalal Panui

The "vacant space" created after the contraction of God's Infinite Light. At first, there was no Divine light whatsoever contained in this space, but almost immediately God infused it with a "ray" of His light, referred to as the *kav*.

D-Tz-Ch-M

An anacronym spelling out the words *Domem* (Inanimate), *Tzomeach* (Vegetative), *Chai* (Animal), and *Medaber* (Human) — the hierarchic domains of Creation that account for all material entities in the physical world. They are all able to dynamically interact with each other due to the unique soul that each possesses, conferring it with existence and its own unique characteristics.

Ein-sof

"The Infinite One," (literally, "No End"). A Kabbalistic term describing the initial revelation of God's concealed Essence. Lacking any better term to describe God's nature, *Ein-sof* at least affords a sense of how the initial manifestation of God's Presence might be grasped. All other parameters are beyond measure. In truth, it would be equally legitimate to describe God's Essence as "No Beginning," but our Sages preferred "No End" as the former is too difficult to comprehend.

Ekyeh

A holy name in the kabbalistic context and possibly an additional name that is forbidden to erase when written Hebrew in context. It is mentioned in these words of God to Moses (Ex. 3:14): "So shall you say to the people of Israel: '*Ekyeh* sent me to you.'" This Name corresponds to the feminine *sephirah* of *Binah*.

Elokim

Another one of the seven holy names of God that are forbidden to erase, it corresponds to the *sephirah* of *Gevurah* (Might) and represents the power to impose limits on the revelation of *Havayah's* expansive light. Hence, its association with the laws of nature.

ERM"A

An acronym of the four Elements: *Eish* (Fire), *Ruach* (Wind), Mayim (Water), and *Afar* (Earth). Based on the classical theory identifying the basic constituents of material reality. A foundational formula in the Kabbalah of the Ari.

Gematria

A system of calculating the numerical value of Hebrew words based upon the unique number associated with each letter of the Hebrew alphabet. Derives from the Kabbalistic belief that God created the world through various combinations and permutations of the Hebrew letters. Employed by the Ari for the purpose of deciphering hidden allusions found in the words of prayer, as well as a tool for interpreting Scripture.

HaAri

Rabbi Isaac ben Solomon Luria Ashkenazi (1534 - 1572), commonly known by the acronym "the ARI (Lion)," often accompanied by the word *hakadosh* (the holy one) or *zal* (of blessed memory). The greatest of the Safed Kabbalists, he articulated a new system of Kabbalah that is known by his name. The main purpose of his system was to describe the spiritual dynamics of the supernal realms that enable the drawing down into the world of Divine life-force. He created a practical and operative infrastructure for drawing down such life-force by identifying exactly its place of origin and the path it takes to its intended destination. This detail is obtained through unique formulas composed of the World, *partzuf* and *sephirah* being addressed. The specific life-force being summoned is identified as well by a combination of Divine Names and gematrias. According to the Ari's system, one who performs a mitzvah or prays with a deep understanding of these complex details will succeed in drawing down upon himself and his surroundings a powerful life-force.

HaRashash

Rabbi Shalom Sharabi (1720-1777), known by the acronym "the RaSHaSH. He emigrated to the Land of Israel from Yemen and distinguished himself as a great Kabbalist. He wrote the seminal work Nahar Shalom, but his major contribution was the preparation of a prayer book that incorporated the Ari's system in practice, enabling many to adopt a routine based on Kabbalah.

Havayah

A moniker used in place of God's ineffable Four-letter Name. Its root, *h-v-h*, means to "confer being." There are other descriptions of this Name: *Shem HaMeyuchad* (The Special Name); *Shem Ben Arba Otiyot* (The Four-letter Name or the Tetragrammaton); *Shem HaMeforash* (The Explicit Name); or simply, *Hashem* (The Name). In contrast to other Divine Names found in Scripture that derive from traits that God manifests, this name reflects on His Essence and is unrelated to any specific act or characteristic. Unlike other Divine Names, it does not take on any possessive suffix, for it represents God in His absolute and "naked" singularity, outside the realm of manifest relationship. Due to the holiness of this Name, one is not allowed to enunciate it as written; rather, when reciting Scripture or blessings, it is pronounced *Adonai*, literally, "my Master," in accordance with God's pronouncement: "Not as I am written, am I to be pronounced."

HaZohar

The foundational text of Kabbalah, just as the Pentateuch is for the Oral Law. Discovered in 13th century Spain, most of its homilies and discourses are attributed to Rabbi Shimon bar Yochai and his disciples from the 2nd century CE. The sources of many of these homilies can be found in the Tannaitic compositions *Sefer HaYetzira* (The Book of Formation), *Sefer HaBahir* (The Book of Illumination), and *Hechalot Rabatai* (The Greater Book of Divine Chambers).

Hishtalshelut

The "unfolding" of Creation. A Kabbalistic tradition portraying the sequence of events that led from God's Infinite Light filling reality to the creation of a "space" in which a succession of realms was allowed to emerge, each less ethereal in nature than the one before, culminating in our own material reality.

Kabbalah

Judaism's mystical tradition with deep roots in the ancient *Hechalot* and *Merkavah* traditions that were the province of a select few. The Ari in the 16th century interpreted, elaborated on, organized, and refined these ancient Kabbalistic traditions, thereby constructing a new and more accessible system of teachings.

Kav	A single, linear, and narrow "ray" of Divine light originating in the *Or Ein-sof* that penetrates the *chalal* formed by the *tzim-tzum*, filling it with Divine emanations. The light channeled through the *kav* is what sustains all of Creation, kind of like a Divine umbilical cord. The further into the *chalal* that the *kav* penetrates, and the greater its distance from its source outside the *chalal*, the less its intensity and force.
Kavanah Kabbalit	"Kabbalistic meditation," as articulated by the Ari, consists of three stages: 1) Understanding the Rashash's explanation of the significance attached to the prospective act. 2) Understanding both the macro and the micro implications of the process to be undertaken, to the extent one could. 3) Meditating on the holy names and the course to be taken by the anticipated life-force as detailed in the prayer book.
Kavanat Manoach	Literally, "the meditations of Manoach," the father of Samson. The title given to the set of Kabbalistic meditations performed upon eating as laid out by the Ari in his interpretation of Manoach's encounter with the angel of good tidings (Judges 13:11-19).
Kelim	The metaphysical "vessels" that both contain and filter the vestiges of God's Infinite Light so that they may be introduced into the finite realm of Creation These vessels themselves are constructed from Divine light, but of a coarser and less refined variety than the light which they contain.
Klipot	"Shells." As the shards of the shattered vessels descended into the Four Worlds of *ABY"A*, they brought about the formation of inferior spiritual entities in need of restoration, referred to as *klipot*.
Maaseh Breishit Maaseh Merkavah	"The Work of Creation" and "The Work of the Chariot" — two ancient mystical traditions, the first dealing with the hierarchy of created realms that unfolded over time and the second dealing with God's intervention in the world post-Creation. Appears first in the Mishna Hagiga (2,1). The Mishnah was redacted at the end of the 2nd century preserving the oral traditions of the Pharisees from the Second Temple period (516 BCE – 70 CE). Eventually these traditions were supplanted by the Zoharic tradition of Kabbalah and its interpreters.

Matbea *Berachah*	"The Format of Blessing." A reference to the standard wording of the blessings instituted by the Sages, it also refers to the series of meditations that are based on that wording. These meditations are especially important insofar as they serve as a prototype for all other Kabbalistic meditations.
Mochin (*Chabad*)	Literally, "brains" or "intellect" — a term that Kabbalah uses to indicate the Divine force that advances Creation to its full potential, just as human intellect is an indicator of man's potential for growth. *Mochin deKatnut* are "immature" when they have yet to exert maximum influence on Creation, and *Mochin de-Gadlut* "mature" when they do. In terms of the *sephirot*, *mochin* refers to the spiritual energy embodied in the three "cognitive" *sephirot*: **Ch**ochmah ((Wisdom), **B**inah (Understanding), and **D**aat (Knowledge) — abbreviated as Chabad.
Motzaot Hapeh	The five "outputs of the mouth," referring to the five phonetic classes of the Hebrew alphabet, generated by the five anatomical components of the mouth. They are: The letters *aleph*, *heh*, *chet*, and *ayin* — referred to as the gutturals — formed by the throat; the letters *gimmel*, *yod*, *kaf*, and *kof* — formed primarily by the palate; the letters *dalet*, *tet*, *lamed*, *nun*, and *tav* — formed primarily by the tongue; the letters *zayin*, *samech*, *tzadi*, *reish*, and *shin* — formed primarily by the teeth[103]; and the letters *bet*, *vav*, *mem*, and *peh* — formed primarily by the lips. Our Sages viewed the faculty of speech as essential to man's nature insofar as it allows him to express his innermost thoughts, thus acting as a kind of bridge between man's spiritual and physical sides.
Nefesh *HaMazon*	"The soul of food." The spiritual life-force that inheres in every material entity in the physical world, but most importantly in the food we ingest. This soul is the basic reason for every entity's unique existence. This idea is supported by the theory of panpsychism.
Neshamah	The general term for "soul," the "representative" of the Divine *Ein-sof* in the body, conferring it with life. In its specific Kabbalistic sense as the third level of soul in the body, it is not based in the body itself but emanates from without.

Nitzotzot	"Sparks." Vestiges of the primordial *Or Ein-sof* that descended into the Worlds of *ABY"A* at the time of *Shevirat HaKelim*. Lodged in the shards of the shattered vessels, they provide the Divine energy that sustains the lower worlds. When liberated from these shards, they return to their primordial source, thereby elevating Creation at the same time.
NRNCh"Y	An acronym of *Nefesh*, *Ruach*, *Neshamah*, *Chai*, and *Yechidah* — the five levels of soul that correspond to the five parts of the body: skull, right and left brain hemispheres, heart and liver.
Olam Gashmi	"The physical world," the lowest rung of Creation, the ultimate manifestation of the World of *Asiyah*. This World is permeated with *klipot* bearing within them vestiges of the *Or Ein-sof* in the form of holy sparks, or *nitzotzot*.
Olam HaAtzilut	"The World of Emanation," the highest of the Four Worlds and the initial repository of Divine life-force. As the bridge between God's Infinite Essence and the finite realms of Creation, this World, from our perspective, appears completely Divine.
Olam HaRuchani	"The spiritual world" can refer to any of the Four Worlds which are comprised exclusively of *partzufim* and *sephirot*, with no semblance of physicality.
Or	"Light," the term used to poetically and symbolically describe the Divine energy that manifests itself in all the Worlds of *ABY"A*. Not to be confused with the electromagnetic radiation perceived by the human eye. Kabbalah's ubiquitous use of the term *Or* to describe God's manifestation in Creation derives from its perceptible, yet supremely ethereal, nature.
Orot	Plural of *Or*, a general term used to describe the abundance of Divine life-force that infuses all of the lower Worlds — particularly our own world of physical action.
Or Pashut	"Simple (Uniform) Light," the term used to describe God's Infinite Light as it existed prior to the *tzimtzum*, when it uniformly filled all of reality, precluding the possibility of any finite being.

Pardes	Literally, an "orchard." The figurative term employed by the Sages when alluding to the field of Divine mystery and Kabbalistic contemplation. The origin of the term can be found in the Talmudic account of the "four who entered the orchard" of mystical contemplation (*Chagigah* 13b).
PRD"S	Pronounced *pardes*, an acronym for **p**eshat (simple meaning), **r**emez (allusive meaning), **d**rash (hermeneutic meaning), and **s**od (mystical meaning) — the four levels of Scriptural interpretation. Corresponding to the Four Worlds of *ABY"A*, the term first appeared in *Tikkunei Zohar*.
Partzuf (*partzufim*, pl.)	"Persona," a Kabbalistic configuration of the ten *sephirot* that is conferred a metaphorical human face comprised of eyes, ears, nose, and mouth. The six *partzufim* are referred to as: *Atik Yomin* (Ancient Days), *Arich Anpin* (The Long Countenance), *Abba* (Father), *Ima* (Mother), *Zeir Anpin* (The Small Countenance), and *Nukva* (Female). Recasting the *sephirot* into *partzufim* allows them to operate holistically while at the same time interact dynamically with each other.
Reshimu	An Impression or afterglow of God's Initial Light left behind after the tzimtzum transpired. The reshimu is the fabric into which all existence is imprinted. Bears a resemblance to the Cosmic Microwave Background (CMB) which uniformly fills the cosmos.
Sephirot	Divine "Emanations." Ten metaphysical expressions of the Divine that serve as conduits of His life-force, dynamically directing and guiding the world as bridges mediating between *Ein-sof* and a bounded, material Creation. The word *sephirah* resembles the English word "sphere," as in "sphere of influence," which is an apt description of the effect that the *sephirot* have on Creation. The ten *sephirot* are: *Chochmah* (Wisdom), *Binah* (Understanding), *Daat* (Knowledge), *Chesed* (Kindness), *Gevurah* (Might), *Tiferet* (Beauty), *Netzach* (Victory), *Hod* (Splendor), *Yesod* (Foundation), *and Malchut* (Kingship).

Sephirot HaIgulim	"Circular Sephirot" refers to the configuration of the *sephirot* as agents of God's general supervision over Creation, such as through the laws of nature. These are the *sephirot* that sustain Creation in a pre-determined fashion, without regard for the behavior of its human occupants. Every point on the circumference of a circle is equidistant from its center, with no hierarchical significance for the human standing outside of it.
Sephirot HaYosher	"Linear Sephirot" refers to the configuration of the *sephirot* as agents of God's particular supervision over each and every individual. Operating as vectors, these *sephirot* exhibit the qualities of both verticality and direction. These are the *sephirot* that the Ari generally addresses in his system of Kabbalah.
Sha Nehorin	The "370 Lights" that are radiated by the *partzuf* of *Arich Anpin*. Cited in both the Zohar and the writings of the Ari, these 370 Lights have their source above the World of *Atzilut* but are then channeled through the ten *sephirot* of that World, the number 300 alluding to the three higher *sephirot* called *mochin* and the number 70 alluding to the 7 lower *sephirot* called *midot*. The number 370 is two times the gematria of the Name *El* when spelled out in full. As the Name associated with God's attribute of *Chesed* (Kindness), these Lights serve as agents of God's mercy and kindness as they propagate through the Four Worlds.
Shefa	A "bountiful flow" or abundance. This is the basic term applied to the Divine life-force that sustains and advances Creation, generally as a force of blessing or benefit that can be either spiritual or material. *Shefa chitzon* (outer *shefa*), which is associated with the autonomous laws of nature, uniformly sustains Creation regardless of human behavior. *Shefa pnimi* (inner *shefa*) manifests itself in accordance with human behavior, bestowing additional life-force upon those whose actions are directed toward that end.
Shem Malei	"Full Name," the system of spelling out a Divine Name so that each of its component letters is spelled out in full. For example, the Nam *El*, which is composed of two letters, would have those two letters spelled out in full like this: ***aleph-lamed***.

Shem Malei d'Malei	"The fuller form of Full Name," whereby each of those two fully-spelled letters has its own component letters spelled out as well, like this: *aleph-lamed-peh* (*aleph* in full) *lamed-mem-dalet* (*lamed* in full).
Shem Pashut	"Simple Name," the standard spelling of a Name without any extensions or elaborations.
Shemot HaKodesh	"The Holy Names" of God, as they appear in the Hebrew Bible: *Havayah* or *Kah, Adonai, Elokim, Tzevaot, Shaddai, El*, and *Ekyeh*. According to Kabbalah, there are several other permutations of Divine Names whose role is to generate a new spiritual reality capable of creating an intimacy between the Infinite One and His creatures. We know next to nothing about His essential nature, but His Names at least serve as "garments" that afford us a certain appreciation of His plan for Creation.
Shevirat HaKelim	"The Shattering of the Vessels." A central element of the Ari's Kabbalah, describing what happened immediately after the *tzimtzum* when the *kav* entered the "vacant space" and channeled God's Light into the waiting "vessels." Unable to contain the force of this Light, the vessels shattered into a multitude of shards (Klipot). Vestiges of the Light, referred to as *nitzotzot* (sparks), were trapped within these shards and together they formed the basis of Creation's evolving structure. Paradoxically, this catastrophic occurrence is what facilitates the necessary restoration of reality through the process of freeing the sparks from their captivity in the shards and restoring them to their supernal source.
Sod	"Mystery." Something profound and obscure that is meant to be revealed to a select audience — to "those who fear Him," as in the verse (Psa. 25:15), "The mystery of God is for those who fear Him, and His covenant to inform them." "Secret" would be an inappropriate translation insofar as it implies something that is forbidden to reveal.
Tikkun	"Restoration" Tikkun is THE mission of mankind in general and of each individual alone. In Kabbalah, the term has a much more specific connotation, relating to a series of spiritual maneuvers including extracting the sparks from their *klipot*, elevating them, and returning them to their proper place. A successful *tikkun* results in Divine life-force channeling its way from the supernal realms into our own material reality.

Torah Shebeal Peh	*Tikkun* takes place in three stages: 1. An exact identification of the spark to be extracted, based on specific formulas provided by the Ari. 2. *Birur* (extraction) — identifying and isolating the spark from its entanglement in the shard. 3. Releasing the spark from the shard in which it is trapped and elevating it to the uppermost realm.
Torah Shebichtav	"The Oral Torah." The vast range of laws not found explicitly in Scripture, including those conveyed to Moses orally at Sinai; those derived from Scripture by the Sages through special hermeneutic rules; and special decrees and ordinances instituted by the Rabbis over the course of centuries. According to tradition, Moses received the written Torah on Mount Sinai together with an oral explanation of its commandments, including their mystical significance. These were passed down orally from master to disciple through the course of Jewish history, eventually being committed to writing in the form we know today as *Mishnah*, *Talmud*, *Midrash*, and the Kabbalistic tradition.
	"The Written Torah." The Bible — consisting of the Pentateuch, the books of the Prophets, and additional Writings — is a compendium of sacred texts that are the most ancient and foundational bases of Judaism. According to tradition, the five books of the Pentateuch were dictated to Moses by God during the Israelites' forty-year sojourn in the Wilderness. The remaining books of the Bible were conveyed through prophecy over the course of later generations.
Tzelem Elokim	"The Image of God," a reference to man who was created in God's "image and likeness" (Gen. 1:26), rendering him the "crown of Creation" for whom all else was created. I have suggested in this book that man was invested with this Divine character after God breathed the "breath of life" into *Homo sapiens*.
Tzimtzum	"Contraction," the term used in Kabbalah to describe God's first step toward creating the world: the withdrawal of His Infinite Light so as to create a space in which to generate an extrinsic reality. The Ari elaborated greatly on this idea, although its roots are much more ancient.

Tziur HaOtiyot
"Picturing the [Hebrew] Letters." A powerful form of guided imagination employed by the Kabbalistic meditator in his attempt to envision, with eyes closed, various permutations of God's holy names as called for in specific meditations.

Yichudim
"Unifications." The act of unifying a male *partzuf* with its female counterpart, having been separated at the time of *Shevirat HaKelim*. The result of these "unifications" is the generation of new Divine life-force in the world.

Zeir Anpin (Z"A)
"The Small Countenance," the *partzuf* that was formed from the totality of elements in the World of *Atzilut*. This male *partzuf* constitutes the interface between the uppermost realms and corporeal man in the World of *Asiyah*. Most of man's Kabbalistic service deals directly with this *partzuf*, including bringing about its "unification" with its female counterpart, the *partzuf* of *Nukva*, thereby generating new Divine life-force in the world.

GLOSSARY OF ENGLISH TERMS

Agnosticism
A philosophical outlook according to which it is impossible for man or science to prove or negate anything regarding a divine reality which lies beyond the realm of science or our senses.

Aesthetics
A branch of philosophy that deals with questions of how to characterize beauty. In our context, it relates to the spiritual role played by taste, smell, and the presentation of food, as alluded to in the verse (Gen. 2:9), "The Lord God made sprout from the earth every tree that was a delight to behold and good for food."

Animism
An anthropological belief that attributes to every element in Creation a distinct spiritual essence (call it soul or spirit) that defines and sustains it. It recalls the Kabbalistic belief in a unique soul inhering in every constituent of the four domains of Creation: inanimate, vegetative, animal, and human.

Athropomorphism
A psychological term indicating the attribution of human traits to non-human entities. Kabbalah often describes metaphysical forces in anthropomorphic terms (i.e. the *partzufim*) so as to render them more understandable — "Torah speaks in the language of ordinary people."

Aesthetics
A branch of philosophy concerned with the nature and appreciation of art, beauty, and good taste. In the context of this book, it relates to the color, taste and smell of the food as alluded to in the verse, "every tree that was a delight to behold and good for food" (Genesis 2:9).

Appetizer Approach
An expression coined by Rabbi Mordechai Attiah, implying that one should relate to Kabbalistic meditations as if they are spiritual "appetizers" — do what you can, however insignificant you think it is. One should immediately implement a Kabbalistic meditation regardless of the level of understanding achieved. Under no circumstances should one delay implementation until having mastered the practice in all its depth and breadth.

Atheism
The rejection of belief in the existence of God or any other ethereal being.

Atomic Number
An identifier of every chemical element which is equal to the number of protons found in the nucleus of its atom. I suggest in the book that an element's atomic number is the most intimate physical expression of the unique soul with which the Creator conferred it.

Cosmology
A branch of science whose aim is to investigate the origins and evolution of the universe, from the Big Bang to present day. Derived from the Greek *cosmos* (universe) *logia* (study of).

Dark Energy
According to current accepted scientific theory, dark energy constitutes approximately 70% of the universe's mass-energy. This energy resembles the Zohar's concept of *butzina d'kardunisa*, "the candle of darkness." The latter refers to the Creator withdrawing His Infinite Light so that Creation could reveal itself. Just as one can only contemplate the sun when its light is obscured, so did the concealment of God's Light (darkness) enable the revelation of Creation (the candle).

Dualism
A philosophical view maintaining that spiritual and mental phenomena exist independent of physical phenomena, and are no less authentic. In terms of the mind-body relationship, it views consciousness and the soul as being independent of the brain's neurological activity. Theologically, it implies that the natural universe exists alongside the Infinite Creator Who sustains it.

Gastronomy
The study of the relationship between food and culture. From the Greek *gastro* (stomach) *nomos* (custom).

Great Chain of Being
An ancient doctrine, referred to in Latin as Scala Naturae, which defines the hierarchical structure of all matter and life, beginning with God at the top and followed by the angels, man, animals, plant life, and minerals. According to its proponents, this hierarchy is fixed and ungiven to change, in contrast to the Four World hierarchy of Kabbalah which sees upward mobility along the chain, otherwise known as "Elevation of the Worlds," as the key element in the restoration of reality.

Hedonism
A theory of life that posits physical pleasure as the central factor in determining one's potential courses of action.

Homo sapiens
Literally, "wise man" in Latin (*homo* = man, *sapiens* = wise). According to Darwin's theory, *Homo sapiens* was the last in the developmental chain of the hominid family.

According to the Kabbalistic approach presented in this book, while *H. sapiens* is genetically identical to a human being, the soul that conferred man with a Divine image was only imparted by God breathing the "breath of life" into Adam.

Hylomorphism
A philosophical thesis that divides every existing entity into two basic constituents: matter and form. The connection between the two is what confers that entity with lasting existence. The dynamic interplay between matter and form is what is responsible for changes in the thing itself. From the Greek *hylo* (matter) *morph* (form).

Immanent
A philosophical term indicating a sense of intimacy with the Infinite source of Creation, Who is constantly sustaining it in all of its aspects, even the most insignificant.

Introspection
A psychological term signifying the contemplation of one's inner life: one's soul, thoughts, feelings, needs, memories, etc. The Sages associate it with the process of *cheshbon nefesh*, "spiritual accounting." From the Greek intro (inward) spec (look).

Kreb's cycle
A metabolic pathway that serves to produce energy from the organic compounds in living creatures. In the book I compared the process of metabolizing food into energy with the process of elevating the spiritual essence of our food — the *nitzotzot* — into the soul of the one eating.

Materialism
A philosophical approach that negates the existence of a spiritual realm, viewing physical matter as all that exists, both comprising and driving the universe.

Mindfulness
A psycho-spiritual practice whose goal is to increase one's awareness of what is occurring in the here-and-now. Awareness, consciousness, and mindfulness are all related phenomena.

Mysticism	A field dealing with matters that are not accessible to the human senses or measurable with instrumentation. Derived from the Greek *mystikos* (concealment). Mysticism deviates from science which occupies itself with measuring and quantifying the physical world.
Observer effect	A counter-intuitive phenomenon in quantum physics whereby the act of observing subatomic particles unavoidably alters the nature of their behavior when unobserved. One of the aspects of quantum physics that violates the rules of classical physics. I suggest in the book that quantum "strangeness" supports the possibility of a Divine force, which cannot be measured or characterized, sustaining and guiding all living organisms.
Panpsychism	An ancient philosophical theory which maintains that all matter has a nonphysical mind-like aspect and that reality is beyond the grasp of understanding. Panpsychism argues that consciousness is the essential characteristic of the existing world. It shares a lot with *Dualism* insofar as both approaches oppose materialism.
Philosophy	The study of basic concepts engaging human awareness, such as existence, reality, soul, consciousness, logic, ethics, causality, knowledge, and language. Derived from the Greek, meaning "love of wisdom."
Physiology	The branch of science dealing with the physical and bio-chemical functioning of living creatures. In this book I draw a number of connections between physiological processes and their spiritual source according to Kabbalah.
Quantum biology	A field of study that identifies and investigates quantum phenomena that are observable in the biological realm, being as the same subatomic particles found in the physical realm operate there as well.
Quantum Mechanics	The accepted theory in physics describing the basic physical characteristics of nature at the level of atoms and subatomic particles. I suggest in this book that the counter-intuitive aspects of quantum mechanics hint at the possibility of a Divine force existing outside of the cosmic framework.

Transcendent	A theological-philosophical term which places God outside the realm of physical law and beyond human comprehension. In order to overcome this distance and achieve a religious experience, one must resort to mystical practices such as prayer or meditation.
Uncertainty principle	A counter-intuitive, fundamental principle of quantum mechanics that asserts the impossibility of simultaneously measuring with any exactitude certain particle variables (such as position and momentum), owing to their acting both as particles and waves at the same time. I suggest in this book that the counter-intuitive aspects of quantum mechanics hint at the possibility of a Divine force existing outside of the cosmic framework.

NOTES

1   Rabbi Yehuda Getz (born 1924 in Tunis, Tunisia—died 17 September 1995 in Jerusalem) was the rabbi of the Western Wall for 27 years and served as the head of the Beit El Kabbalist yeshiva from 1973-1995

2   Search for REThink - debate with Rabbi Sacks and Richard Dawkins.

3   Based on a commandment found in the Book of Exodus 21:23–27 expressing the principle of reciprocal justice measure for measure, otherwise known as the law of retaliation (Latin: lex talioni).

4   BT *Bava Kama* 83b It is taught in a baraita - Rabbi Dostai ben Yehuda says: The phrase: "An eye for an eye" (Leviticus 24:20), means *monetary* restitution.

5   Phylacteries, or *tefillin*, are two small leather boxes with straps containing parchments inscribed with verses from the Torah. One is placed upon the head while the other is wrapped around the arm. They are worn in the course of weekday morning prayers.

6   The *etrog*, or citron, is one of four species that are held together and shaken during the Succot holiday. Although the verse does not identify the *etrog* as the required "fruit of a citrus tree," the oral tradition does, resulting in its universal use

7   See also Maimonides' introduction to *Guide for the Perplexed*.

8   See prof. Isaiah Tishbi (1908–1992), Responsa of R. Moses de Leon on matters of Kabbalah, Part 1, p. 64

9   *Mishneh Torah, Hilchot Yesodei HaTorah* 4:13: "Only one who has filled his stomach with 'bread and meat' should wander the 'orchard.' 'Bread and meat' refers to knowing what is permissible and what is forbidden in regard to the other commandments."

10   Ibid.: "We do not teach it in public."

11   Ibid.: "One who is wise and understands … for not everyone has a broad mind with which to comprehend."

12   United Nations Food and Agriculture Organization: Food Balance Sheets

13   See Wikipedia: *List of diets.*

14   Bratman & Knight (2000). *Health Food Junkies: Overcoming the Obsession with Healthful Eating.* Broadway.

15   Food and Agriculture Organization, World Health Organization: *Obesity & overweight.*

16   Boston Medical Center (bmc.org,), Nutrition and Weight management Center.

17   The Pentateuch (Five Books of the Torah), first part of the Old Testament.

18   Kitamura et al. (2010). US National Library of Medicine, H, Niijima A 2010

19   Guinness World Records, March 2015: *YouGov poll.*

20   *Scientific American* (September 2013): The Food Issue

21 Kitamura et al. (2010). US National Library of Medicine, H, Niijima A 2010

22 Marieb, E. (2010). Human anatomy & physiology (8th ed.). Pearson, pp. 945-947

23 See BT *Berachot* 40a: "Concerning the tree from which Adam ate, Rabbi Meir said: It was a grapevine, for nothing causes man to wail like wine, as it states (Gen. 9:21), 'He drank from the wine and became drunk'; Rabbi Nechemiah said: It was a fig tree, for the source of their ruination was also the source of their remedy, as it states (ibid. 3:7), 'And they sewed together a fig leaf and made for themselves belts'; Rabbi Yehudah said: It was wheat, for it is only after tasting grain that an infant knows how to say Mommy and Daddy.'"

24 *Midrash Tadshe* 7 (a small midrash which begins with an interpretation of Gen. 1:11 authored by Rabbi Pinchas ben Yair in the 4th century.

25 Even regular water tastes sweeter after being stolen

26 *Sifra Vayikra* 20:26

27 See *Stanford Encyclopedia of Philosophy* (2007): Purpose of Philosophy. The word philosophy derives from the Greek "love (philos) of wisdom (*sophia*)."

28 *Petichat Eliyahu HaNavi* in the introduction to *Tikkunei HaZohar*

29 *Zohar, Chelek* 2, pp. 23b-24b. The Book of the Zohar is a central work of the Kabbalistic tradition. It is attributed to Rabbi Shimon bar Yochai, a 2nd century Tanna, but first came to light in the 13th century.

30 Ibid. *Shaar* 39, *Derush* 3.

31 *Medaber*, "the one who speaks," is a synonym for man, based on the ancient Aramaic translation of Genesis 2:7, where man's creation as "a living soul" is rendered as "a talking spirit," intimating that the very essence of man is his ability to speak — to formulate thoughts and impart them to fellow humans — a trait exclusive to the human species

32 See Ball, P. (2004) *The Elements: A Very Short Introduction*. Oxford University Press, p. 33

33 Carl Sagan was an American-Jewish astronomer, cosmologist, astrophysicist, astrobiologist, and author.

34 *Shaar HaMitzvot* 41b.

35 See Chapter 10: Between Science and Faith.

36 Written in the 4th century BCE. Aristotle distinguishes between four types of differences among living things: Differences in particular body parts (numbers I – IV); differences in lifestyles; types of activity (numbers V, VI, VII, and IX); and differences in specific characteristics (number VIII). See also: Singer, Charles (1931). *A Short History of Biology: An Introduction to the Study of Living Things*. Clarendon Press.

37 See Russel, Bertrand (2004). *A History of Western Philosophy*. Routledge, p. 289.

38 Lovejoy, Arthur O. (1936): *The Great Chain of Being: A Study of the History of an Idea*. Harvard University Press.

39 Eisley, Loren (1961). *Darwin's Century*. New York: Doubleday Anchor, p. 8. Loren Eisley was a professor of anthropology and the author of many books in the field.

40 Tradition attributes this prayer to Joshua bin Nun. See Responsa of the *Geonim Shaarei Teshuvah* 44 in the name of Rabbi Hai Gaon; also Rabbi Avraham Miranda (1804). *Yad Neeman*. Saloniki.

41 Shaar HaMitzvot 42b

42 This passage implies that that eating animals also brings about an elevation of the Worlds, since the soul of the *chai* ascends to the next level. For an elaboration of this matter, see Chapter 9: What To Eat, "Vegetable or Meat — Is There a Preference?"

43 See Chapter 10: Between Science and Faith, "The Existence of the Soul."

44 Mora, Camilo et al (2011). How many Species Are There on Earth and in the Ocean? *PLOS Biology*.

45 *Shaar HaKavanot, Drush Yom HaKippurim, Drush 1.*

46 *Sefer Baal HaTurim, Orach Chaim 207.*

47 *Sefer HaLikutim, Parshat Ekev.*

48 See Chapter 5: The Foundational Principles of the *Shevirah* and the *Tikkun.*

49 Named after the German-Jewish biochemist, Hans Krebs, and for which he received the 1953 Nobel Prize in Medicine.

50 King et al. (2007). *Dictionary of Genetics*: The Krebs Cycle. Oxford University Press.

51 *Shaar HaMitzvot 42b.*

52 The words of the blessing are taken as an allusion to the Four Worlds of Tikkun (restoration) whose names are: Atzilut, Beriah, Yetzirah and Asiyah. A fuller exposition is provided in Chapter 5, but for now it is sufficient to simply recognize that the blessing refers to these four worlds.

53 See Chapter 6: A Practical Guide to Meditations for Eating, "Everything Starts with Aleph."

54 See Chapter 3: The Structure of the Universe and the Food Chain.

55 Anecdotally, the Rabbi who impressed me with his eating habits (as mentioned in the forward) looked to me to be in his early 40s, when in fact he was 69 years old at the time.

56 https://www.livescience.com/16660-big-bang-origins-universe-birth.html Wall, Mike (2011). *The Big Bang: What Happened at the Birth of Our Universe.*

57 Hawking, S.W (1981) The Boundary Conditions of the Universe. *Pontifical Academy of Sciences*, pp. 563-574. Hawking, S.W. (2018). A Smooth Exit from Eternal Inflation. *Journal of High Energy Physics.*

58 Introduction to *Otzrot Chaim.*

59 BT *Chagigah* 13a.

60 A photon is a basic energy particle lacking mass that moves at the speed of light, expressing behavior that is in contradiction to the classical laws of physics.

61 Human incapacity to describe, much less understand, the essence of the Creator is axiomatic across the board for all Kabbalists and scholars of pshat (straightforward and simple) as it states in Isaiah Chapter 55, 8 "For My thoughts are not your thoughts, neither are your ways My ways, saith the LORD". Indeed the very verb *bara*, to create,

62   *Etz Chayim, Shaar 1 Anaf* 1

63   *Sefer Kerem Shlomo* on *Etz Chayim, Shaar* 1 *Anaf* 2 *Ot* 8

64   *Sefer Yetzirah* (The Book of Formation) is a Kabbalistic work that describes how the world was created through the agency of the twenty-two Hebrew letters and the ten sephirot. Tradition ascribes its authorship to our forefather Abraham, perhaps even originating with Adam. It was apparently passed on as oral traditions and first committed to writing in around 200 CE.

65   See *Etz Chayim, Shaar* 30 *Drush* 42.

66   This principle is elegantly and succinctly described in the classical Kabbalistic work *Pardes Rimonim* (5,4) "The reason it is revealed is because it is hidden and the reason it is hidden is because it is revealed."

67   See BT Chullin 60b.

68   *Shaar HaKavanot*, introduction to *Drushei Shabbat*.

69   *Midrash Aggadah* and *Radak* on Gen. 24:1.

70   See Chapter 10: Between Science and Faith.

71   *Adam Kadmon*, or "Primordial man," is the Kabbalistic term applied to the Divine state that existed at the intersection between God's Infinite light and the emanation of the Four Worlds of *ABY"A*. It represents God's fundamental desire to create. The term primordial is used here in the sense of antecedent and certainly NOT in the Neanderthal, prehistoric context.

72   See *Etz Chayim, Shaar* 8 *Perek* 3, 14:3 15:4 et al.; *Shaar HaKavanot, Drushei Shacharit*; *Shaar Maamarei Rashbi, Parashat Breishit*; *Shaar* Ruach *HaKodesh* 2:5 et al.

73   Rabbi Moshe ben Nachman (1194-1270) was a great Sephardic sage, halakhist, commentator, philosopher, Kabbalist, and physician.

74   BT *Kiddushin* 71a.

75   ibid.

76   The Hebrew word for "name," *shem*, also connotes renown or reputation as in the verse (Isa. 56:5), "I shall grant them…a place of honor and renown (*shem*) that is better than sons and daughters; I will grant them eternal renown (*shem*)."

77   *Shulchan Aruch, Orach Chaim* 215:4: "Whoever recites an unnecessary blessing is guilty of uttering the Name of Heaven in vain"; ibid. *Yoreh Deah* 276:9: "It is forbidden to erase even one letter of the seven unerasable Names;" ibid. 13: "One must excise the parchment on which the Name is written and bury it. One should never inscribe the Name other than in a Torah scroll lest it be treated disrespectfully. Hence, we are careful not to write out the Name of God in correspondence"; *Rambam, Hilchot Sefer Torah* 10:10: "It is a *mitzvah* to designate a place in which to house the Torah scroll and to honor it and glorify it to the greatest extent."

78   Reference to God's Name through use of the generic shem appears hundreds of times in the Bible.

79 Introduction to *Tikkunei Zohar*.

80 *Shemot Rabbah* 3:6.

81 See Bar Lev, R. Yechiel. *Yedid Nefesh – Mevo l'Kabbalah*, p. 129: also Sharabi, R. Shalom. *Nehar Shalom*, p. 3.

82 See *Etz Chayim, Shaar 6 Perek 2*.

83 The value of the letters added to the base-letters Y-H-V-H

84 The value of the letters added to the base-letters Y-H-V-H

85 BT *Niddah* 45b; see *Etz Chayim, Shaar 26 Perek 3*.

86 See Chapter 5, under heading: "Sparks, Shards, and Shells."

87 *Shaar HaMitzvot, Parashat Ekev* p. 41 on. The *hamotzi* blessing, which is made over bread at the start of a meal, reads as follows: Blessed are You O Lord our God, King of the universe, Who brings forth (hamotzi) bread from the earth.

88 See Chapter 5: The Foundational Principles of the Shevirah and the Tikkun, under the heading, "The Mechanism for Tikkun Olam."

89 *Etz Chayim, Shaar* 8:1; *Shaar HaHakdamot* 13b; *Zohar, Chelek* 2, p. 249a.

90 For elaboration, see *Perek TNT"A* in *Etz Chayim*.

91 This term embraces the entire mystical tradition beginning with the *Hechalot* literature through the Zohar and up to the writings of the Ari.

92 *Shaar HaMitzvot, Parashat Ekev* p. 42a

93 *Shaar Ruach HaKodesh* p. 6b: "And afterward, the brain achieves *birur* through the eating meditation, which is a very important meditation — that is, the manoach meditation."

94 See *Shaar Maamarei Rashbi, Chelek* 4 (*Sifra Ditzniuta* [*Parashat Terumah*]) where the letter *aleph* is associated with *Chochmah*. See also Proverbs 4,7: "The beginning of wisdom (*chochma*) is to acquire wisdom (*chochma*)." The word "beginning" could also allude to the letter *aleph*, the beginning letter of the alphabet, which would render the verse, "*Aleph is chochma.*"

95 See BT *Berachot* 61a; also *Sefer HaLikutim, Parashat Chayei Sarah*.

96 My teacher, Rabbi Attiah coined the definition of a 'novice' regarding these meditations - as one who has been practicing them for up to thirty years!

97 Sharabi. R. Shlomo (Rashash). *Benayahu ben Yehoyada, Chelek Kavanot Pratiyot* p. 15b.

98 See *Shaar HaMitzvot, Parashat Ekev* p. 44.

99 For elaboration, see Chapter 10: Between Science and Faith, on the verse. "From my flesh, I shall envision God."

100 Similar to what we wrote regarding picturing the Name *Havayah*. See *Mishnah Berurah* 1:4: "One should constantly imagine that one is standing before the Holy Blessed One Whose Glory fills the entire Earth. It is written in the name of the Ari that one should constantly picture the Name *Havayah* before one's eyes, punctuated like the word *yirah* (awe). This is the secret behind the verse (Psa. 16:8): 'I have set *Havayah* before me always,' and it is of great advantage toward acquiring *yirah*."

101 Sharabi. R. Shlomo (Rashash). *Siddur Benayahu ben Yehoyada* p. 15, ed. Rabbis Shaul Dwick and Yaakov Ajami.

102 See Chapter 5: The Foundational Principles of the *Shevirah* and the *Tikkun,* under the heading, "The Mechanism for *Tikkun Olam*."

103 The implication of this correspondence is that the grinding of the top jaw against the lower jaw is spiritually comparable to the act of unification between male *Chochma* and female *Bina,* resulting in the creation of new life-force. See *Shaar HaKavanot, Drushei Pesach, Drush 6; Shaar Maamarei HaRashbi; Pri Etz Chayim, Shaar Rosh Chodesh; Shaar HaMitzvot, Parashat Ekev; Etz Chayim, Shaar 6:1; Otzrot Chayim, Shaar HaAkudim.*

104 Indeed, even the animal sacrifices in the Temple are referred to as God's *lechem,* insofar as they are the means by which we seek to appease and come close to Him.

105 Such as *Shaar HaMitzvot, Parashat Ki Tetze; Etz Chayim* p. 68; *Shaar HaHakdamot* p. 53.

106 Sharabi, R. Shalom (Rashash). *Nehar Shalom,* p. 20b.

107 *Midrash Tanchuma, Parashat Tazria 5.*

108 BT *Berachot* 35a.

109 Luzzato, R. Moshe Chaim (Ramchal). *Shaarei Ramchal,* p. 34.

110 *Shaar Ruach Hakodesh* p. 8b.

111 This summary is based on *Shaar HaKavanot, Drushei Kavanot Haberachot* and *Nehar Shalom* p. 20, col. 3.

112 The term *mochin* — literally, "brains" or "intellect" — is a term that Kabbalah uses to indicate the Divine force that advances Creation to its full potential, just as human intellect is an indicator of man's potential for growth. Hence, *mochin* are "immature" when they have yet to exert maximum influence on Creation, and "mature" when they do. In terms of the *sephirot* and their influence on the human soul, *mochin* refers to the Divine energy associated with the three "cognitive" sephirot: *Chochmah* ((Wisdom), *Binah* (Understanding), and *Daat* (Knowledge). In this context, *mochin d'katnut* should be understood as a "constricted" Divine consciousness, whereas *mochin d'gadlut* represents an "expanded" Divine consciousness.

113 A Biblical *mitzvah* is one that has its source in the Five Books of the Torah — such as keeping the Sabbath or donning *tefillin.* A Rabbinic *mitzvah* is one that derives from a decree of the Prophets or the Sages of the Sanhedrin —such as lighting Sabbath or Hannukah candles. An optional *mitzvah* is one which is not obligatory, but which still constitutes a *mitzvah* when performed — such as wearing *tzitzit* (a fringed four-cornered garment) or ritually slaughtering an animal for its meat.

114 Based on *Siddur HaRashash.*

115 This unification is depicted as the combination of two holy Names: *Havayah,* corresponding to *Aba,* and *Ekyeh,* corresponding to *Ima.* The comingling of the letters of these two Names, as referenced in Chapter 6, simulates the conjugation between male and female in the physical realm and hence generates the birth of new *mochin.*

116 These are the sparks that fell into the lower Worlds as a result of the "shattering of the vessels." The number 288 is 4 times 72, which is the *gematria* of the Name *Havayah* associated with the *partzuf* of *Abba* (see Chapter 5) According to a Kabbalistic tradition, 202 of these sparks were already elevated at the time of the Exodus, leaving us with 86 yet to be elevated (the *gematria* of the Name *Elokim* which also equals *hateva*, "Nature").

117 From *Ze'ir Anpin* to *Abba* and *Ima* to *Arich Anpin* and finally to *Atik Yomin*.

118 Kaplan, R. Aryeh (1978). *Meditation and the Bible*; (1986). *Meditation and Kabbalah*.

119 See Kaplan, ibid.; Verman, Mark (1997). *The History and Varieties of Jewish Meditation*; Jacobs, L. (1976). *Jewish Mystical Testimonies*.

120 See Wang (2017). The association between attention deficit/hyperactivity disorder and internet addiction. *BMC Psychiatry Journal*; Rajneesh (2001). *Awareness: The Key to Living in Balance*.

121 Prof. Joyce Schenkein,

122 Wilmer et al. (2017). Smartphones and Cognition: A Review of Research Exploring the Links between Mobile Technology Habits and Cognitive Functioning. *Frontal Psychology*.

123 National Centre for Biotechnology (2018). Neuroscience of Mindfulness Meditation. *Studies in Neuroscience, Consciousness, and Spirituality*: Vol. 2.

124 See Daube & Jakobsche (2015). Biochemical Effects of Meditation: A Literature Review. *Scholarly Undergraduate Research Journal at Clark (SURJ)*: Vol. 1; Krishnakumar, Hamblin, et al (2015). Meditation and Yoga can Modulate Brain

125 See Chalmers, David (1997). *The Conscious Mind*. Oxford University Press, p. 225; Smith, Ward (2011) *Who Me? Choosing Radiance, A Better Way of Living*. Xlibris Corp. p. 94; Ferrari, Michael ed. (1998). *Self-Awareness: Its Nature and Development*. Guilford Press, pp. 12-13.

126 Descartes, Rene (1637). *Discourse on the Method; (1641) Meditations on the First Philosophy.*

127 BT *Berachot* 26b.

128 *Breishit Rabbah* 42:8; BT *Bava Batra* 15a.

129 See Proverbs 12:25: "When worry is in a man's heart, he should speak it out (*yesichena*, from the same root, *siach*).

130 BT *Berachot* 30b.

131 *Tur Orach Chaim, Hilchot Tefilah* 98.

132 Rabbi Schneur Zalman of Liadi (1966). *Ma'amorim Ketzarim, Inyonim*, p. 133.

133 Rabbi Chiya, one of the greatest Babylon Talmudic Sages, lived in between the Tannaitic and Amoraic eras (180 - 230 CE). It is told that Elijah the Prophet considered him and his sons as equal to our holy forefathers

134 Shmuel was a Babylonian Amora of the first generation (165 - 254 CE).

135 JT *Berachot* 2:4.

136 BT *Berachot* 31a.

137 Based on the verse (Isa. 29:13): "With its mouth and its lips [Israel] has honored Me, yet its heart is distant from Me; their fear of Me is like a rote human dictate."

138 See Walsh, Shapiro (2006). The meeting of meditative disciplines and Western Psychology. *American Psychology*, pp. 227-239; Cahn, Polich (2006). Meditation states and traits: EEG, ERP, and neuroimaging studies. *Psychological Bulletiin*, pp. 180-211; Merriam-Webster Dictionary. Definition of "Meditate."

139 Creswell, JD (2017). Mindfulness Interventions. *Annual Review of Psychology*, Vol. 68: 491-516.

140 See Chapter 5: The Foundational Principles of the *Shevirah* and the *Tikkun,* under the heading, "The Holy Names of God."

141 See Deblitzky, S. *Petach Enayim HaChadash*, vol. 1 p. 9, in the name of the Kabbalist Rabbi Mordechai Hadayah.

142 BT *Berachot* 5:1; *Shulchan Aruch Orach Chaim* 93:3, *Misnah Berurah* 6.

143 BT *Berachot* 23a.

144 *Shulchan Aruch Orach Chaim* 98:1.

145 Ibid. *Misnah Berurah* 93:2; 185:1.

146 BT *Berachot* 5:1

147 Rabbi Israel Baal Shem Tov. *Keter Shem Tov* (1999), chap. 68.

148 Rabbi Avraham Yeshaya Karelitz1878-1953)), one of the greatest Talmudic scholars of his time. He lived in Israel as was referred to as the *Chazon Ish*, the title of his scholarly works.

149 BT *Berachot* 31b.

150 Ibid. 24b.

151 Ibid. *Rashba, Bach*, et al.

152 A term first coined by the early medieval commentator and Kabbalist, Ramban, in his commentary on Lev. 19:2.

153 BT *Taanit* 5a; *Shulchan Aruch Orach Chaim* 170:1.

154 Ibid. 170:7-8, *Mishnah Berurah* 22.

155 Partially digested food which is regurgitated into the mouth in order to be chewed again.

156 A proper ritual slaughter, referred to as *shechita*, is deemed necessary so as to eliminate undue suffering on the part of the animal. See *Minchat Chinuch, mitzvah* 451.

157 See *Sefer HaChinuch* 35: "God wished that every species in His Creation propagate amongst themselves, and that one species should not mix with another. He also wished that human seed should be identifiable and not mixed together [through illicit relations]."

158 See *Rambam, Moreh Nevuchim* 3:48.

159 Perhaps this hints as to why genetically modified food (GM) should be avoided.

160 BT *Yoma* 39a.

161 Ibid. *Rambam*.

162 *Sefer HaChinuch* 362.

163 See Levinger, Israel (2014). *Shechitah v'tzaar baalei chaim.* Jerusalem, where he argues that *shechitah* is the quickest and most humane form of slaughter.

164 See BT *Sanhedrin* 59b.

165 BT Chullin 16b: "…initially [in the Wilderness], the Israelites were forbidden to consume "craved meat" [meat not sanctified as an offering]."

166 *Mishneh Torah, Hilchot Yom Tov* 6:18; *Shulchan Aruch Orach Chaim* 529:2.

167 Pinkas Haraaya, pinkas א chapter 6

168 See Chapter 5: The Foundational Principles of the *Shevirah* and the *Tikkun,* under the heading, "Perfecting the World (*Tikkun Olam*) Through Human Action."

169 Ibid.

170 The implication is that one should only eat meat if one is wealthy enough to have his own livestock. A person struggling financially should make do with simpler fare.

171 *Encyclopedia Talmudit* vol. 13, "*Chazir*"; Recanati on Lev. 23:2; *Rabbeinu Bachya* ibid. in the name of *Midrash Tanchuma.*

172 Yosef Chaim ben Eliyahu, the *Ben Ish Chai* (1898). *Ben Yehoyada* vol. 4 on Tractate *Nazir* 23a.

173 BT *Bava Batra* 75a.

174 *Mishneh Torah, Hilchot De'ot* 4.

175 The head of the last Sanhedrin, lived in the 1st century BCE.

176 *Vayikra Rabbah, Parashat Behar* 34.

177 See Chapter 10: Between Science and Faith.

178 Sievert et al. (2019). Effect of breakfast on weight and energy intake. *British Medical Journal.*

179 See BT *Sotah* 2a.

180 See BT *Taanit* 11a; *Nedarim* 9b.

181 See Horowitz, Yeshaya Halevi. *Shnei Luchot Habrit, Maamar* 7:12.

182 BT *Taanit* ibid.; *Nedarim* 10a; *Nazir* 19a, 22a; *Bava Kama* 91b.

183 BT *Nazir* 19a.

184 JT *Kiddushin* 4:12.

185 BT *Yoma* 76b. Rava was a Babylonian rabbi (280 – 352 CE)

186 *Mishneh Torah, Hilchot De'ot* 3:1.

187 BT *Berachot* 57b.

188 *Mishneh Torah* ibid. 3:2-3.

189 One can substitute the terms: "laws of nature" or "matter" → "science" and "Torah" and "spirituality" → "faith."

These terms are often used interchangeably insofar as they represent the same basic phenomena.

190 Rees, Martin (2001). *Just Six Numbers*. Chapter 3: "The Large Number N: Gravity in the Cosmos." Basic Books.

191 2020 Nobel Prize winner in Physics, born to a Jewish mother.

192 https://www.youtube.com/watch?v=yDqny7UzyR4. Roger Penrose — Is the Universe Fine-Tuned for Life and Mind? minute 1:35.

193 Rees ibid.

194 Elaine Howard Ecklund of University at Buffalo, The State 196University of New York

195 John Searle is a professor in the philosophy of mind and of language who taught at the University of California, Berkeley.

196 Dawkins, Richard (2006). *The God Delusion*. Mariner Books, p. 158.

197 A 2006 BBC interview about his book, *The God Delusion*.

198 See Lewis & Barnes (2016). *A Fortunate Universe: Life in a Finely Tuned Cosmos*. Cambridge University Press.

199 https://www.youtube.com/watch?v=noj4phMT9OE. Mathematical Challenges to Darwin's Theory of Evolution.

200 Eckland et al. (2016). Religion among Scientists in International Context. *Socius:Sociological Research for a Dynamic World*.

201 See Meyer, Stephen (2021). *The Return of the God Hypothesis*. HarperOne.

202 Author of 34 books, including *Quantum Physics and Theology: An Unexpected Kinship*.

203 See Greenstein, George (2023). *Quantum Strangeness*. The MIT Press. Anecdotally, a particle physicist I spoke to admitted that after many years in the field, their initial sense of astonishment and amazement begins to dull !

204 Dirac, P.A.M. (1962). *The Principles of Quantum Mechanics, 4th Edition*. Oxford University Press, p. 3.

205 Einstein et al. (1935). Can Quantum-Mechanical Description of Physical Reality Be Considered Complete? *Physical Review*. Vol. 47, pp 777-780. Einstein referred to this phenomenon of entanglement as "spooky action at a distance."

206 Sen, D. (2014). The uncertainty relations in quantum mechanics. *Current Science*, vol. 14 pp. 203-218.

207 See Nikulo, Alexy (2018). Absurdity of quantum mechanics and the crisis of physics. *Russian Academy of Sciences*.

208 Das Wesen der Materie" [The Nature of Matter], speech at Florence, Italy (1944) (from Archiv zur Geschichte der Max-Planck-Gesellschaft, Abt. Va, Rep. 11 Planck, Nr. 1797)

209 See Feynman, Richard (2017). *The Character of Physical Law*. MIT Press Cambridge, Massachusetts, 1995), 129. Also there is a Youtube video of Feynman saying exactly that here: https://www.youtube.com/watch?v=w3ZRLllWgHI

210 Krauss, Lawrence (2012), *A Universe from Nothing*. Atria Books.

211 The Theoretical and Computational Biophysics Group at University of Illinois, Urbana-Champaign.

212 Polkinghorne, John (2007). *Quantum Physics and Theology*. Yale University Press, Chapter 1: The Search for Truth.

213 *Mishneh Torah, Hilchot Teshuvah* 5.

214 See Keysar & Navarro-Rivera (2014). Chapter: A World of Atheism: Global Demographics. The Oxford Handbook of Atheism. Oxford University Press, pp. 553-586; also the General Social Survey of the Pew Research Center (https://gss.norc.org/.)

215 This is the position of Lord Rabbi Jonathan Sacks in his book *The Great Partnership: God, Science, and the Search for Meaning* (2011).

216 This is the position of Professor Gerald Schroeder in his book *Genesis and the Big Bang* (1990) and in other publications.

217 See Muller. Richard (2008). *Physics for Future Presidents*. Chapters 3,4. W.W. Norton & Co.

218 Sacks, ibid. "Introduction."

219 Scruton, Roger (2001). *Short History of Modern Philosophy*. Routledge, p 191.

220 A similar Aristotelian approach is called hylomorphism.

221 Koch, Christof (January 2014). Is Consciousness Universal? *Scientific American.*

222 See Goff, Philip (2017). The Case for Panpsychism, *Philosophy Now;* Weisberg, Josh (2018). The Hard Problem of Consciousness. *Internet Encyclopedia of Philosophy* (https://iep.utm.edu/hard-problem-of-conciousness/https://iep.utm.edu/hard-problem-of-conciousness/)

223 See Chapter 4: The Secret of Growth and Development, under the heading, "The Kabbalistic Explanation of Growth."

224 *Shaarei Kedushah, Chelek* 3 *Shaar* 1.

225 See Kuhse & Singer ed. (2009). *A Companion to Bioethics*. Wiley-Blackwell, pp. 294-5.

226 Tylor, Edward (1871). *Primitive Culture.*

227 Rabbi Shabtai Sabato is the head of Yeshivat Maor Tuviah in Mitzpeh Yericho, Israel.

228 *Tikkunei Zohar* 14b.

229 Gerald Schroeder holds a PhD in nuclear physics and earth and planetary sciences from MIT and was a lecturer in the physics department for seven years.

230 Computed by Douglas Theobald, Department of Biochemistry, Brandeis University.

231 Adam Yashar, Drushei ABY"A; see also Etz Chayim, Shaar 42, Perek 1.

232 See Clayton, Ewan (2019). *Where did writing begin?* The British Library Website; also Walker, C.B. (1989). *Cuneiform: Reading the Past*. University of California Press.

233 Balter, Michael (May 2005). The Seeds of Civilization. Smithsonian Magazine.

234 Dr. Senta German from article on Khan Academy website.

235 Schroeder, Gerald (1990). *Genesis and the Big Bang*. Bantam; (1997). *The Science of God*. Free Press; (2002). *The Hidden Face of God*. Free Press.

236 Krauss, Lawrence (2013). *A Universe from Nothing*. Atria.

237 According to this, the word for "nothing" in Hebrew — *ayin* — may allude to God as well. Hence, the verse in Psalms (121:1), "From where (*ayin*) will my help come?" may alternatively be read as "From God (*ayin*) will my help come."

238 *Etz Chayim*, p. 1: "When it rose in His Will to create the Worlds and emanate the emanations…"

239 See Lemonick, Michael D. (2001). *Echo of the Big Bang*. Princeton University Press.

240 Haberman, Joshua ed. (1994). *The God I Believe In*: Conversation with Arno Penzias. Free Press, p. 175.

241 *Shaar HaMitzvot, Parashat Ekev.*

242 As noted earlier, one can substitute "laws of nature" or "matter" for "science" and "faith" or "spirituality" for "Torah." These terms are often used interchangeably insofar as they represent the same basic phenomena.

243 Mason & Hunt (2001). *Liberty, Equality, Fraternity: Exploring the French Revolution.* Penn State University Press, p. 21.

244 See Duncan, Jonathan (2022). *The Dukes of Normandy, From the Times of Rolls to the Expulsion of Kking John. Legare Street Press; Classical Journal* Vol. 11, No. 5 (Feb. 1916), pp. 293-297.

245 See Ferrone, Vincenzo (2015). *The Enlightenment: History of an Idea.* Princeton University Press; Hibbert, Christopher (2014). *The French Revolution.* Penguin Press, pp. 29-31.

246 See Chapter 3: The Structure of the Universe and the Food Chain, under the heading "The Ladder of Being."

247 See Lieven, Dominic *(1993). Nicholas II: Emperor of all the Russias. John Murray;* Verner, Andrew (1990). *The Crisis of the Russian Autocracy: Nicholas II and the 1905 Revolution. Princeton University Press; Steinberg & Khrustalev (1995). The Fall of the Romanovs: Political Dreams and Personal Struggles in a Time of Revolution. Yale University Press; Wortman, Richard (2006). Scenarios of Power: Myth and Ceremony in Russian Monarchy. Princeton University Press; Figes, Orlando (1997). A People's Tragedy: A History of the Russian Revolution. Viking.*

248 *BT Avot 4:13 with Rambam's commentary.*

249 *Mishneh Torah, Hilchot Sanhedrin 2:1.*

250 *BT Mishnah Sanhedrin 4:2.*

251 *BT Mishnah Horayot 3:8.*

252 Maimonides, Introduction to his commentary on *Avot.*

253 Isaacson, Walter (2007). *Einstein: His Life and Universe.* Simon and Shuster, "Einstein and Faith" page 169 (April 5): 1947

254 BT *Menachot* 29b.

255 See Chapter 5: The Foundational Principles of the *Shevirah* and the *Tikkun*, under the heading, "The Holy Names of God."

256 *Etz Chayim, Shaar* 18 *Perek* 5; *Shaar HaMitzvot, Parashat Ekev.*

257 The implication of this correspondence is that the grinding of the top jaw against the lower jaw is spiritually comparable to the act of unification between male *Chochma* and female *Bina*, resulting in the creation of new life-force. See *Shaar HaKavanot, Drushei Pesach, Drush* 6; *Shaar Maamarei HaRashbi; Pri Etz Chayim, Shaar Rosh*

Chodesh; Shaar HaMitzvot, Parashat Ekev; Etz Chayim, Shaar 6:1; *Otzrot Chayim, Shaar HaAkudim.*

258 I heard this metaphor from my teacher, the Rabbi and Kabbalist Mordechai Attiah.

259 Indeed, even the animal sacrifices in the Temple are referred to as God's lechem, insofar as they are the means by which we seek to appease and come close to Him.

260 See Chapter 5: The Foundational Principles of the *Shevirah* and the *Tikkun,* under the heading, "The Unification (*Yichud*) between Male and Female."

261 *Sefer HaLikutim, Parashat Breshit, Perek* 2.

262 Such as *Shaar HaMitzvot, Parashat Ki Tetze; Etz Chayim* p. 68; *Shaar HaHakdamot* p. 53.

263 See *Zohar, Chelek* 1:4, *Chelek* 3:133b; *Etz Chayim, Shaar* 15 (*Shaar HaZivugim*) *Perek* 2.

264 This association is based on the verse (Psa. 52:3), "The kindness (*chesed*) of God (*Kel*) is all day long."

FULL MEDITATIVE OVERVIEW

STAGE	PICTURED LETTERS	MEDITATIVE THOUGHTS
1. PREPARING ONE'S teeth לֵ"ב Lev (32)		$Yod (10) + Vav (6) + Vav (6) + Yod (10) = 32$
2. VIEWING THE FOOD מֵ"ו Mooh (46)		$Yod (10) + Vav (6) + Yod (10) = 26$ (Upper jaw) $Yod (10) + Vav (6) + Dalet (4) = \underline{20}$ (Lower jaw) **46**
3. PLACING THE FOOD IN ONE'S MOUTH נֵ"ז Nach (58)		$Yod (10) + Vav (6) + Vav (6) + Yod (10) = 32$ $Yod (10) + Vav (6) + Vav (6) + Dalet (4) = \underline{26}$ **58** = *ochel* (food)
4. CONTEMPLATING THE FOOD לחֵ"ם Lechem (78)		$Yod (10) + Vav (6) + Vav (6) + Yod (10) = 32$ $Yod (10) + Vav (6) + Vav (6) + Dalet (4) = 26$ $Yod (10) + Vav (6) + Dalet (4) = \underline{20}$ **78** = *lechem* (repast)
5. CHEWING THE FOOD דֵ"ק Dak (104)		$Yod (10) + Vav (6) + Yod (10) = 26$ $Yod (10) + Vav (6) + Dalet (4) = 20$ $Yod (10) + Vav (6) + Vav (6) + Yod (10) = 32$ $Yod (10) + Vav (6) + Vav (6) + Dalet (4) = \underline{26}$ **104** = *dak* (finely ground) Meditate on chewing the food finely so that the sparks of holiness may be released from the *klipot*.
6. SWALLOWING THE FOOD פֵּ"ד Pad (84)		$Yod (10) + Vav (6) + Vav (6) + Yod (10) = 32$ $Yod (10) + Vav (6) + Vav (6) + Dalet (4) = 26$ $Yod (10) + Vav (6) + Yod (10) = \underline{26}$ **84** = Meditate on the guttural letters of the Hebrew alphabet: א, ח, ה, ע *aleph* (=1), *heh* (=5), *chet* (=8), and *yin* (=70) = **84**
7. DIGESTING THE FOOD שֵׁ"ע Shah (370)	מֵ"ו נֵ"ז לחֵ"ם דֵ"ק פֵּ"ד	Reconjure the previous five meditations in their stated order. Their respective *gematrias* — 46, 58, 78, 104, 84 — add up to 370, the number of "lights" radiating from the face of *Arich Anpin* and which fill the Four Worlds, advancing their restoration.

Appendix A

Stage 1: Preparing One's Spiritual Teeth

This first meditation in the series, centers around preparing the utensils used in the process of eating, chief of which are one's teeth. Hence, the Ari instructs us as follows:

> One should meditate on this form of the letter *aleph*: א , whose *gematria* is 32, alluding to the 32 teeth in one's mouth, which correspond to the 32 "pathways of *Chochmah* (Wisdom)" by which the *birur* (extraction) takes place.

The 32 teeth in one's mouth are the first anatomical parts to be engaged in the process of breaking down food into its various components. As we have often stated, behind every physiological function there exists a corresponding spiritual force responsible for it. In this meditation, we are preparing our spiritual "teeth" for the work of extracting the sparks and freeing them from the *klipot*. The *sephirah* responsible for executing this *birur* is *Chochmah*. Both the Zohar and the Ari state in many places that "the 32 teeth correspond to the 32 pathways of *Chochmah* by which everything is refined in the realm of thought." The ensuing *sephirah* of *Binah* (Understanding) continues and advances the action of *Chochmah*.[256]

The final step in our meditation is to picture the letter *aleph* as portrayed in the chart, א, with two *yods* connected by a diagonal *vav* split in two. The *gematria* of two *yods* (10+10) plus a double *vav* (6+6) is 32, corresponding to the number of teeth as well as the pathways of *Chochmah*. This serves to crystallize in our mind, by way of visual imagery, the essence of our meditation.

APPENDIX B

STAGE 2: VIEWING THE FOOD

The next two meditations revolve around the letters of the name Manoach, the Biblical figure, who the Ari sees as the source for his eating meditations. The objects of preparation at this stage are our two jaws that power our teeth as they begin to clarify the sparks within our food.

In the first step, one should gaze upon the food and imagine the letter *aleph* in its common form, as two *yods* (10+10) connected by a single diagonal *vav* (6): א. This produces the standard *gematria* of the Name *Havayah*, 26, corresponding to the upper jaw. Immediately following, one should imagine the letter *aleph* with the lower *yod* replaced by a small *dalet*, ד, resulting in a *gematria* of 20 (10+4+6), corresponding to the lower jaw. The upper and lower jaws correspond as well to male and female. That is why the *aleph* associated with lower jaw has a *dalet*, the letter that Kabbalah associates with the female.[257]

The combined value of these two *gematrias* (26+20) is 46, which is the value of the first and third letters of the name Manoach: *mem* (40) and *vav* (6).

Forty-six is also the added value of the Name *Havayah* when spelled in the *malei* form corresponding to the *sephirah* of *Chochmah*, whose *gematria* is 72. Subtracting the base value of 26 from 72 leaves us with the added value of 46. *Chochmah*, as we have seen, is the *sephirah* responsible for the work of *birur*.

א = 26 = *Havayah* = upper jaw (*Chochmah*)

א = 20 = *Havayah* = lower jaw (*Binah*)

APPENDIX C

STAGE 3: PLACING THE FOOD IN ONE'S MOUTH

In this meditation we also commence by imagining the two *alephs*, one with a lower *yod* and the other with a lower *dalet*. However, instead of the singular diagonal *vav*, we imagine these *alephs* with their *vav* split lengthwise.

The first *aleph* is composed of both an upper and a lower *yod* (10+10) connected by a double *vav* (6+6), its *gematria* equals 32, as in our first meditation. The second *aleph* is composed of an upper *yod* and a lower *dalet* (10+4) connected by a double *vav* (6+6), its *gematria* equals 26. Together, the two letters produce a *gematria* of 58, which is the value of the remaining two letters in Manoach's name: the *nun* (50) and the *chet* (8).

In addition, as can be seen on the chart, 58 is also the *gematria* of the word *ochel*, "food," as well as the combined value of the two holy Names — *Kel* (31) and *Havayah* (26) — which are associated with the process of rectifying our food.

"Wait a second," you may ask, "*ochel* actually equals 57, as does the combination of the two Names!" "So, eat a little more," I might say jokingly, but the truth is that the system of *gematria* allows for adding an additional value of 1 signifying the entirety (*kolel*) of the *gematria*. Think of a carpenter building a table. Before completing his product, he has four legs and a top, once completed, he has a whole table. Even though not an additional gram of wood was used in the process, the overall value of the completed table, both monetarily and functionally, is way beyond what its individual parts were worth.[258] The addition of the *kolel* in calculating a *gematria* is not arbitrary. It is only applied to cases where the words being calculated have an "added value" relative to their constituent letters. There is a reverse rule, called "without the *kolel*," which is applied when the constituent letters are considered to be more important than the whole word.

With this meditation, we complete the association between the extraction of the sparks in our food and the Biblical figure of Manoach, Samson's father, who lived in 1450 BCE.

א = 32

א = 26

_____

58 = *ochel* (food), as well as *Kel + Havayah*

APPENDIX D

STAGE 4: CONTEMPLATING THE ACTUAL FOOD IN ONE'S MOUTH

At this stage, we shift our focus from ourselves and how we are about to execute the *tikkun*, to the food that is the object of the *tikkun*. As the Ari instructs us (*Shaar HaMitzvot* 43): "Meditate on the food that it should be completely rectified."

This meditation is associated with the word *lechem*. Although *lechem* is commonly translated as "bread," in Biblical sources it can refer by association to any major source of nourishment or satiation[259]. Hence, the Psalmist praises God for the "*lechem* that nourishes the heart of man" (Ps. 104:15), echoing Abraham's words to the angels: "I will fetch a portion of *lechem* so that you may sate your hearts." Sating or nourishing the heart requires more than just a portion of bread.

Hence, it seems logical to apply the term *lechem*, which is the focus of this stage of meditation, to any significant source of nourishment and not just bread. We begin the meditation by picturing three forms of the letter *aleph*, all of which have appeared in earlier stages. The first *aleph* appears like this: א. It is composed of two *yods* (10+10) connected by a double *vav* (6+6), producing a *gematria* of 32. The second *aleph* looks like this: א. It possesses an upper *yod* and a lower *dalet* (10+4) connected as well by a double *vav* (6+6), equaling 24. The final *aleph* is the same as the previous one except that its *vav* is not split: א. Hence its *gematria* is 10+4+6, equaling 20. The combined value of the three *alephs* is 78 (32+26+20), the *gematria* of the word *lechem*. It is also the value of *Havayah* (26) times three, corresponding to the three *alephs*.

The term *lechem* in Scripture is often interpreted by our Sages as a pseudonym for one's wife. When Jethro rebukes his daughters for having neglected to invite Moses into their home, he states, "Go call him so that he may eat *lechem*" (Ex. 2:20), which our Sages take to mean "so that he may marry one of you" (Ex. R. 1:32). They base themselves on an earlier account. We are told that when the Egyptian overlord Potiphar appointed Joseph over his household, "he left all that he had in Joseph's hands, concerning himself with nothing, except for the *lechem* that he ate" (Gen. 39:6). When Potiphar's wife subsequently attempts to seduce Joseph, he refuses, saying, "[my master] has denied me nothing but you, since you are his wife" (ibid. 39:9), making clear what the word *lechem* alludes to.

In context of our meditation, the feminine character of *lechem* suggests the involvement of the feminine *sephirah* of *Binah* in this stage of the *tikkun*. The object of *tikkun*, in our case the food we are eating, is always Kabbalistically associated with the female, as opposed to the executor of the *tikkun* who is associated with the male. Insofar as the *birur* of eating is mediated through the *sephirot* of *Chochmah* and *Binah*, this would be the stage where our thoughts should shift to the role of feminine *Binah* as it unites with male *Chochmah* for the purpose of extracting the holy sparks from our food and drawing down Divine life-force.[260]

$$\aleph = 32$$
$$\aleph = 26$$
$$\aleph = 20$$
$$\overline{}$$
$$78 = \textit{lechem} = \textit{Havayah (26)} \times 3$$

Appendix E

Stage 5: Chewing the Food

This meditation is performed while chewing our food and grinding it finely with our 32 teeth. In this stage, we begin the process of breaking down the food and rectifying it both physically and spiritually. The Ari instructs us as follows:

> One should meditate on grinding the *lechem* very finely with the 32 teeth so that the [sparks of] holiness may be released from the *klipot*, thereby refining the food in accordance with the *gematria* of Manoach which equals 104, spelling *dak*, "fine" [as in finely ground].

We have waited for this point in our book where finally it is possible to taste some food, referred to broadly as *lechem*. A careful reading of the Ari's above instruction provides a revolutionary answer to the question, "Why do we eat?" On the face of it, the question appears strange; certainly, we eat because we are hungry and want to live and accrue strength (and of course, because the food is tasty). Kabbalah, however, offers an altogether different reason: We eat in order to release the sparks of holiness from the *klipot*, as well as to spiritually restore ourselves and the food we are eating! The sensations of hunger and thirst exist so as to drive us toward this work of restoration.

The appropriate imagery for this stage of meditation involves the three *aleph* forms pictured in the preceding stage together with an additional *aleph*, the standard one possessing two *yods* and a single *vav* equaling 26. The meditation begins with our picturing this standard *aleph* together with its variant: א, in which the lower *yod* is replaced with a small *dalet*, producing a *gematria* of 20. Together, these two *alephs* (26+20) possess the numerical value of the letters *mem* (40) and *vav* (6) in the name Manoach.

In the next step, one pictures these same two *aleph* forms, except with their *vavs* split in two. א **and** א. With the additional *vav*, their *gematrias* now equal 32 and 26, totaling 58, which corresponds to the remaining two letters of Manoach's name: *nun* (50) and *chet* (8). We now have a cumulative *gematria* for all four *alephs* of 104, which in addition to equaling the name Manoach also equals *dak*, "finely ground," the objective to be pursued at this stage of eating and the level of *tikkun* pursued by Manoach himself.

There is a spiritual "grinding" that occurs parallel to the mastication of our food for the purpose of extracting its nutrients. The friction created by the upper palate working against the lower palate is treated in Kabbalah as expressive of a process called *betishah*, "chafing." Its purpose is to elicit new life-force through meditating, like the flame produced by striking a match or the new life produced by the chafing of male and female in the act of cohabitation.

$$\aleph = 32$$
$$\aleph = 26$$
$$\aleph = 20$$
$$\aleph = 26$$
_____
104 = man*oach* = *dak*

Appendix F

Stage 6: Swallowing the Food

Upon swallowing the food, the Ari instructs us as follows: "One should have in mind that this is the completion of the extraction process that takes place in the stomach as the beneficial part of the food is absorbed into the blood and the waste is expelled."

The food in our mouths descends into the stomach by way of the esophagus, which is a muscular tube connecting the throat to the stomach and which forces the food down by way of peristaltic contractions. The Kabbalists ascribed a great deal of importance to the dual function of the throat, which is responsible not only for facilitating speech but also for facilitating the breakdown and digestion of our food.

The chewing and swallowing of food calls for the involvement of one's mouth, teeth, tongue, palate, and throat. Kabbalah links these five anatomical components to the five phonetic classes of the Hebrew language, otherwise known as "the five outputs of the mouth."

The verse in Genesis (2:7) states, "[God] blew into his nostrils the breath of life and man became a living being." The first-century commentator Onkelos translated the latter part of this verse into Aramaic as "and it became in man an uttering spirit," thereby underscoring man's facility of speech, and the cognitive abilities that enable it, as basic to his nature. man expresses his innermost thoughts and connects with the other through the agency of language, whose five phonetic classes are formed by the oral apparatus identified above: The letters *aleph*, *heh*, *chet*, and *ayin* — referred to as the gutturals — are formed by the throat; the letters *gimmel*, *yod*, *kaf*, and *kof* are formed primarily by the palate; the letters *dalet*, *tet*, *lamed*, *nun*, and taf are formed primarily by the tongue; the letters *zayin*, *samech*, *tzadi*, *reish* and *shin* are formed primarily by the teeth; and the letters *bet*, *vav*, *mem*, and *peh* are formed primarily by the lips. The enunciation of these letters is made possible by the flow of air from the lungs through the windpipe into the larynx, where the vibration of the vocal cords and the engagement of the above structures forms the various sounds of the alphabet.

Kabbalah views these same five structures as central not only to speech, but also to the edification of our eating:

> "These are the products of the heavens and the earth upon their being created (*b'hibaram*)" (Gen. 2:4). The letter *heh* in the word *b'hibaram* alludes by virtue of its numerical value, 5, to the "five outputs of the mouth" [the phonetic classes listed above]. The mystical significance is this: These are the five outputs of the supernal "mouth." I have already informed you that the five forces of *Chesed* (Kindness) enter the body through the throat ... However, the five forces of *Gevurah* (Might), upon entering the throat, are stopped by the mouth and deflected to the outside.[261]

In swallowing, the food passes from our mouth into our throat, the throat being the last station before the food descends into the body's innermost recesses, the stomach and the intestines. According to the Ari's above description, the mouth acts as the gatekeeper ensuring that only positive spiritual forces accompany our food on its way to being elevated and refined. The Hebrew word for swallowing, *beliah*, has a *gematria* of 117, which is the combined value of two holy Names: the Name *Havayah* associated with the World of *Asiyah* (Action), whose *gematria* is 52, and the Name *Adonai*, also associated with that World, whose *gematria* is 65. This suggests that the act of swallowing is one in which we draw down not only our food, but also the spiritual forces from Above into the lowermost World of *Asiyah* where the work of rectifying material reality takes place.

At this stage of meditation, the images to be pictured are three of the four *aleph* forms pictured in the last stage: the two variants of the *aleph* with a split *vav*, whose *gematrias* are 32 and 26, respectively; and the standard *aleph*, א, whose *gematria* is 26. Together they produce a *gematria* of 84, which is the combined value of the guttural letters formed by the throat: *aleph* (1), *heh* (5), *chet* (8), and *ayin* (70), reflecting the centrality of the throat in this stage of *tikkun*.

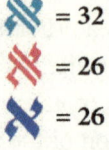

= 32

= 26

= 26

___

84 = *aleph* (1), *heh* (5), *chet* (8), and *ayin* (70), the gutturals

Appendix G

Stage 7: Digesting the Food

This, the final stage of our meditation, combines all the stages that preceded it into a single unified meditation. Unlike the previous stages, the physical aspect — digestion — is automatic and requires no effort on our part. The mental aspect, however, requires us to reconjure the previous five meditations, beginning with the stage of viewing our food. All in all, that entails visualizing five sets of *aleph* sequences and their corresponding *gematrias* in the following order:

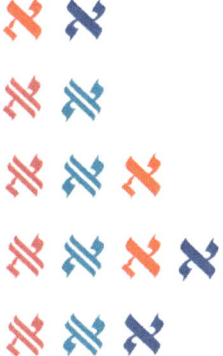

Pursuant to the order of the stages, the *gematrias* that we have meditated upon are 46, 58, 78, 104, and 84, producing a combined value of 370. This is a very significant number in the Ari's Kabbalah. In many of his works[262], the Ari discusses the Divine countenance of *Atik Yomin* (the Ancient Days), the most exalted of the *partzufim*, or "personae," that we have mentioned in the course of this work. *Atik Yomin* works in consonance with its fellow *partzuf*, *Arich Anpin* (the Long Countenance), to emanate and propel 370 "lights" through the Four Worlds. The Ari describes in figurative terms how the *gulgalta* (hoary scalp) of *Arich Anpin* enclothes the *Chesed* (Kindness) of *Atik Yomin* and as a result radiates these 370 lights, 185 from each "cheek." These lights, which originate above the Four Worlds,[263] are the reservoir of Divine life-force that sustains these Worlds while propagating through them for the purpose of rectifying Creation.

The number 185 is the *gematria* of the Name *Kel* when spelled out in full: *aleph* (111) + *lamed* (74). This is the name associated with the Divine attribute of *Chesed* (Kindness),[264] the force of *Atik* that generates the 185 lights radiating from each cheek of *Arich Anpin*. As these lights of *Chesed* descend into the lower three Worlds, they become identified with three Divine Names all based on the Name *Kel*. In the uppermost of these three Worlds, the World of *Beriah* which is not metaphysically related to food, these lights are identified with the Name *Kel Shaddai*. In the intermediate World of *Yetzirah*, which is where food has its metaphysical origin, they are identified with the Name *Kel Havayah*, a Name we have encountered a few times in the above meditations. Finally, in the World of *Asiyah*, where the actual work of rectifying our food through meditative eating takes place, these lights of *Chesed* are identified with the Name *Kel Adonai*.

In context of our meditation, only these last two Names are relevant, each being based on the Name *Kel*, which when spelled in full equals 185. Thus, together they equal 370, the combined value of all 14 *aleph* forms that comprise the focus of our meditation. Through these two Names, we draw down the Divine life-force of our food from its source in the World of *Yetzirah* into our own World of *Asiyah*.

LIST OF ILLUSTRATIONS